CLEAN

Other titles by Tony Spooner

Coastal Ace

In Full Flight

Faith, Hope and Malta GC

Warburton's War

CLEAN SWEEP

Tony Spooner DSO, DFC

Best Wishes

Ivor Broom

A Goodall paperback
from
Crécy Publishing Limited

First published in hardback by Crécy Books in 1994
This edition published in 2001

ISBN 0 907579 18 3

Printed by The Guernsey Press Co. Ltd., Guernsey, Channel Islands

A Goodall paperback

published by

Crécy Publishing Limited
1a Ringway Trading Estate, Shadowmoss Road, Manchester M22 5LH

Contents

Foreword

It is always interesting to speculate on the part that luck plays in one's life or whether there is some pre-ordained destiny. I personally have a feeling that one makes one's own luck or at least the lucky ones are those that take full advantage of what might come their way. But destiny must surely play some part and the fact that, in the course of our nation's history, Ivor Broom happened to be approaching manhood when the Second World War started must surely have had more to do with destiny than luck. For I do not believe anyone who has taken part in war and seen one's comrades, all in the flower of their youth, killed can describe the circumstances as luck.

Ivor Broom was at the centre of the Royal Air Force's operational activity for most of the war. He became one of our most experienced operational pilots, deservedly highly decorated, and followed with a distinguished peacetime career in the Royal Air Force, in the process never losing the 'common touch' which made him such a widely respected commander and such a popular officer.

The story of his life makes fascinating reading, at the same time giving a snapshot of life in the Royal Air Force through an eventful period of history both in wartime and in the years that followed. If he had not been swept forward and upward by the tides of war would he have climbed the ladder from clerk in the Tax Office in Ipswich to be a high official in the Inland Revenue? I suspect that, with the drive, dynamism and personality that made him so successful in his Air Force career, he would have almost certainly diversified into other more adventurous avenues.

I hope you enjoy reading this book about Ivor Broom's life as much as I have done. He sets a fine example to us all.

Sir Michael Beetham GCB, CBE, DFC, AFC, FRAeS
Marshal of the Royal Air Force

Acknowledgements

This book could not have been written as it is without the generously given help of a number of people and especially without the massive assistance personally provided by Air Marshal Sir Ivor Broom. He opened up his files, went through photograph albums, proofread and corrected drafts, checked facts at the Public Records Office, loaned his RAF log books, suggested a score of names, addresses and contributed to its accuracy on a hundred or more occasions. There were times when he was carrying out much of the research and most of the work but — and it is important — at no time did Ivor attempt to influence the tone and tenor of the book. Sir Ivor, greatly assisted at times by his Lady Jessica, concentrated upon the compilation and correctness of facts. No biographer could have hoped for better assistance.

In addition, and at the risk of unintentionally omitting a name or two, sincere thanks are also due to:

Eric Atkins, for an unusual Malta recollection; Herb Baker, a Canadian who also recalls Ivor as a Sgt pilot in Malta; R J Beagley, for a photograph and comment of Ivor as an Air Marshal; Sir Michael Beetham, for the excellent Foreword; Frank Bowen-Easley, for valuable Canberra and Brüggen material; Tommy Broom, for so many recollections that parts of this book almost became the story of not one, but two Brooms; Tony Browne, for a personal recollection; Ulf Burberry, for many useful Canberra contributions; Eric Chandler, a WOP/AG on Blenheims in Malta; Len Fearnley, a Blenheim researcher and historian; Arnold Field, a former DG of the UK National Air Traffic Services who worked with Sir Ivor in developing these; Sir Robert Freer, who succeeded Sir Ivor as AOC 11 Group; Al Glazer, a Canadian and room-mate of the newly commissioned P/O Broom; Mike Henry, another Malta Blenheim aircrew survivor;

William Hoy, who knew Ivor at Manby and West Malling; Bill Jinks, who served under Ivor with 163 Squadron on Mosquitoes; P B 'Laddie' Lucas, for an extract from his book *Thanks for the Memory*; Frank Lilley, another who served under Ivor on Mosquitoes and who has retained contacts; Bob Lyndall, for providing a useful address; Norman Mackie, who flew alongside Ivor with 571 Squadron on Mosquitoes; Frank Newton, who recalls Ivor at Bomber Command Development Unit; Sir John Nicholls and Sir Ian Pedder, both of whom were young Spitfire pilots and who, in Singapore, learned much from their 'veteran' 25-year-old squadron commander; Makis Panas, a Greek with intimate knowledge of Argostoli; 'Fiery' Phillips, for a colourful account of a historic arrival at West Malling; Roy Ralston, for significant Mosquito memories; F Robinson, for memories of Pathfinder Group days; Dickie Rook, who flew alongside Ivor with 114 Squadron on Blenheims; Norman Searle, with fond memories of Ivor and Jess at Brüggen; Stan Slater, 213 Squadron; Terry Staples, who worked alongside Ivor at 114 Squadron and at 13 OTU, Bicester; Arlette Tedder, a WAAF Officer known as 'Harry' who was much impressed by a flight with Ivor in Singapore and who kindly lent photographs; Graham Warner, for his invaluable help; Malcolm Webber, 213 Squadron; Tom Williams, a Malta Blenheim pilot who will never forget Ivor, after being only inches away from an early demise; Bob Wootton, another young Spitfire pilot who accompanied Ivor on a Singapore to Hong Kong formation flight; Thanks are also due to Clive Williams, Editorial Director of Crécy Books, for taking such a personal interest in the work: also to my wife, Anne, for careful proof-reading and occasional typing assistance.

Introduction

Whereas there can be no doubt but that Air Marshal Sir Ivor Broom was a great pilot both in peace and war, and not every Second World War ace pilot could adapt to a peacetime regime, Ivor is unique in one respect.

The teenage Ivor was not madly keen on aeroplanes. He was not one who had been inspired by Britain's many aviation successes such as to win three times the Schneider Trophy and to hold the world speed record. Britain had also pioneered many air routes with record flights and led the world in international air mail services at very cheap rates. Ivor had applied to join the RAF in 1940 simply because at the time he was working in an office in Ipswich and was therefore in a position to be impressed by RAF aircraft as they flew overhead on their way towards the German enemy.

As Ivor has confirmed, the probability was that, if he had been in an office in (say) Portsmouth or Aldershot, then he probably would have applied to join either the Navy or Army.

This is supposition but what is certain to anyone who has studied Ivor Broom's long career in the RAF which extended from being an AC 2 in 1940 to a retiring Air Marshal thirty-seven years later, is that whichever Service he did join, then he would have risen to the very top.

Ivor's undoubted success owes much to the basic values that he learned at his mother's knee. There he learned honesty, judgment and tolerance. These, and other Christian values together with an above average intelligence, have enabled him to meet successfully whatever challenges came his way: and some of those challenges, when operating Blenheims and Mosquitoes in wartime and when in charge of atom bomb-carrying aircraft in peacetime, were truly formidable.

It is heartening to be able to write about a person such

as Air Marshal Sir Ivor Broom KCB, CBE, DSO, DFC & two bars, AFC. Although he himself was not initially inspired by the gallant airmen who in 1940 had hit the headlines before him, perhaps the story of his life might inspire the younger readers of today?

CHAPTER ONE

Early Days

I vor Gordon Broom was born in Cardiff on 2 June 1920. He was the only son of parents who had lived in the Principality for enough generations to regard themselves as Welsh: hence the first name of 'Ivor'. The 'Gordon' points to Scottish forebears and came from his mother's side.

Between the ages of four and thirteen, Ivor's parents moved three times in the Welsh valleys before settling in Porth where his father became the Superintendent/District Manager for the Prudential Assurance Company. This meant that Ivor spent a great deal of his childhood in the Rhondda Valley which, during the General Strike of 1926 and the depression years of the 1930s, must have been an area of anger, poverty and uncertainty.

Ivor's principal school was the Boy's County School at Pontypridd but he learned much at his mother's knee. In a Christian home the simple virtues of honesty, tolerance and fair play predominated. His father must have practised what he preached as a lay preacher at many local Baptist chapels. These virtues were to stand Ivor in good stead for the rest of his life: among them was a lifelong avoidance of both tobacco and strong drink. For years Ivor was strictly TT but he will now occasionally take a glass of wine if the social occasion appears to warrant it. He is certainly not one of those abstainers who will refuse to drink to a friend's health on a worthy occasion. Also he has never minded in the least if others indulge. His understanding of others is almost a hallmark of Ivor Gordon Broom.

From a happy stable background, even if lacking luxuries, the boy showed typical Welsh dedication to learning and he took his schooling seriously. Moreover he showed an above average aptitude and when in his teens and, at the time when he was beginning to wonder what to do after leaving school, he was rather at a loss. In the Welsh valleys, this was not unusual as the depression of the thirties hung like a shroud over the whole area and the prospects for jobs for school leavers were slight.

However, not for the first time in his life, someone in authority over him had detected the latent potential within the youth and gave him a nudge forward. An understanding headmaster at the County School, a man whom Ivor greatly respected, suggested to the parents that the boy might sit the Civil Service Examination. This was a fairly stiff test but it could open doors to a stable future. At that time it was the ambition of fond mothers to try to get sons placed in nice 'white collar' jobs with prospects. Mining was the number one occupation but not the kind of job that ambitious parents sought for their sons: especially with massive unemployment all around. It was also a harsh life and one which was quite remarkably poorly paid at that time. On the other hand a good Civil Service job really opened doors towards a 'job for life.' Provided a successful applicant kept his nose clean and worked steadily he could be reasonably sure of employment with occasional promotions until reaching the age of sixty-five at which point he would be retired with a pension. In the Rhondda Valley no proud mother could wish for much more in the terrible conditions all around.

Ivor successfully passed the stiff examination and, leaving school at seventeen, he first started working in the tax office at Banbury in Oxfordshire. Here he assimilated himself into a now English environment, played rugby football as he, alongside every Welsh boy, had been taught, attended the local Baptist Church and generally made a good promising start. His parents must have been proud of him even if, having no voice, he did not sing in the local choir!

Ivor made an almost ideal Civil Servant being punctual, tidy, sober and industrious. Having got his foot on the first rung of the ladder, he was then moved to Ipswich and it was soon thereafter that the power-mad German Fascist dictator, Adolf Hitler, marched the huge army he had created into Poland on the flimsiest of pretexts. As Britain had a Mutual Assistance Treaty with Poland, it meant that within forty-eight hours

I

Britain and Germany would again be at war; only twenty-one years after the 'War to end all wars' had terminated.

Ivor Broom at first made no move to abandon the job for life for which he had worked so assiduously. Nor at once did it seem necessary. For a few days the population held its breath while awaiting the rain of bombs which the experts had predicted; and which had devastated civilian populations during the 1936–39 Spanish Civil War. Millions of children were evacuated to less vulnerable areas, windows were all papered up, everyone carried their gas mask at all times and air raid shelters were dug in every town and village. However, no bombs rained down and the war more or less stagnated while Germany and her new ally, the USSR, carved up the unfortunate Poles. There were the privations of petrol and food rationing and the annoyance of a complete black out covering the whole country. The British Expeditionary Force was rushed to France along with a large number of RAF units but, only at sea where the German U-boats immediately began to menace Allied convoys, were the British fighting Services seriously stretched. Britain and France awaited the blow which never fell. It was the period of the 'phoney' war and in quite remarkably quick time the British people adjusted to it.

All the Services were rapidly expanded and, thankfully, the additional RAF aircraft which had been ordered during the immediate pre-war years, were rushed into production via the established manufacturers and the newly built 'shadow' factories which had sprung up.

This period of unreality with a country at war but with little signs of it, was soon to be shattered in the spring of 1940. First the Nazi war machine, the Wehrmacht, invaded Norway; forestalling a British intention to do likewise as both sides realised the importance of its coast line bordering the North Sea. In a lightning campaign of brutal efficiency Norway was over run. A similar fate befell a British force which had been rushed to seize Narvik, a port in northern Norway. From start to finish it was all done in a few weeks in April 1940 with deadly thoroughness.

Worse was to befall the Allies. Even before Norway was

under total control, the German Army and Air Force, working in unison, swept into and through Holland and Belgium and assailed the 'impregnable' Maginot Line of forts which the French had built (at enormous expense) in order to check any possible threat from her old enemy across the Rhine. By swift actions and daring moves, the impregnable forts were bypassed or over run and the Nazi war machine swept into France almost unopposed. The onslaught began on 10 May and within three weeks Paris was reeling. The tanks rolled rapidly forward while overhead a Luftwaffe of 3,530 operational 'planes, supported by nearly 500 JU 52 transport aircraft, pulverised any form of opposition. It was something that the world had never before seen nor imagined. The Wehrmacht seemed irresistible.

Probably the Norwegian seizure, coupled with the British defeat at Narvik, was sufficient to arouse most Britons that the phoney war was about to be replaced by a most deadly one; especially perhaps among those living in the areas which for 200 years, from the 9th to 11th century, had been part of Danelaw.

Ipswich was one such place where an affinity, if only in place names, still existed. Without doubt, the blitz which had hit Holland, Belgium and France had a devastating effect upon all in Britain. Now everyone with red blood in their veins dropped everything else to do their bit for King and Country. The 'job for life' in a tax office appeared of minor relevance. The attack against Western Europe commenced on 10 May 1940 and it was on the next day, 11 May, that Ivor Broom went to the nearest recruitment office and said, 'I want to join up and become a pilot in the RAF.'

By then he had become familiar with the sight and sound of Blenheims and other RAF aircraft flying low overhead as they went on their way to attack his country's enemy. Their closeness and seemingly awesome power was impressive. Ivor felt a desire to become one with them — a challenging undertaking but his die was cast. In the first place would they take him and, if so, how would he cope? Time alone would tell.

CHAPTER TWO

Learning to Fly

A t first Ivor Broom's attempt to join the RAF as a pilot went well. He attended an interview at which he must have given the right impression and certainly his educational standards met the fairly high requirements for a pilot. All that was needed was a medical examination which was known to be a demanding test.

One item of this caused such surprise that other doctors were summoned to look inside Ivor's mouth because his teeth showed not a single filling! Clearly Ivor's strict but kindly upbringing must also have included a sound choice of foods with sugar and sweets kept under control.

However, for all his obvious good health, Ivor was turned down on a minor point. He had a swollen TB gland in his neck that didn't please the 'quacks', as all RAF doctors were disrespectfully called. It was, however, something that could fairly readily be fixed and after a visit to the local hospital, Ivor was able to be re-examined four weeks later and this time was passed as 'fit for pilot training.' Ivor cannot recall ever having been asked to undergo any proficiency or reaction tests — the so-called Cambridge Tests. Possibly in the period immediately following the fall of France (June 1940), many niceties were put on one side. The call was for pilots; fit young men like Ivor Broom who were keen on games, well educated and prepared to give their lives if need be to fight and fly for the country.

Although Britain had woken up belatedly to the threat that Germany and her large air force — the Luftwaffe — posed in the late 1930s and although the RAF had been enormously increased by such inspired schemes as the RAF's Short Service Commission, an Auxiliary Air Force scheme, and the RAFVR*,

---

* The Royal Air Force Voluntary Reserve gave to young, well educated, physically fit men a maximum of twenty-five hours flying per year in light RAF aircraft. On the outbreak of war all were called up and immediately incorporated into the RAF but with an 'RAFVR' tab.

the numbers of eligible young men who in 1940 were fit to be trained as pilots had swamped the training facilities available. Flying training in thousands cannot be turned on or off like a tap. It requires airfields, training aircraft, instructors and the necessary back-up facilities on the ground. By 1940 these facilities had become overstretched and Ivor, although now fully accepted by the RAF for pilot training, was sent home for a couple of months before a place for him could be found.

It was not until August, with the Battle of Britain still raging over south-east England, that Ivor was ordered to report to an Aircrew Reception Depot at Babbacombe in Devon. Here he became an Aircraftman Second Class (AC 2) and was duly kitted out. Little else happened there but Ivor does remember that it was a most pleasant place.

AC 2 Broom and his colleagues were then sent to an Initial Training Wing at Aberystwyth, where they were the first intake. A variety of lectures were given as well as a fitness programme as, regrettably, many of the young men of Britain in 1940, having suffered years of the depression were under-nourished and in need of a physical build up. Ivor recalls taking part in drills on the promenade among the many holiday-makers much to the latter's delight. He was now attired in the standard RAF blue serge and promoted to the rank of a Leading Aircraftman (LAC) but, to mark him out as an aircrew trainee, his forage cap bore a white flash.

Some idea of the state of alarm then existing in Britain, can be gained by an incident which happened at Aberystwyth in September 1940. The Battle of Britain was poised to go either way and an invasion of Britain was generally thought likely to take place at any time. One night Ivor and all his fellow trainees were roused from their beds and told that the invasion had started. They were further told to get dressed and packed ready to move to Liverpool at a moment's notice. At Liverpool they would be put on board a ship and sent immediately to America or Canada where their training as pilots would continue. After sitting on their beds for some time, fully 'kitted' out, the news came through that the invasion had not started and all went back to normal.

II

It was not until October 1940 that Ivor Broom at last commenced flying training when, as a member of a group of would be pilots, he was posted to No. 13 Elementary Flying Training School at White Waltham near Maidenhead. It was, due to the school's proximity to London, a curious place to begin to learn to fly as the tail end of the Battle of Britain raged, almost overhead on some days. In the clear autumn skies, the condensation which the fighters trailed behind them criss-crossed the heavens, while below the de Havilland 82A Tiger Moths of Ivor and his colleagues were gently carrying out their first flying exercises.

Before even being allowed to sit in the cockpit, Ivor Broom's first encounter with an RAF aircraft was when he was taught how to swing the propeller of a Tiger in order to get the Gypsy engine to fire and start. It was a necessary training drill as the aircraft had no self starter or brakes and if the propeller was incorrectly handled, the engine was liable to start up quickly and slice off a hand, or even the head, of its prop swinger!

Ivor's flying training got off to a bad start. He was assigned to Sgt Hymans as his instructor but, as happens on occasions, the two of them did not gel. It was generally recognised that a young lad ought to be able to fly a first solo after about ten hours of dual instruction in the air and many able pilots who 'got the message' right away were let loose on their own in as few as six hours or thereabouts. After nine hours of dual, Ivor was not even close to being sent solo and was clearly heading for rejection. It must have been a worrying time with others already flying solo. A simple cure for the problem was to try the pupil with another instructor and in Ivor's case the chief instructor of the intake, F/Lt Mills, took over. He rapidly realised that Ivor had little, if any, idea of what he was trying to do. 'We started again from scratch and were soon making good progress.'

Ivor's first solo — an event which no pilot ever forgets — took place on 13 November 1940. Almost a month had gone by since his first dual lesson in the air but from then onwards, with confidence reborn, thanks to F/Lt Mills, Ivor began to catch up with his fellow pupils. Just like the kindly headmaster who, some time before had come to Ivor's rescue at a time when his future was looking uncertain, so now had F/Lt Mills.

Ivor's first solo was not, however, without incident. Soon after the instructor had unfastened his harness, climbed out and left a rather surprised pupil pilot all alone in the aircraft, Ivor successfully took off only to find himself caught in the slipstream of a powerful Fairey Battle of the ATA* which was also doing a circuit and landing. This rather unnerved him and he had to make three attempts to approach and land before finally committing himself to making a controlled return to Mother Earth. As any experienced instructor can confirm, this was an impressive performance rather than an alarming one. It showed that Ivor Broom could keep his head in an unexpected situation and that he was capable of unhurried judgment. It would have been easier and might have looked better to have tried to come in and land at once even after experiencing the other aircraft's slipstream. Ivor was not concerned with what it might look like. He simply waited until it felt right to land.

Due to his slow start, Ivor and a few others were told one day to take their machines up and get in some extra hours flying. Perhaps from boredom of flying around locally, Ivor and three others strayed further afield than usual and got themselves lost! Sighting an airfield, they landed to ask where they were. They had landed at Northolt in north-west London. Having no maps they were advised to fly south until sighting the Thames and then to turn west so that they could find Maidenhead and more familiar territory.

On their return, Ivor and his fellows were hauled before the CO and given a Red Endorsement in their personal flying log books. When reprimanded for flying over a Prohibited area around Northolt, Ivor protested that he did not know that he was flying over a Prohibited area. 'Of course you didn't know. It's a secret area!' said the CO.

Notwithstanding his eleven and a half hours of dual before

---

* The Air Transport Auxiliary (ATA) delivered new aircraft from the factories to the RAF units. Many, from the fastest fighters to the biggest bombers, were delivered by women pilots. ATA pilots were seldom given dual instruction; just pilot's notes. It was not unusual to have to fly more than one aircraft type on the same day. They did a wonderful job.

going solo and his (rare) Red Endorsement, Ivor Broom was passed out at the end of November as 'Average' ie. not labelled with the stigma of 'Below Average.' Some idea of how far behind in number of hours he had fallen can be seen in his log book. In all, between 15 October and 29 November 1940, he had flown 47.35 hours of which 22.20 hours being dual instruction as further dual was always continued long after a pupil's first solo. Yet, during the period of 23–29 November, LAC Ivor Broom flew on twenty-six separate occasions and logged nearly sixty percent of his total solo hours in that one week.

Only for his Link Training exercises was Ivor tagged as a 'Below Average' student. This was accompanied by a comment that 'he would improve with more practice.' But once again lack of time may have played a part as Ivor had not completed a full Link course. He clearly had much to catch up due to a slow and shaky start with an incompatible instructor. However he did make the grade and proceeded to the No. 14 Service Flying Training School where he would come much closer to flying one of the 'real things' with which the RAF and Luftwaffe were locked in battle. Britain was still fighting for the mastery of the air and it was a fight for her very life especially as she was now, after the fall of France, alone.

No. 14 SFTS was at Cranfield and, instead of the tiny single engined Tiger Moths powered by one 120hp engine, pupils were now taught to fly the much bigger twin-engined Airspeed Oxford with their two Cheetah X engines of several times greater power. It was a challenging task for one who had only his first flight eight weeks earlier but, provided the pupil made the grade, the Oxford was a good aircraft to learn to master just as the Tiger Moth had been previously. This is because neither is easy to fly. By comparison, those who learned to fly the Avro Anson, as their first twin-engined aircraft, learned precious little as it was the most viceless and simple to fly of any type in the entire RAF.

One of Ivor's most lasting impressions was of having to crank up the engines of the Oxfords in the cold of winter which was now upon them. He was once asked if he was ever really frightened when in the RAF. After much thought he recalled the times when during that winter he had to climb up on to the ice-covered wings of an Oxford and hand crank the propellers to get the engines started. 'That really scared me. I was terrified of slipping off into the whirling propellers as the engines fired up.' This, and not any daring Blenheim or Mosquito operation, was Ivor's most frightening recollection of the Second World War!

By then Ivor had come to terms with flying aeroplanes and he experienced no great difficulty in mastering the rather unpredictable characteristics of the Airspeed Oxford. It was a type with which liberties could not be taken without risk. After 5.40 hours of dual from F/O Courtney, Ivor successfully flew solo on his first twin-engined aircraft. It was to be a long time before he was again to fly a single engined type of any kind. It was not until he had been flying Oxfords for about two months that any exercises included single-engined landings. These could be very hazardous in that type and it was 'just bad luck' if a pupil should happen to be faced with this at an early stage of his training. The war required pilots to be produced as rapidly as possible and, sadly, many fell by the wayside in the course of their hurried training. It was not quite a matter of the survival of the fittest but mighty close to it. By the end of the war 3,865 lives had been lost in the RAF due to flying training and another 7,345 to technical training. Fortunately, just after his first solo in an Oxford, Ivor was wisely shown how to abandon it. Aircraft per se were, at most times during the Second World War, available in plenty but pilots were generally a lot more scarce and valuable. 'When in doubt, jump out' was, therefore, a sound policy.

Formation flying now took up a sizeable part of Ivor Broom's flying training. This was largely due to the still prevailing pre-war belief that bombers in formation could cope successfully with attacks by enemy fighters. All RAF bombers then in service were equipped with tail guns and/or turrets with up to four guns. The theory was that if a formation of bombers flew in close proximity to one another, their combined rear fire power would defeat that of the attacking fighters. Sadly this did not work out in practice and it took the loss of nearly every Fairey Battle in France and subsequent heavy losses by Blenheims and Wellingtons operating in daylight, before the lesson was truly learned. Even by the end of the war the RAF had no bomber capable of holding its own against enemy fighters which attacked from underneath or used superior speed to dive through a formation. Until the fast unarmed Mosquito type arrived, RAF bombing either had to be attempted in daylight at almost zero feet or carried out during the hours of darkness. However, the habit of teaching bomber aircraft pilots to fly in close formation — one which added to the number of training accidents — remained and persisted throughout Ivor Broom's months at No. 14 SFTS.

Ivor now had to pay more attention to navigation as another part of the course at Cranfield was to carry out cross-country flights to other distant airfields. Some emphasis was also given to flying by instruments in the knowledge that bombers would often have to seek the protection of clouds. There the only way of maintaining control would be by instruments. However, by the time that Ivor came to leave Cranfield, his total instrument hours were only eighteen and of these nearly thirteen had been dual instruction.

Night flying was still largely ignored although by then Bomber Command had resorted to a policy of mainly night bombing. Ivor's total here was just 3.05 solo. Night flying was known to be dangerous and it was largely left to the Operational Training Units to bring pupils up to the required standards in the operational types in which they would be flying. This made some sense as if a pupil was posted to a Blenheim squadron and attended a Blenheim OTU in preparation, there would be virtually no night flying requirement. Whereas if he was posted to a Wellington or larger type OTU in preparation for night bombing, it then became the responsibility of that OTU to provide the required night training.

LAC Ivor Broom spent four months at Cranfield from mid-December 1940 to mid-April 1941. The undoubted high-spot was that at the end of the course, as well as being passed out as an 'Average' twin-engined pilot, LAC Broom was awarded his RAF Wings and thereafter became Sergeant pilot I G Broom, No. 1252084. This also meant that his pay shot up from 7 shillings and 6 pence per day (37.5p) to a princely 12 shillings and 6 pence (62.5p).

In wartime the granting of the much coveted RAF pilot's brevet was merely an administrative action and 'Wings' Parades with bands, seats for relatives, an imposing Air Marshal and flowery addresses were dispensed with. Ivor just went to Stores, drew a 'Wings' badge and Sergeant stripes and sewed them on as best he could. On his course he can only remember a Jimmy Corfield who was later killed during a daylight raid in which Ivor also took part.

As a Sergeant pilot with 'Wings' badge now showing, Ivor became one of those whom the public had taken to their hearts. All pilots with 'Wings' were assumed to be Battle of Britain pilots who had shot down dozens of the enemy. Ivor first became aware of this on a visit to London when strangers would come up to him and wish him luck. It was an embarrassing situation for one who had not flown an operational aircraft nor fired a gun in anger. When in London and using the Underground at night, he observed the thousands who were bedded down and who were using the system as a gigantic air raid shelter. As he passed their crowded rows, he would receive smiles and hear such shouted cries as: 'Give it to them', 'Well done lad' and 'Shoot one down for me.'

Britain in the 1940–41 period, when she stood very much alone, was a heartening place in which to be living and it made the youthful Sergeant pilot Ivor Gordon Broom determined that when he was given a chance to 'give it to them', he would not be found lacking.

CHAPTER THREE

OTU and Blenheims

S gt pilot Ivor Broom's final training stage before he could be let loose against the enemy was at No. 13 Operational Training Unit at Bicester. At all the OTUs, the trainee pilots had to come to terms with the type of aircraft they would soon have to operate. They also met up with the crew with whom they would be sharing the dangers of future operations and, coming from their respective training units, they would probably also be newcomers to actual war. In Ivor's case he found himself with Sgt Bill North, navigator and Sgt Les Harrison, who would be the Wireless Operator-cum-Air Gunner (WOP/AG).

Although Ivor had not been in the RAF for long, it was well known that most Blenheim aircrew had little chance of surviving for over long. The statistics were that a Blenheim crew stood a twenty-five percent chance of surviving their first tour of operations but such figures were never released. In any event, as Ivor has cheerfully admitted, he was endowed with the supreme optimism of youth and it never occurred to him that he might be adding to these mournful statistics.

Much has been said and written about the Blenheim light-to-medium twin-engined bomber and, as this is being written, it is still capable of making headlines. During the summer of 1993 the last of the type to be reconstructed made its maiden flight after years of dedicated re-build by devoted admirers of the 'plane. It flew well, too.

Whatever may be said for or against the aircraft, all who flew it came to love its flying and handling qualities although these do not mask the fact that from its first inception in 1935, the Blenheim has attracted controversy.

The aircraft type owes its origins to the initiative of its designer, Frank Barnwell of the Bristol Aircraft Company and to the patriotism of a millionaire newspaper proprietor, Lord Rothermere. The Blenheim bomber of the RAF in the Second

World War was the eventual outcome of an attempt by the well-known Bristol firm of aircraft manufacturers to compete with a number of emerging USA aircraft which had been designed to cash in on the high speed executive civil aircraft market developing in the 1930s. A few millionaires and large corporations were beginning to take air transport seriously and wanted their own 'planes for swift private travel. Accordingly in 1935 the Bristol company built a prototype of what was called the Bristol 135. This was a mid-wing twin-engined aircraft capable of carrying about six passengers at speeds of up to 280mph for 1,000 miles and powered by two Bristol Aquila engines of about 500hp each. This, also, was a revolutionary design having sleeve valves instead of the usual poppet type.

Lord Rothermere, proprietor of the successful *Daily Mail*, and a very ardent pro-British and pro-British Empire enthusiast, bought the prototype for £18,500, christened it 'Britain First', gave it to the Air Ministry and immediately began to campaign for it to be re-designed as a much needed fast bomber for the RAF. Through his newspapers, he was able to alert the public of Britain's need for such an aircraft.

The prototype bomber first flew on 25 June 1936 and at that time it was considerably faster than the RAF's front line fighter the Gloster Gauntlet which was a biplane with a fixed pitch wooden propeller, a fixed undercarriage, no brakes and no takeoff or landing flaps to enhance performance. By contrast the Bristol design had a three-bladed metal propeller, a retractable undercarriage, brakes, flaps, supercharged engines and was an all-metal monoplane. In every aspect it was years ahead of anything that the RAF then possessed. Yet the country was being made aware almost daily that the new dictators of Europe, Benito Mussolini of Italy and Adolf Hitler of Germany were building up large air forces of modern 'planes and, by 1936, were trying out their latest designs by aiding another Fascist, General Franco, in his efforts to overthrow the Socialist Government of Spain in that testing Civil War (1936ñ39).

To its credit, the Air Ministry, riding on the wave created by the *Daily Mail*, acted swiftly. The Bristol 135 was re-designed and initially designated the Bristol 142M. It was also provided with more powerful conventional radial engines, the Bristol Mercury of 840hp, and put into large scale production. This modified design was soon to be named the Blenheim after the small Austrian town that provided the location, in the early 18th century, for the battle won by the first Duke of Marlborough and perpetuated since by the palace which was built and named after it.

Ironically during the Second World War the Blenheim was to be used extensively against a Germany which by then had incorporated the whole of Austria into its Reich. However, the Blenheim aircraft lacked the range to penetrate as far as the town of its name.

The RAF placed a (then) massive order for 150 Blenheims, which was soon to be increased to one of 600 and, by the start of the war 2,000 had been ordered and a shadow factory at Coventry, managed by Rootes, makers of the Humber and Hillman cars, was hastily erected to increase the rate of supply.

Almost before the first examples began to flow from the Bristol Company, an enhanced model of the Blenheim was planned. This Mark IV, by contrast to the original Mark I, had increased cockpit length and is sometimes referred to as the long-nosed Blenheim. The extra section was to provide the navigator with a better position and one from which he could also act as bomb aimer. It was curiously off-set from the centre line in order to allow the pilot, who sat on the left (port) side of the aircraft, an unimpeded forward view during take-offs and landings.

The military version, by the addition of guns, a mid-upper turret and other military requirements was now heavier and less streamlined but the extra power of the engines enabled it still to fly at about 250mph, which was about twice the speed of the RAF's torpedo-carrying bomber, the Vickers Wildebeest, which looked as if it had strayed from the First World War!

By the 3rd September 1939, when the Prime Minister, Neville Chamberlain, announced to all in Britain via his 1100 hrs broadcast that 'A state of war exists between Britain and France against Germany at 11.15 hours', the RAF had received about 1,000 Blenheims of which about 100 were of the later Mark IV model. As this version came on stream, the Mark I was phased out. As a bomber the Blenheims could uplift 1,000lb weight of bombs and usually carried four 250lb bombs but occasionally two 500lb ones or a cluster of smaller types.

The history of the Blenheim bombers in action during the Second World War, at the time when Sgt pilot I G Broom arrived at 13 OTU in order to learn to fly them on operations as soon as practicable, namely mid-July 1941, was one of great bravery but terrible losses.

At the outbreak of war, by which time the RAF had more Blenheims than any other aircraft type, about a dozen squadrons were sent to France either under 2 Group, or as part of the Advanced Air Striking Force (AASF) or, as was the case of 53 and 59 Squadrons, as Army Co-operation units.

During the period of the 'phoney' war — September 1939 to May 1940 — they were used in France as reconnaissance rather than bombers as virtually no bombing took place across the frontiers. However, the squadrons in England had a sharp baptism of fire. As early as the afternoon of 3 September 1939, Blenheims were sent out to reconnoitre and to take photographs of the German naval bases followed, the next day, by the first attempted assault on Germany by Blenheims. A small number set forth to bomb German capital ships at anchor in the Wilhelmshaven docks; an important naval base facing the North Sea. Few managed to find the target and of those which did most were shot down or damaged. Blenheims even in the tight formation which the pre-war pilots had been at such pains to perfect, were no match for the Me 109s and larger but slower Me 11 Os which, alerted by German radar, had attacked them. The damage they did was largely caused by a Blenheim which was brought down and crashed into the cruiser *Emden*.

The RAF thereupon largely abandoned, for the time being, the idea of bombers attacking German positions by day, especially as Germany hitherto had shown no intention of bombing British military establishments. Strangely, this was, to some extent, still a Gentleman's war with the RAF crews being given strict instructions not to drop bombs if civilians appeared to be in danger and Germany giving the shot-down RAF crews ceremonial funerals with full military honours and coffins draped with the Union flag. It was indeed a period of the 'phoney' war.

In France, it was also noticed that several Blenheims sent on reconnaissance missions towards Germany failed to return. Generally these flights were made at quite high altitudes as the aircraft, with its supercharged engines, could operate near to 20,000ft,

However, these disasters paled to relative insignificance once the German onrush through Belgium and Holland began in May 1940. At once the Blenheims were used to try to halt the advance by bombing the bridges which lay ahead of the swiftly advancing German armies. It was then that the true inadequacies of the type were fully revealed. Losses of over fifty percent on some raids occurred and no air force could tolerate such casualties for long; especially as the cream of the RAF's pre-war trained pilots were lost. Of the many Blenheims which flew in the defence of France in May 1940, few ever saw service in Britain again.

The sad truth, when it was learned that Blenheims stood little chance against the Messerschmitts at height, was that low level attacks, where the vulnerable undersides would be less exposed, was the only likely alternative but it was then discovered that German low-level ack-ack fire could be equally devastating. If the aircraft bunched together, for mutual protection from their many air gunners, they then made a splendid target that AA ground gunners could hardly miss. Conversely if they opened up to make life difficult for the AA gunners, the Me 109s dealt with them with ruthless efficiency. Perhaps the biggest disaster was on 17 May 1940, when twelve Blenheims of 82 Squadron were dispatched to attack the advancing enemy. Sadly only one returned and it was so badly damaged that it never flew again. When it was realised that Blenheims were unable to halt the Germans and France could not be saved, the attacks ceased.

However, respite for the Blenheim crews was short lived as within months, while the Battle of Britain raged over south-east England, Hitler and his generals were planning the invasion of Britain, their 'Operation Sealion.' When the build-up of invasion barges in the enemy held ports just across the English Channel began, the Blenheim squadrons were once again thrown into the fray. Still flying at low-level, they were sent to bomb the massed ranks of barges and other vessels which crowded the enemy's ports. Again the losses were calamitous but, at that time, everything and anything that could fly was being thrown at the enemy.

It is not generally known that during the crucial months when the Battle of Britain was being fought Bomber Command lost a greater number of aircrew than did Fighter Command. For one thing, every Blenheim lost meant the loss of three aircrew. For another, a Blenheim hit at low level gave the crew little chance of being able to bail out and if they did manage to gain enough height to do so, they fell on hostile soil whereas the fighter pilots were often able to live and fight again even after having to descend by parachute. It is always preferable to be defending over Home territory than to be attacking Away.

As if this was not enough it was decided, after the heat of the Battle of Britain had died down, and as 1941 came into being with the threat of invasion no longer uppermost in mind, that the Blenheims could instead be used to attack — again at low level — enemy shipping as it moved along the shores of Germany, Holland, the Friesian Islands and Channel coasts.

The change of targets did not lead to less dangerous operations as the Germans soon learned to protect their coastal traffic by sending ships in convoys well protected by Flak ships, destroyers and other well-armed craft. For the third or fourth time, Blenheim losses became calamitous and even Winston Churchill would soon be remarking upon them.

This was the state of the war and the fate of the Blenheim aircrews when Ivor Broom and his new crew commenced their training at No. 13 OTU at Bicester in May 1941. Not that it seems to have worried Ivor in the slightest. What kept pilots going throughout the Second World War was an almost unshakeable belief that it was not going to happen to them. It was symptomatic that the expression always was that 'poor old so-and-so got himself killed.' The implication being that it was some error on the poor chap's part. Also the frequent postings in and out of a squadron meant that there was a constant change of personnel in the Messes. Aircrews avoided close friendships outside their own crew and, in effect, there was little difference between a casual acquaintance being posted away to another RAF station, and knowing that a person had been killed or was missing. In neither case was it likely that the person would be encountered again. Hence the loss was never grievous. Only if a well-known CO or similar was killed was the loss personally felt. However, by and large, it was the more experienced COs etc, who survived.

For all its losses, the Blenheim played a major role at a time when it seemed that ultimate victory was hard to imagine. It ceased to be used on operations from the UK quite early in 1942 as more suitable types became available but continued to be used in the Mediterranean for about a year thereafter and in the Far East until the end of the war. By then over 6,000 had been built mainly in the UK but also in Canada where it was named the Bolingbroke after being modified to better withstand the extremes of climate. Most were Mark IVs but a later version, the Mark V, or Bisley, was also produced. The amount of armour plate and number of guns were increased and, to counter the added weight, more powerful versions of the Mercury engines were fitted; with Canadian versions having Pratt & Witney radials. Improved turrets and propellers came to be fitted but, sadly, it was never far from being a vulnerable aircraft when on operations due large to the tasks which it was asked to perform.

In all, Blenheims served ninety-four squadrons and also fought with the Finnish air force against the Russians in a 1940/41 campaign which has become almost lost to memory as the tides of history have washed by. Blenheims served Fighter, Bomber, Coastal, Training Commands and Army Co-op units. They played a long-range fighter role although very ill-equipped for the task because, at the time, there was no other type capable of even pretending to fill the bill. It served as a night fighter for the same reason and was the first aircraft anywhere to be fitted with night fighting radar. It carried out the first offensive raid of the war and a pilot, F/Lt Doran, was the first to be awarded both a Distinguished Flying Cross (DFC) and a bar to this gallantry award. A Blenheim destroyed the first German U-boat (11 March 1940) and later the first Japanese submarine to be sunk by the RAF (7 July 1942).

Three Blenheim pilots were awarded Victoria Crosses; Wing Commander Hugh Edwards, leading a raid from the UK, Wing Commander Malcolm, in North Africa, and F/Lt Scarf in the Far East. Blenheims saw action in France, Norway, over Germany, Malta, North Africa, Canada, and became almost the RAF's standard bomber in the Far East where it was used up to 1945. By then its weight had risen to about 17,000lb which was about twice that of the first Blenheim Is to be delivered to the RAF. It was fitted at various times with a variety of machine guns; in the wings, alongside the engines, underneath (to fire forwards or in some cases backwards), in a pack under the nose and in its turret. It produced perhaps the most aggressive pilot of the war in Basil Embry who was twice shot down, twice taken prisoner, twice escaped and got back to UK — personally strangling his guard in one case and hiding in a manure heap on another occasion. This character rose to Air Marshal rank with *four* DSOs — and generally was seldom out of the news. Love it or hate it, the Blenheim, if only for its loss record, was, and still is, a 'plane which some will remember to their dying day; one that came too soon for many.

However, in May 1941, the ever optimistic Ivor Broom was *delighted* to be posted to a Blenheim OTU! Was it not the sound and sight of these same aircraft which had initially brought him out of a tax office in Ipswich to the position he now held; that of a Sgt pilot with 'Wings' on his tunic and impatient to get at the enemy?

The Blenheim was not difficult to fly: probably less so than the Oxford and, after only one period of dual instruction, Ivor, on the 28 May 1941, was allowed to take up the aircraft by himself. Within a week he was taking part in the now customary formation practice and even had one detail of flying the newer Mark IV. His crew members did not join him until he was familiar with the aircraft both by day and, very briefly, by night. Thereafter they practised both high, but mainly low level, bombing and the WOP/AG made himself familiar with the wireless set on which, in bad weather, much would depend for a safe arrival and his ability to get Ivor reliable homing bearing (QDMs). The crew also engaged in cross country flights to check the skills of the navigator.

The three young Sergeants were preparing themselves for battle.

CHAPTER FOUR

114 Squadron

'**W**ar changes men just as motherhood changes women.'

Certainly this was true for many a young man in the RAF during the Second World War and the three youthful Sergeants who made up Ivor Broom's Blenheim crew with 114 Squadron, help to confirm the point.

While Bill North his navigator, who was a schoolmaster pre-war and went back to his calling afterwards to rise to a position of headmaster in Sheffield, was not affected, careerwise, by the war, Les Harrison, the WOP/AG was.

Pre-war, Les was a delivery boy for Sainsburys in London. Post-war he joined the Metropolitan Police and within five years was an inspector, retiring as a Chief Superintendent. The war changed life for many and shook up the established patterns. The RAF was the making of many; the difficulty was to survive to enjoy the metamorphosis.

At the end of his course at 13 OTU at Bicester, Ivor passed out with another 'Average' assessment. It had lasted a bare six weeks and he was now classified as a competent Medium Bomber pilot, with a total flying time, since first getting into an aeroplane, of 180.80 hours made up in the following way:

Type	Dual	Solo	Total	Period
DH 82A	22.20	25.15	47.35	15/10/40–8/12/40
Oxford	38.10	40.05	78.15	19/12/40–14/4/41
Blenheim	8.15	47.15	55.30	28/4/41–7/7/41
TOTAL	68.45	112.35	180.80	

To become an operational pilot deemed fit to take on the Luftwaffe in the air had taken less than nine months, including a spell of leave before proceeding to his OTU. He had flown less than 50 hours solo on any type and his total hours at night were just 2.10 in an Oxford and 55 minutes in a Blenheim. It was very inadequate in every respect but Ivor and his colleagues had become 'victims' of the lean years which the 1930s politicians had imposed upon Britain's RAF. Ivor and his colleagues were also being rushed into action to replace the carefully-trained pre-war pilots who had been slaughtered by having to fight in Blenheims and Battles against the much superior Messerschmitt fighters flown by young German 'veterans' who had honed their skill during the Spanish Civil War.

Ivor and his crew found themselves posted to 114 Squadron. He had no choice as although, pre-war, trainee pilots were offered a choice of Bomber, Fighter or Coastal Command (not that they always got their choice but that is the way of all Services!) this was another nicety which had been hastily dropped. During the 1940s, the demand had been for fighter pilots. By 1941, with the Battle of Britain fading into memory, the prior task was to build up a huge Bomber Command. 114 was a Blenheim bomber squadron of 2 Group.

Strange as it may seem, despite the Blenheim's appalling casualty rate, Ivor Broom would have opted to join a Blenheim squadron if given a choice! Obviously, since he had been trained to fly twin-engined aircraft, he would have chosen a twin-engined unit and he regarded the Blenheim as a more exciting prospect than the alternative Wellington, Hampden or Whitley bombers. It was faster and it operated in daylight whereas the others appeared to be almost lumbering giants which operated at night and night flying was something that, throughout his training, had been regarded as dangerous and therefore was to be avoided. Also the Blenheim losses had not been made public while its few successes had been lauded to the skies; as Ivor himself was shortly to experience. At the time when Ivor and his crew joined 114 Squadron, the unit was based at West Raynham in Norfolk but was on temporary detachment at Leuchars, close to the famous golf course of St Andrews in Scotland. It had been redeployed there in order to carry out some special North Sea sweeps on the look out for U-boats. This was a one-off assignment which was probably most welcomed in the squadron as normally the dozen or so Blenheim squadrons of 2 Group were being used in three quite different ways.

One type of operation was for a small number of Blenheims to attack, from about 8000ft with bombs, a military target just across the Channel while being accompanied by a huge fighter formation. The idea was to compel the Luftwaffe fighters to arise to attack the bombers and so enable Fighter Command to drop down hard upon the Me 109s and Fw 190 enemy fighters. The Blenheims were, in effect, being used as 'bait.' Britain's main concern at that time was to give every kind of help she could to the hard pressed Russians who, ever since Germany had turned upon the USSR in June 1941, had become our principal ally. With Germany now in full control of all Europe as far as the Pyrenees, Britain could only realistically help Russia in the air and at sea. It was hoped that the nightly bombing of Germany and these 'bait' raids by Blenheims would force the Germans to keep a large part of her fighter forces in Europe and so give the Russians a much needed respite. These 'bait' operations were known as 'Circuses.' The very fact that the RAF was now trying to lure the Luftwaffe to fight — and to fight over their own airfields — was an indication of how events had changed since the grim days of August and September 1940 when the Battle of Britain was poised to go either way and when the enemy's Channel ports were crammed full of invasion barges. The thought was now one of how to get at the enemy: not how best to defend.

Another form of 2 Group operation, as has been mentioned earlier, was to use Blenheims to attack enemy coastal shipping as it plied along the German and Dutch coasts. These mast-high attacks were murderous on both sides.

The third kind of operation was to arrange an occasional 'spectacular.' These were daring daylight raids carried out at low-level against military targets in Europe beyond the strictly limited range of the Spitfires and Hurricanes. Consequently, once these Blenheims had crossed beyond the Channel, they would be on their own. Their object was two-fold; to destroy vital war installations and to 'tell the World', especially the Russians, that Britain, far from being on her knees as German propaganda was proclaiming, was ready and willing to take the offensive into the German heartland by day as well as by night.

There was always the fear that Russia might, in her plight, apply for peace, in which case the whole weight of the Wehrmacht would be turned against Britain. With such a daunting prospect always in view, almost any losses of Blenheims seemed justified.

One such 'spectacular' had been when 139 Squadron had attacked the big German town and port of Bremen on 4 July 1941. Of the fifteen aircraft that departed, twelve reached the target flying at literally 'nought feet' and four were shot down. The leader was the Australian Hughie Edwards and it was for this attack that he was able to add the Victoria Cross to the Distinguished Flying Cross he had already been awarded. He led the formation in so low that he had to fly under the high tension cables. The formation also had to contend with a balloon barrage as well as the usual deadly flak and Messerschmitts. Another similar raid had been launched against the big steel works at Ijmuiden in Holland and just before Ivor, Bill and Les joined 114 Squadron, the biggest-yet low level Blenheim raid had been launched against the docks and shipping at Rotterdam. This time thirty-six aircraft took part. The crews claimed seventeen hits on ships and escaped with the loss of only four aircraft. Massive publicity had been given this raid. It was the kind which made Ivor almost leap for joy upon learning that he would be posted to 114 Squadron. The mighty Blenheims had done it again! Later that port was again the object of another 'spectacular' and it was one which was to have important repercussions.

Ivor's first two operations with 114 Squadron were two of the unusual anti-submarine patrols from Leuchars down to West Raynham and back. They made an almost perfect introduction to Ops as records show all too clearly that a crew on its first operation was especially vulnerable. In their enthusiasm to get to grips with the enemy after so many weary weeks of training, they were apt to throw all caution to the wind. Alternatively they discovered that their training did not cover the actual conditions which they now encountered or they simply made mistakes through lack of flying experience.

Inexperience with the Blenheim may well have cost Ivor and his crew dearly on his next operation which was his first 'Circus.' He and others from 114 were detailed to bomb the French Channel port of Le Trait. Overhead and alongside were a vast array of Spitfires and Hurricanes awaiting a Luftwaffe reaction. However as the Blenheims proceeded towards the target, Ivor, who was at the rear of the formation, fell further and further behind. Even with the throttle wide open, his aircraft lacked the speed to keep up but fortunately a couple of Hurricanes noticed his plight and fell behind to keep him company.

The formation duly bombed the port and Ivor, because he lagged behind, was in a good position to observe their accurate strikes. Generally on these missions the formation bombed simultaneously on the command of the experienced leader. Although Ivor was 'easy meat' for any enemy fighter due to being on his own, none came near him.

It was on the way home, after Ivor had also dropped his bombs, that he discovered that he had been flying throughout with the Air lever in 'Warm' position. This had an adverse affect on performance and when he moved it to the 'Cold Air' position, the machine leaped forward and soon caught up with the others.

If this mistake had been made during either a shipping strike or a 'spectacular', the chances against any such laggard getting home would have been slight. As any operational pilot of the Second World War who survived a large number of sorties could confirm, luck played an important part in their survival.

Ivor cannot recall a single Blenheim being lost on 'Circus' operations and remembers feeling absolutely safe with so many fighters around and above him. It was also widely thought that the Spitfire was more than a match for the Me 109s or even the Fw 190 although the truth was that the types were very evenly matched and at times the Me 109s held the advantage as they could always out-dive the Spits.

The only other operations that month were two which were aborted. In one the target was in Holland but was only to be attacked if the leader considered that there was cloud sufficiently close at hand to enable the Blenheims, if needs be, to take cover. The weather was clear so the formation turned tail. In the other it was bad weather which caused the operation to be abandoned. Bad weather was always a threat as the aircraft had very inadequate means of returning safely to base under conditions of low cloud or poor forward visibility. The fact that instructions were being issued for formations to return to base if conditions were not quite right for an attack, shows that some regard was now being paid to aircrew survival. Perhaps someone was getting alarmed?

On 2 August Ivor and his crew took part in their one and only shipping strike from England. However, as was not too unusual, the Blenheims swept along the enemy coast without sighting any target to attack. It is perhaps just as well that no enemy ship was sighted as, on this type of mission whenever ships were sighted and attacked, Blenheims were inevitably lost. Although 2 Group could claim to have attacked 401 ships between March and July 1941, they had lost sixty-eight aircraft in the process. Before August was out, another seventy-seven Blenheims had also managed to launch attacks on enemy ships but of these twenty-three never came back: a thirty percent loss.

Although Ivor and his colleagues failed to find any ship to attack, the sortie of 2 August was not without excitement. While scouring the Friesian Islands, they ran into a formation of Arado 196 seaplanes; possibly on a reconnaissance mission. The groups milled around for a short while but, since neither made an efficient fighter aircraft, no harm was done to either side but it was the first enemy aircraft that Ivor Broom and his crew had seen.

In between operations, the crews continued to become better equipped to manage their aircraft. They practised bombing, they made flights to other RAF stations, they indulged in local flying, instrument approaches and tested out the wireless frequencies. These extra training details were necessary but were also costly in personnel. Because Blenheims were 'hot ships' manned by hastily trained crews, accidents were all too frequent. One survey shows that of the 869 Blenheims delivered to the squadrons within a period of about a year, about 195 were lost or written-off due to accidents. As another 395 were lost in action and others damaged, only fifty-two ever reached the stage where they could be struck off the operations list as 'Time Expired.' British weather always had to be treated with respect and because the aircraft had no sophisticated radio landing aid, few crews were prepared to enter into or fly above the clouds. This meant low flying whenever the weather was bad and this, in poor visibility, was hazardous enough without the addition of balloon barrages and trigger happy home gunners prepared to shoot first and ask questions afterwards.

Then came 12 August 1941. Grouse shooting traditionally commences on that date but for 114 Squadron it was to be remembered for other reasons.

For days a rumour had spread that a special operation was planned especially when all other operations were cancelled. The Squadron concentrated upon producing maximum serviceability making the crews even more aware that something was 'in the wind.' A powerful rumour was that there would be a spectacular attack upon an enemy factory in the Paris region. This was rather unnerving as they all knew that the Spitfires could not accompany them anywhere near as far as that: and they would have to fly the last 100 miles or so unescorted and, worse still, have to fly back unescorted after the attack when all surprise would have been lost. It was a prospect which filled some with gloom especially those crews who were close to the number of operations (30) when they would be 'rested' and posted away.

Once or twice the operation, whatever it might be, was 'on' only to be cancelled. This did not help to reduce tension although none of these mournful speculations seem to have bothered the ever optimistic Ivor Broom.

Finally, on 12 August, the day dawned when the special job definitely would take place. The conditions were at last right and, according to custom, the crews trooped into briefing — soon all would be revealed.

By now even the new crews knew where to look. There was a big wall map behind the officer giving the briefing and the crews' initial attention was directed to it and the piece of red tape which stretched from the start point, usually West Raynham, to wherever it was that the target would be.

As the map was exposed an audible intake of breath could be heard. The red tape crossed the Channel, crossed over Holland, passed close by the Ruhr and terminated near Germany's fourth largest city — Cologne. Cologne had been raided many times by the night bombers but it was far beyond any target that day bombers had attempted to reach. This was to be the spectacular of all 'spectaculars.' It would also be by far the largest number of Blenheims that 2 Group had, or ever would, launch in daylight. Fifty-four aircraft would be attacking.

The plan, officially known within 2 Group as Operation No. 77, was fraught with danger. To reach Cologne, aircraft would have to fly for 150 miles over occupied or enemy territory, almost entirely without fighter support and, even if an element of surprise could be achieved on the way to the target, there was no hope of having any such advantage on the 150 miles back, when, as like as not, a number of the attackers would have been damaged and unable to keep up with their colleagues.

Given that Blenheims at low level could cruise at only about 200mph on their way to the target and a bit faster when less laden on the way back and when maximum power could be used without fear of running out of petrol, it all added up to about an hour and a half of extremely hazardous flight — ninety minutes of sheer anxiety.

There were two specific targets, both power stations, just outside the city itself. Eighteen Blenheims from 21 and 82 Squadron were to attack the power station at Quadrath while

Blenheims from 18, 107, 114 and 139 Squadron were to attack the main target, the power station at Knapsack where the biggest steam generators in the world were housed. This power station produced over half a million kilowatts of electricity and was the major source of power over a wide industrial area. It produced about twice the power generated by the famous Battersea Power Station in London.

To the RAF's credit, the planners had made enormous efforts to protect the bombers. A large number of Spitfires were detailed to accompany the bombers as far as the Dutch coast and another large number would be awaiting the return of the survivors in the same area. In addition a small number of Westland Whirlwind twin-engined fighters, a new type with a slightly longer range, would rendezvous with the Blenheims outbound and stay with them almost as far as Antwerp.

In addition and in an effort to prevent enemy fighters being in position to attack the outbound Blenheims, a number of diversionary and other schemes had been devised. One of these involved a small number of B-17 four-engined, American built, Flying Fortresses, of which Bomber Command had acquired a handful. One or two were detailed to attack enemy airfields in Holland and as far away as Emden. These attacks were timed to take place about one hour before the time, 12.30, when the Blenheims would be dropping their bombs on Quadrath and Knapsack. The thinking was that the German fighters would rise to attack the big bombers and thus, one hour later, be either refuelling or returning to their airfields and not able to rearm in time to get at the Blenheims.

Nearer the Belgium/French coasts, a different misleading ploy would be effected. This was timed to take place when the Blenheims would be crossing the Dutch coast near Flushing. At that moment Hampdens, from 5 Group Bomber Command, would be staging a Circus type raid near the French port of Le Trait. This, too, should have the effect of drawing enemy fighters away from the path of the attacking Blenheims.

As a final diversion, other Flying Fortresses would be bombing the town of Cologne itself from about 30,000ft as this was the only bomber that could reach such heights. This, it was hoped, would draw the Me 109s and Fw 190s away from the low level attackers operating nearly 6 miles lower down.

For the time when the Blenheims would be returning, another 'Circus', this time in the Calais area, had been planned and would be carried out by Blenheims of 226 Squadron accompanied by the usual massive fighter support. 226 Squadron also provided two more Blenheims to act as navigation leaders for the Spitfires over the North Sea as they would be beyond range of their Sector Controllers. Sadly these two Blenheims encountered Me 109s and were shot down although they did lead the Spitfires to the correct interception point and thus enabled them to escort the returning Blenheims back to UK.

The 114 Squadron attackers included Sgt I G Broom and his crew. By then they had been assigned a regular aircraft, a Blenheim IV:V-6391, identified by its letter 'V' (for Victor). This was boldly painted on its sides along with the squadron marking of RT. In full, therefore, the aircraft was smarked 'V-RT' on its port side with an RAF roundel placed between the 'V' and the 'RT.'

To Ivor Broom, who almost alone seems to have had no qualms about this memorable raid, the operation for him was uneventful except that he was fascinated by the sight of the Dutch people waving and cheering as his aircraft swept by literally at house top height. He recalls that the reception given him by the Dutch people brought home to him what the war was all about and made it seem all worth while. The Dutch, below, were occupied by a brutal foreign power.

Ivor knew when his aircraft had crossed over the frontier with Germany because suddenly the people below no longer waved! A curious way of obtaining a navigation fix! His target, the huge Knapsack complex of power stations and cooling towers was easily recognised (which may be why it had been chosen as Krupps factory at Essen would have been a better known one and a few miles less to fly). He dropped his bombs and, noticing that others were also on target, turned for home. During this time he never saw an enemy fighter and points out, 'There probably was a lot of flak but inside an aircraft with engines flat out, you do not hear flak. So, unless it happens to hit you or you see black puffs of smoke bursting around you, there is no way of telling if it is there.' There was much smoke around both from the power generator's normal discharge and also from bursting bombs and this may have helped to obscure any near misses from flak.

It appeared that the raid caught the enemy partially by surprise and although twelve of the fifty-four Blenheims were lost, it remains uncertain as to what caused the losses*. It seems likely that at least two were lost in a collision and that flak probably accounted for many of the others. The dreaded fighters apparently did not arrive until at least well after the attack — if at all.

The raid has been described in dramatic terms by some of those who took part. A WOP/AG Eric Chandler has written:

Nothing was sighted until near the enemy coast-line on the way home. Ahead I sighted a row of dots in the sky and knew that the Messerschmitts had at last found us. I 'drew a bead' on one as it approached rapidly but before I could fire he was waggling his wings as if to say, 'Don't shoot — I'm a friend not a foe.' I've never been so pleased in my life to see a Spitfire.

However, all was not then plain sailing. The aircraft in which Eric was flying received three severe jolts. It had been hit and one engine began to fail. His pilot managed to get the aircraft back to base before all power was lost and, upon examination, the cooked remains of three seagulls were discovered in the engine cowling. To paraphrase Eric's comments, 'To have been brought down by a Messerschmitt would have been understandable but by a seagull, that would have been a major disgrace!'

The raid was regarded as so much routine by Ivor Broom

* P/O Jimmy Corfield was one of those shot down. Ivor and he had been through all their training together and Jimmy had been one of the unfortunate four to have been given the Red Endorsement. His brother, also a keen RAF pilot, has researched his death and discovered that he was shot down by Adolf 'Dolfo' Galland, the famous German leader and ace. The two have corresponded about the event.

that he makes no comment in his log book other than his usual brief account of the operation, 'Low level raid on Knapsack power station at Cologne.' In all he had been 4 hours 30 minutes in the air: much of it unescorted at 50ft over hostile territory.

Another pilot describes the scene:

> Over Germany we flew below the level of the houses. My observer called me up when we were seven minutes from the target and, at that moment, another Blenheim squadron crossed us. They were on their way to bomb the other power station. The air was alive with British bombers.

It was just as well that the Messerschmitts had been led astray as a few months earlier when 82 Squadron had sent a force of a dozen aircraft to bomb Aalburg airfield in Denmark from high level, they had run into Messerschmitts which had shot down eleven of them. The only survivor was one which had turned back with engine problems. This was the second time that the unfortunate 82 Squadron had lost eleven out of twelve. Fifty-four Blenheims, 150 miles into Germany and without a fighter escort, would have presented the German fighters with an almost unprecedented chance to slaughter not just one Blenheim squadron of 2 Group, but half a dozen.

In the debriefing which followed, the newspaper reporters were, for once, allowed to be present. Consequently, as was intended, the Press made much of this daring raid and it was boosted up to be a great triumph. As one of the Blenheim pilots was the well-known Test cricketer, Bill Edrich, the Press tended to concentrate upon him with headlines such as, 'Germany hit for six.'

The Blenheims carried two 500lb bombs and all who returned were adamant that with such a big target so easily identified by the towers and tall chimneys, it was impossible not to have dropped accurately. Quite complicated dropping instructions had been worked out with different formations dropping from 50 to 1,500ft so as to reduce the chances of collision over the target area.

It so happened that when a number of Blenheims were

over the power stations, a gunner from an adjacent aircraft took a dramatic picture which showed smoke belching from Knapsack power station from dropped bombs. The picture also showed a sky full of flak bursts and the rear part of a Blenheim in the immediate foreground. This aircraft was sufficiently close for its RAF letters to be identified as 'V-RT.' The picture was featured in a number of British newspapers and periodicals such as the prestigious *Illustrated London News* and it was reproduced around the world, as British propaganda was quick to cash in on details of the raid and this photo. This was the aircraft flown by Sgt pilot Ivor Broom.

Later the well-known RAF artist, Michael Turner, produced a dramatic painting of the Knapsack power station attack, almost beneath one of the low flying Blenheims, and which aircraft did he depict? It was V-6391 again with 'RT-V' clearly showing on its starboard side. None mentioned Ivor Broom nor had Ivor regarded it more than just his eighth operation but his aircraft was viewed and admired by millions around the world!

The loss of twelve Blenheims was tragic but the boost it gave to the British peoples and others including, it was hoped, the Russians then in full retreat, was very considerable. It showed that Britain, although having been put on one side to be dealt with later by Hitler, was prepared to risk much to succour her desperately fighting ally which at that time was having to absorb the full fury of the German war machine as it marched, daily, closer and closer to the key cities of Moscow and Leningrad.

The message to Germany was that essential military installations, within the industrial heart of Germany, could be attacked in broad daylight. How many extra AA gunners and fighter aircraft were added to bolster up the defences of that part of Germany was never known but every one was one less that Russia would have to face. In all probability the damage was not that great and power stations, even if totally destroyed — and neither of these were anything like being totally destroyed — can be covered by others to some degree. As Britain herself knew, a determined people will repair structures with amazing rapidity while the general population was prepared to go without light and power for a period.

The Knapsack raid, by which name it is generally known (although the other power station was nearly as big), was almost the last of the daylight 'spectaculars.' Later that month Rotterdam was attacked for a second time and another dozen Blenheims were lost although this was a much smaller effort. The attack took place on 28 August and, not for the first time, Winston Churchill himself became involved in the pros and cons of such raids.

The AOC of 2 Group, Air Vice-Marshal D F Stevenson, had been dubbed 'Black' Stevenson by some who considered that he was casting his crews into, if not fire, then into too warm spots.* On the next day Churchill was to write in a memorandum:

Such losses [as the twelve Blenheims lost over Rotterdam] might be acceptable in attacking *Scharnhorst, Gneisenau* or a southbound Tripoli convoy ... While I greatly admire the bravery of the pilots, I do not want them pressed too hard.

He went on to compare the actions of the Blenheims with the notorious Charge of the Light Brigade. With his sense of history, coupled with the widely held belief that the Charge of the Light Brigade was a waste of human material, it was not hard to deduce that the PM, in a subtle way, was casting doubts upon the policies of 2 Group. He implied that lives were being cast away for glory rather than for military gain.

By the end of the next month, A V-M Stevenson was being replaced and 2 Group flew no more 'spectacular' raids. Within a few more months, the RAF had ceased, entirely, to send Blenheims from the UK against the enemy. Enough was enough!

Sgt pilot Broom's period with 114 Squadron was also drawing to a close but before he left the Unit, he carried out

---

* Also known as 'Butch' or 'Butcher'.

another low-level raid on an enemy installation but it was hardly a spectacular one. On 21 August he was among the formation which attacked the big steel works at Ijmuiden, a few miles north-east of Amsterdam. As this was almost within Spitfire range and as it was on the Dutch coast and therefore could be approached entirely from over the sea, the risks were slight by comparison with the Knapsack venture. As it was a low level attack the bombs, carried by the Blenheims, would have been triggered by fuses with an eleven seconds delay built into them. This was always the case with such attacks as the eleven seconds gave the aircraft time to be clear of the explosion. Without the time delay, it was likely that the low-level attacking aircraft would blow itself up as well as its target. The big Ijmuiden steel works were the subject of several attacks as they constituted an important part of the Nazi industrial strength which now included factories in Belgium, France, the Netherlands as well as those seized pre-war in Czechoslovakia and Austria. Much of Europe was now turning out arms for Hitler and his work force had been enormously increased by the millions of slave workers who had been forcibly obliged to work in these manufacturing plants. This is why Britain was doing all she could to harass Germany from the West while Panzer armies continued to drive deeper and deeper into Russia.

This particular Ijmuiden raid turned out to be the last (and 12th) operation for Ivor Broom and his crew while serving 114 Squadron. However, they spent the last week of August carrying out a number of 'Army Co-operation Exercises' which were probably laid on to enable ground gunners to practice aiming at low-flying fast aircraft. They might even have been exercises just to get new army recruits familiar with the sight and sound of low-flying bombers as they screamed overhead almost low enough to part their hair. Until actually experienced, this could be very frightening to youths who only months before may have been clerks, shop assistants, labourers or just schoolboys. Ivor recalls that when they were briefed about these by the West Raynham Station Commander, G/Capt The Earl of Bandon, he described it as a chance 'to prang the

Pongos.'* A Pongo being the rather derogatory slang that the RAF used when referring to their Army brethren.

After a spell of leave, Ivor, still with the same crew, found that they were to be posted overseas. Although, initially, the destination was unknown it was quite a thrill as none of them had been outside Britain other than in their aircraft — and that didn't count! Guesses were made — probably the Far East but, possibly, the Middle East.

First they picked up a new aircraft and spent a couple of days testing and checking it. It was a Blenheim Mark IV fitted with long range tanks. Next they had to fly it to Portreath in Cornwall which, by then, had become an RAF airfield from where most aircraft destined for overseas, *via* Gibraltar, departed.

At that time few, if any, RAF bombers were flown direct to the Middle East non-stop as they lacked the range. Also it was taking a risk to fly over Nazi-controlled Europe. The standard way of reaching the Middle East, where a large Air Force was being maintained, was to fly from Portreath in Cornwall to Gibraltar and then, after a short rest, Gibraltar-Malta and, again after a rest, Malta-Egypt. But even these flights required bombers to be fitted with extra long range fuel tanks.

At Portreath, a surprise awaited Ivor and his crew. A number of Blenheims would be making the journey and a leader was required: someone with experience to shepherd the others. Sgt pilot I G Broom, because he had taken part in a dozen operations with 114 Squadron and had flown all of fifty-five hours in Blenheims, was found to be the pilot with the most experience!

The flight from Portreath had its dangers and not only from the enemy. It taxed the range of the aircraft even with the extra tankage and required careful navigation for a route which was entirely over water. This was because neither Spain nor Portugal, both allegedly neutral countries in the conflict, were to be overflown. The Luftwaffe kept a sizable long-range fighter

---

* 'Paddy', the 5th Earl of Bandon, had been the popular CO of 82 Squadron when it first lost eleven out of twelve of its aircraft. He did much to rebuild the Unit and restore morale.

force in Western France — it was there to give extra protection to the U-boat bases of Brest, Lorient, St Nazaire and La Palice — and so the route, across the Bay of Biscay, had to be well out to sea. After passing Cape Finisterre (north-west Spain), the coasts of Spain and Portugal could, if given good visibility, be kept in sight until, rounding the south-east of Iberia, the crew headed due east towards Gibraltar via the Straits of that name.

After overcoming these navigation problems, another difficulty was the landing at Gibraltar by which time the fuel would have been almost spent. It required a landing by a tired crew on the short narrow strip of land that separates Gibraltar from mainland Spain. This had been turned into a runway which later would be extended by building out into the sea as it used every inch of the land available. It was necessary to approach Gibraltar with great care so as not to, inadvertently, over-fly any part of Spain. Quite apart from Spain's permanent resentment against Britain for retaining the Rock on her doorstep, it was now under the Fascist General Franco who leaned heavily towards Germany, being personally indebted to Hitler for the help that he had been given during the Spanish Civil War of 1936–39. Indeed it was a surprise that Spain had not openly declared war on Hitler's side. Consequently Spanish gunners overlooking Gibraltar were more than eager to fire at any RAF 'plane that happened to stray over her frontier as this was considered a legitimate target.

Although the landing strip was adequate in length for Blenheims, being a type which did not require long runways, its proximity to the huge towering Rock, made approaches and landings tricky. Frequently they had to be made cross-wind and, more often, the aircraft would be caught in a low-level gust or eddy as the wind swirled around the great Rock. Wind shear was always an airman's enemy and could bring a 'plane down in seconds. A graveyard of crashed bombers lined the landing strip as if to remind the tired pilot that extreme caution was necessary!

The flight had taken seven hours and forty minutes and was by far the longest that the lone pilot on board had ever undertaken. However, Ivor and his small flock all arrived safely largely due to Bill North who was proving to be an able and reliable navigator. Bill's navigational skills were an asset that Ivor would shortly be needing and would play a big part in the successes to come.

After a couple of days enjoying the shops, food and drinks in a colony which seemed to be as full of goods as it ever was, in strict variance with the tightening rations and paucity of goods available in the UK, Ivor and his cohorts departed on the next long leg of his journey to the Middle East and possibly beyond.

For the Gibraltar-Malta leg, the fuel tanks were filled to the brim. Again navigation would play a part as the whole flight would have to take place over the waters of the Mediterranean although, provided the visibility was good, there would be occasional glimpses of the mountains of Africa to the south and perhaps those of Sardinia to the north. The Italian island of Pantelleria would also have to be skirted around when approaching Malta. Throughout, especially when nearing Malta, enemy aircraft might be sighted. However, none were seen and again Bill North's navigation rose to the occasion for after an uneventful flight of seven hours, Ivor Broom safely brought the Blenheim aircraft Z7618 on to Luqa's runway. This being Malta's largest airfield and the one used by transit bombers *en route* to Egypt.

In all Ivor had led a flock of six Blenheims safely all the way from UK. However, on the last leg to Malta, one of the others pulled alongside and indicated by gestures that he was heading off in a slightly different direction. The briefing had contained orders to keep strict radio silence and Ivor was unable to deduce or ascertain his reasoning. Bill North was a competent navigator and Ivor was happy with the course that they were on. In any event in daylight, if badly off course, land on one side or the other was bound to show up soon. That was the last that Ivor or anyone else saw of this Blenheim as it landed up in Sicily and the crew were incarcerated as prisoners of war!

At night, this was not too uncommon as the crafty Italians,

having been forewarned by spies overlooking Gibraltar that a formation was *en route* to Malta, did their utmost to lure doubtful navigators towards Sicily by contacting them on the RAF frequencies and giving them false bearings to follow. Sadly, they caught quite a few Wellingtons and other aircraft by this ruse including one in which a senior General was travelling on his way to take up an important command in the Middle East.

But before Ivor and his crew could even start to plan the next stage of his journey, an event took place which was to change the entire course of the life of pilot Ivor Broom. Fate had intervened — fate in the person of the pugnacious Air Officer Commanding Malta, Air Vice-Marshal Hugh Pughe Lloyd.

CHAPTER FIVE

Hi-jacked!

The three Sergeants had speculated regarding their final destination and the general opinion was that since they had been provided with RAF maps as far as Singapore, this British outpost was their most likely destination. This kind of natural logic did not however always prevail in postings by a still rapidly expanding Service as it was not unknown, for example, that some had been kitted out with tropical gear, only to be posted to Iceland!

Singapore was then a British possession and, with its vast Naval base was one of the Empire's bastions in the Far East with both an impressive army and RAF presence there to back up the Royal Navy's great base. There had been rumblings of a possible conflict in the Far East between the USA and Japan as both regarded the Pacific Ocean and its islands as their particular sphere of influence. Japan had invaded China and, ever since November 1935, had steadily been taking it over — piece by piece and in the process had been inflicting appalling atrocities upon the vanquished citizens. Japan's aggressive operation had incurred the wrath of the civilised world causing the USA to impose economic sanctions and especially to deny her the oil and iron ore which was needed to continue the war against China. It was thought that, with Holland now enslaved by Nazi Germany, Japan might seize the opportunity to invade the Dutch East Indies with their plentiful oil supplies. In this event Britain would do all, within her powers, to assist her Dutch ally. Consequently, with the Battle of Britain won and Germany now locked in a gigantic struggle with the USSR, the RAF was reinforcing its Singapore and other Far East stations with more modern types such as the Blenheims.

The position of Malta was very different. This island group*, also then a British possession with a strategically

---

* Malta is a group of three inhabited islands but the group is generally known as 'Malta' as it is by far the biggest and most important of the three.

important Naval Base, was already under an almost constant air attack. At first by the Italian Regia Aeronautica, immediately following upon the decision of the Italian Dictator Benito Mussolini, taken on 10 June 1940, to enter the war on Hitler's side and later by the Luftwaffe too, after Germany had been obliged to prop up the faltering Italians in their attempted campaign to seize Egypt.

It was only after September 1940, when the huge Italian armies had first cautiously crossed into Egypt, that Malta really became of vital importance in the Second World War. Any war in the North African desert depended almost entirely upon what supplies could be brought to an area which produced virtually nothing as, in 1940, no oil had been discovered in that part of the world. British supplies to her Army defending Egypt, also a country then under British dominance, would normally pass through the Mediterranean. Axis supplies to Tripoli, the only major port in Libya or Tripolitania — both then Italian Colonies — would have to run the gauntlet past Malta. The island stands at the cross roads of the Mediterranean, blocking either the north-south or the east-west sea routes.

Pre-war thinking was that if Britain was at war with Italy, a likely prospect after Mussolini's defiance of the League of Nations and his seizure of first Abyssinia and then Albania, then Malta could not be defended. It lies only 55 miles from Sicily where the Italian Dictator, having built up a big force of fast modern bombers, the SM 79s, had established half a dozen air bases from which to launch them. Consequently in 1940, Malta lacked RAF airfields* and fighters. However, by improvisation the RAF, by using at first hastily assembled Royal Navy Sea Gladiators which happened to be in packing cases on the island, had quickly demonstrated that the vaunted Regia Aeronautica was far from being the deadly force that it portended to be. A few Hurricanes were swiftly added to Faith, Hope and Charity (the names given to the original Gladiators) and Malta held firm.

---

* In 1940 the Royal Navy alone had a small military airfield at Halfar for its Fleet Air Arm (FAA) aircraft but a much larger one was nearing completion for the RAF at Luqa.

Later the arrival, in Sicily, of General Geisler's X *Fliegerkorps* of the Luftwaffe gave the enemy a material advantage over the small RAF presence in Malta which then consisted of only two Hurricane I fighter squadrons and, occasionally, a Fulmar or two off a Royal Navy carrier, plus a Blenheim squadron from the UK and a Wellington squadron from the Middle East.

Happily for Malta, the dominant Luftwaffe in Sicily was largely withdrawn after 22 June 1941 when the perfidious attack by Germany upon her Russian ally was launched. As soon as it was appreciated that Malta again only had the Italians to overcome in the skies, it was arranged for a Blenheim squadron to fly to Malta for a period of approximately one month at a time: the one relieving the other. They were drawn from 2 Group and, after a detachment of 21 Squadron had proved the feasibility of the operation, 139 Squadron then arrived in May '41 to be relieved by 82 Squadron. Next came 110 Squadron to be relieved in mid-July by 105 Squadron. 107 was in the process of relieving 105 at the time when Ivor Broom was testing and checking Blenheim Z7618 immediately prior to his departure from Portreath.

By the time that 105 Squadron arrived in Malta, the Axis convoys which carried all the supplies, men, oil and even some food to General Rommel, whom Hitler had placed in charge of all German-Italian armies in North Africa, had become well defended. They now posed as big a threat to any attacking Blenheim as had the well-defended shipping plying along the Dutch/German coasts. Although Blenheims were scoring many successes against these convoys, they were also losing crews at an alarming rate.

By then a new forceful AOC had arrived to take charge of all RAF and Fleet Air Arm operations from Malta. This was Air Vice-Marshal Hugh Pughe Lloyd, widely known as just 'Hugh Pughe' after his rhyming Christian names. Hugh Pughe had been Senior Air Staff Officer in 2 Group under AOC 'Black' Stevenson and was every bit as offensive minded as that tough character. His orders, on taking over command in Malta, were to stop the supply ships reaching Rommel. This meant stopping the convoys reaching Tripoli as this was the only port of any size in the whole of Libya and Tripolitania. Air Vice-Marshal Hugh Pughe Lloyd was determined to carry out his instructions.

Thanks to excellent intelligence reports, backed by ULTRA intercepts and first class aerial reconnaissance provided by the Luqa-based 69 Squadron, the AOC knew when the convoys were at sea. With the Wellingtons to bomb the departure ports as well as Tripoli, with Swordfish of 830 FAA Squadron torpedoing the ships at night and with the Blenheims attacking by day, the enemy losses were heavy. On top of which, with the Luftwaffe occupied elsewhere, the Royal Navy moved in a light striking force — Force K — which supplemented the great carnage already being achieved by the U Class submarines based in Malta. Since Rommel had to be sent a regular tonnage of supplies, the ships carrying these, and the escorting Italian destroyers, both became more and more heavily armed.

105 had flown in on 28 and 30 July. Twelve Blenheims had left the UK but one had crashed in Portugal en route. The eleven were commanded by Hughie Edwards, VC, DFC, now promoted to Wing Commander. Almost at once they began to hit ships but to lose aircraft in the process. By 11 August they had lost one Flight Commander S/Ldr Goode, DFC, and two more crews were lost later that week. Hughie Edwards departed for another assignment at the end of the month, whereupon Wing Commander Scivier, AFC, took command of 105 Squadron. He was known to Ivor as he had been in charge of the conversion flight at 13 OTU, Bicester, when Ivor was being taught to fly the Blenheim.

Sadly the losses continued with two Blenheims hitting the masts of the ships they were attacking and three more fell to Italian fighters protecting a stricken ship which the Blenheims were trying to finish off. Others simply failed to return from missions.

To make good the losses, Hugh Pughe had to take desperate measures and a young Sgt pilot, Charney*, was hastily commissioned and almost immediately promoted to S/Ldr to

---

* The author had taught him to fly pre-war at the Liverpool Flying Club.

fill a vacancy caused by another loss. Sadly, during almost the same week, S/Ldr Charney was also lost.

The situation is well described by S/Ldr John Greenhalgh, a Hurricane pilot who had been promoted and given a ground job at Air Headquarters in Valletta. He has written:

I was sent up to Luqa to command the Blenheims … the squadrons had suffered frightful casualties and acting promotions from Pilot Officer to Squadron Leader were quite common … I never flew a Blenheim but, although instructed not to fly, I did make a few sorties as a navigator … in one we were badly shot up, the gunner was killed but we managed to get back to Malta. We were lucky.

This then was the position when Sgt pilot I G Broom successfully led his flock of new Blenheims into Malta during the evening of 18 September 1941. But, of the eleven crews who had flown in with 105 Squadron two months earlier, only two now remained.

Air Vice-Marshal H P Lloyd was never one who played safe or abided strictly 'by the book.' Nor was Malta a place where the book ruled. It had survived in the first place by breaking all the rules and defending itself with the Admiralty's Sea Gladiators and, ever since the days of Faith, Hope and Charity had shown that Malta could be defended, it continued to improvise. Castor oil was used for hydraulic fluid, thick rope instead of tail wheels, Hurricanes as night fighters and the AOC was adept at seizing aircraft which arrived in Malta to refuel on their way to the Middle East and beyond. In Hugh Pughe's eyes almost any means justified the ends and his 'end' was to stop supplies going to the armies which were opposing the British 8th Army in the North African desert. If Rommel had been able to overcome this army Egypt would have fallen into German hands and a clear way to the Arabian oil fields would have been opened.

With the situation prevailing the outcome was obvious and Sgt Ivor Broom, who had successfully guided a flock of Blenheims to Malta, was very clearly too good a man to be allowed to go further. He, his Blenheim and crew were immediately incorporated into the sad remnants of 105 Squadron ... 'just for a week or two while 107 get themselves operational.'

Normally upon joining a new unit, and especially when first arriving in a strange country, a crew is given time to acclimatise, to become familiar with the airfields and local landmarks and generally to assimilate themselves into the new environment. However the RAF in Malta was not run on normal lines. Petrol was always in short supply and was not, therefore, expended on training flights. As enemy fighters were always liable to appear suddenly overhead, all daytime flying was reduced to the absolute minimum. Due to the almost daily raids upon the three military airfields which by 1941 had been developed, it was folly to keep aircraft doing nothing when at any time they could be destroyed by bombing or low-level strafing.

After only the briefest low-level bombing practice upon the deserted rock Filfla off the south-west tip of Malta — a short twenty-minute flight — Ivor and his two crew men found themselves on operations with 105 Squadron. Less than two days had lapsed since they had departed from the luxuries of Gibraltar.

The three possible operations which the Blenheims carried out — and carried out with grim determination — from Malta were:

— A low-level strike against a ship or convoy in a known position, as verified by aerial reconnaissance or positive Intelligence methods.

— A sweep in the hope of sighting enemy ships, acting upon less positive Intelligence and without verification.

— An attack against a land objective in Tripolitania or Sicily, such as ships in harbour, barracks or industrial targets, such as oil storage tanks or chemical plants.

If a shipping sortie turned out in practice tote unproductive and if the Blenheims were sufficiently close to enemy held territory, then they had a carte blanche permission to bomb and strafe virtually anything of military value that they might find over land. Hugh Pughe did not believe in wasting petrol without getting results!

Whether, in hi-jacking Ivor and his crew in Malta, Hugh Pughe knew that he was co-opting a fellow Welshman into his team, is unknown but, in such matters, his judgment proved to be unerring and he chose with uncanny precision as events were to show.

Ivor Broom's first operation from Malta — and his 15th overall (the two long flights to get to Malta officially counted as 'operational flights') — is as memorable as any. Six Blenheims, three each from 105 and 107 Squadrons, were detailed to bomb the German/Italian barracks at Horns on the coast near Tripoli. They flew as one close formation but in two 'vics.' The Blenheims of 105 Squadron were led by Wing Commander Scivier in person. Those of 107 were led by Sgt Bill Jackson. Ivor's position was on the immediate port side of his Wing Co, with the other 'vic' on his port. This meant that he was hemmed in on both sides.

W/Cdr Scivier was a squadron commander who led from the front and only the day before he, accompanied by W/Cdr 'Bunny' Harte, the CO of the newly-arrived 107 Squadron, had attacked a ship in the face of murderous fire from the six destroyers which were defending it. One engine of Scivier's aircraft was hit and set on fire but he somehow managed to get the Blenheim back to Malta and be sufficiently undaunted to lead the remnants of his squadron into action the next day.

As the six Blenheims approached the coast of North Africa, with all eyes searching for the Horns barracks, the two leaders almost simultaneously realised that they were about to cross the coast a little too far to the west of their target. Quickly they both turned their 'vics' to port to correct their approach. At low level, all turns are difficult for a pilot of a 'vic' who happens to be on the inside of the turn and Ivor found himself almost squeezed between Scivier's aircraft and the ground. However, he managed to extricate himself from under his leader and within seconds was over the target and dropping his bombs.

With an aircraft in a banked turn to port, its starboard wing restricts vision on that side. Tom Williams flying on the starboard side of Sgt Jackson's formation therefore had no knowledge that the 105 'vic' on his right had turned into and across the three 107 aircraft. A mid-air collision resulted with Williams's starboard propeller almost slicing Scivier's Blenheim in two. Other parts of the two Blenheims also came into contact and Ivor, out of the corner of his eye, saw his Wing Commander's aircraft dive straight down into the target area just below them. He assumed that the other aircraft must have met a similar fate.

The four uninvolved aircraft well and truly plastered the target which included oil storage tanks and immediately headed back towards Malta. The bombs had been set with eleven seconds delay fuses which had left the surviving Blenheims time to get away unscathed as the attack had achieved almost total surprise.

Ivor's next actions show both his calmness and leadership qualities which, till then, had not been called for. Although it was his first flight out of sight of Malta and his first with 105 Squadron, he calmly called up the remaining aircraft to advise that, since W/Cdr Scivier was obviously lost, he would take over and lead them back to Malta. The others then willingly fell in behind him.

After gaining height to about 1,000ft and flying a few miles northwards towards Malta, Ivor's rear gunner, Sgt Les Harrison, reported that he could see a fifth Blenheim struggling along behind them and, more ominously, it was being harried by a CR 42 (Italian) fighter. Ivor at once called up the others, told them to continue towards Malta and announced that he was turning back to see if he could aid the lone and damaged straggler. He had no doubt that it was the Blenheim into which his Wing Commander had turned.

It was indeed Tom Williams who, in spite of a battered nose which had hit the protruding upper turret of Scivier's aircraft and prop blades which had been bent back when slicing into the fuselage of the other aircraft, was still struggling to control his stricken Blenheim.

Williams certainly needed help as, when colliding, his pitot tube had been knocked off and the loss of this meant that both his altimeter and air speed indicator were completely unserviceable. Also, due to the nose damage and the bent props, the Blenheim was vibrating like an old Army truck. Fortunately for both Ivor and Tom Williams, the CR 42 sheared off and made no attack upon either of them.

Williams' Blenheim, Z9606, managed to hold together all the way back to Malta although the port engine was now leaking oil and the blister which housed the Browning guns had largely been demolished as this had also caught the other 'plane. It speaks well for the strength of the Blenheim to have survived such a severe contact and to remain basically still in one piece. Tom Williams' immediate reactions must have been razor sharp, too.*

With help from Ivor alongside, Tom Williams managed to land the aircraft safely at Luqa but none of the three occupants ever again operated from Malta.

It was quite a baptism of fire for Ivor Broom but it confirmed, on his first operation from the island, that AOC Hugh Pughe Lloyd had picked himself a winner. Doubtless in the weeks to come, this incident would be remembered by the Air Vice-Marshal.

It would seem that Ivor and his crew had escaped the horrors of 2 Group's low level shipping attacks only to find themselves in a similar situation. It was a case of 'out of the frying pan, into the fire.' But which was the worse: the frying pan or the fire?

With the benefit of hindsight, it transpired that Ivor and his crew were the lucky ones as the other Blenheim crews who were allowed to continue to Singapore, arrived shortly before the Japanese set that part of the world on fire. Almost to a man they were either killed or suffered the fate of being prisoners of the merciless Japanese.

The next operation for Sgt Broom and his crew was a shipping sweep in the Gulf of Sirte in which Tripoli lies. Although no shipping was sighted, the Blenheim crews later enjoyed themselves blasting away at anything that moved on

---

* To this day, over fifty years later, Tom's navigator keeps in touch with Ivor with a card sent annually, to commemorate 'another year on borrowed time.'

the North African coastal road. This always heartened the crews and raised morale.

In the see-saw war which raged for 2.5 years along that North African coast, practically all the action took place on, or close to, the one long road (which Mussolini had built at great cost) which hugged the coast the whole 1,000 miles from Tripoli eastwards until joining the Egyptian coastal road to Alexandria. To the north of it lay the waters of the Mediterranean to the south, a vast sea of sand. The road was always busy with military traffic; everything from motorcyclists to tanks. A road of such length could not be defended and aircraft coming in low from over the sea could launch surprise attacks with bombs and machine guns. Crews never had to wait long before finding a suitable target.

These lightning attacks upon the road were the air gunners' delight. The aircraft was unlikely to be hit by AA fire while, for as long as ammunition lasted, the gunner could blast away at cars, trucks, buses, troops on the march and tanks to his heart's desire. Near Tripoli itself, there was also a coastal railway and bombs would be reserved for stations, trains or barrack blocks.

All Ivor wrote in his log book was: 'Shipping sweep. Nothing sighted. Attacked MT convoy in Tripoli.'

Two days later in Z7853, the aircraft of 105 Squadron which seems to have been assigned to him (did someone more senior grab hold of the almost new Z7618?), Ivor carried out his first low-level attack in the other direction on an airfield in Sicily. Raids upon ground targets in Sicily were more fraught with danger than those around Tripoli. The Regia Aeronautica (and the Luftwaffe if there in strength) kept hundreds of fighters there on half-a-dozen airfields. Sicily probably also had radar and the attackers were liable to find themselves being chased back to Malta by 'planes with much greater speed and fire power.

This particular raid was part of a big overall plan to give whatever help it could to a British convoy from Gibraltar which was then nearing Malta. The island was fast running short of everything it needed and, just as Rommel in the desert needed constant supplies for his *Afrika Korps* and the Italian armies, so also did Malta need to be constantly supplied with all it needed to sustain the population and continue the war. While the Italian bombers did not always threaten, their torpedo carrying SM 79s had proved to be a determined and courageous foe. Also earlier in the war, the Germans had given a number of JU 87 dive bombers to strengthen the Regia Aeronautica and these flown by men of the 96th Gruppo posed an additional threat to the incoming convoy. At such times Malta's defences would be temporarily reinforced by Beaufighters and other aircraft flown in from the Middle East; in this case Beaufighters of 272 Squadron and a few long-range fighter Blenheims of 113 Squadron. Everything available was being used to defend the arrival of the ships and to make life difficult on the airfields from which enemy aircraft might arise to attack the incoming ships. Even Hurricanes fitted locally to carry 40lb bombs were used to attack the Sicilian airfields with some pilots making three sorties per day. In all over two tons of these small bombs were dropped on the airfields at Catania and Comiso. Ivor and his crew were, in effect, doing their bit to ensure that as many ships as possible of the convoy, 'Operation Halberd', reached Malta. With only the *Imperial Star* being lost and with 85,000 tons of supplies unloaded, the great efforts of the RAF paid dividends.

Ivor and his crew flew twice to Sicily on 27 September and, although he had forgotten about it and had to be reminded, on the second operation of that day, his Blenheim was hit by AA fire which shattered the instrument panel only inches in front of his nose! He rarely recalled such 'trifles' in his log book!

The hi-jacked crew had now been in Malta a week during which they had carried out six operational sorties. They had seen their CO crash to his certain death, they had temporarily assumed leadership of a formation, they had bombed a barracks, helped materially to bring back the damaged aircraft of a colleague, had attacked the enemy at low level in both Africa and Europe and had the pilot's instrument panel shattered by ground fire.

Living conditions at that time were tolerable although before long they were to become far worse. Thanks to the Luftwaffe having been withdrawn to fight in Russia, the daily bombing of the island had been left to the Italians. Although the air raid sirens continued to wail several times each day, the damage inflicted was not too serious as some Italian formations clearly had no stomach for the fight. Quite large formations would be built up over Sicily (all watched on Malta radar) and, with fighters around, would head towards Malta where the Hurricanes would be waiting for them. But before the outnumbered Hurricanes could intercept, the bombers would drop their bombs harmlessly into the sea and turn tail back to Sicily. Later that evening Rome radio would announce in their English-speaking broadcasts, how badly the island had been hit. This radio once claimed that the railway marshalling yards outside Valletta had been destroyed and, on another occasion, reported the destruction of military installations at Filfla. Since Malta had no railway and Filfla is only an uninhabited small rock, both claims were curious!

At other times, however, a formation of Italian bombers — usually SM79s or Fiat Br 20s, would come across the island in a tight formation at considerable height. It was as if performing at an Air Display and nothing would deter their excellent formation-keeping; not even when one of the three or five was shot out of the sky. The others would continue as if nothing had happened and would drop their bombs, at times with great accuracy, upon an airfield, fuel storage depot or other military target. One group came so often that they were dubbed 'The Famous Five.'

On the whole the Hurricanes could cope with the Regia Aeronautica although, when the speedy Macchi 202 fighters began to appear in September 1941, they found themselves outpaced. These latest Italian fighters were powered by the same Daimler-Benz engines as were fitted to the Me 109 German fighters and the Mc 202s had the same ability to outdive the British fighters.

Due to their heavy losses by day, the Italians resorted to night bombing but a home-made Malta Night Fighting Unit, using Hurricanes and aided only by searchlights, began to pile up a score against these, too. What Malta lacked — and it was most things — was made good by improvisation. Under their dynamic AOC Hugh Pughe Lloyd, everyone was encouraged to try anything. Hurricanes found themselves being used as fighters-bombers, photo-reconnaissance 'planes and even for the dropping of money, at night, to a spy half way up Mount Etna! In Kalafrana Bay, under strict secrecy, an ex-Norwegian Air Force Heinkel 115 float 'plane was housed and this carried out clandestine missions at night* along with a French Latecoere float 'plane and, later, a three-engined Cant Z506 'stolen' from under the noses of its Italian crew! Swordfish of 830 Squadron FAA were also used to land agents behind enemy lines.** Everything which possibly could be used by the RAF in Malta was used. The AOC saw to this whether it was 'Regular' or not.

At the time of Ivor's arrival in Malta, both food and war supplies were generally getting through. Prior to the loss of the Imperial Star, virtually all ships had arrived whether sailing from Alexandria, as had a March convoy, or from Gibraltar (Operation Halberd). Food was as important as war supplies for Malta was, and still is, one of the most densely populated places in all the world with over a quarter of a million souls occupying an area of only 91 square miles — less than the Isle of Wight. Its rocky surface contains very little arable land and, even before the war, much food had to be imported. The addition of several thousand Service men exacerbated the problem.

The sergeants of 105 Squadron lived away from Luqa at Marsaxlokk near the sea on the south-east of the island. There they seldom saw a bomb or a bomber but on their bus rides to Luqa — often a hair raising experience in itself — they saw many a bomb crater and, while at Luqa, experienced scores of air raid alerts. The RAF personnel at Luqa only took cover

---

* It had been modified locally to carry an agent in one of the aircraft's floats!

** As these biplanes had insufficient fuel to get back, they would be landed at night on a lonely stretch of road where they would drop the agent, refuel by hand from the tins carried and then take-off for return to Malta.

when a red flag was raised to indicate that raiders were almost overhead as, with alerts liable to be in force for many hours each day, little work could have been done otherwise.

At Marsaxlokk, as is a British habit, many of the men made friends with local Maltese and were able to supplement the adequate, but monotonous, diet with eggs, tomatoes etc. Basically the food consisted of whatever was available and, during Ivor's time, this was tins of Maconachies meat and vegetable stew. It was served in every conceivable way; boiled, fried, served in pastry or stewed. When Ivor eventually got back home to the UK and married, he advised his wife that if she ever served him Maconachies M & V stew, she would be divorced! At another time, tins of pilchards appeared at every meal time and there are some who will not touch a pilchard over fifty years thereafter.

Spirits had largely disappeared on the island but a local brewery managed for a while to produce a limited supply of passable beer. The NAAFI had little to offer but the various clubs and dives down Strait Street (known as The Gut), somehow managed to procure, via a dubious Black Market, both food and drinks of a sort: not that Ivor ever touched alcohol or patronised such places.* It was said that Hugh Pughe Lloyd almost encouraged the Black Market. Certainly the proprietors of the clubs and dives were extraordinarily good and generous to the RAF whom they regarded as saviours of the Island.

Sea bathing was good even if barbed wire had at times to be scaled and mined areas avoided. Malta has no sandy beaches except in the bare north-west but, especially when water also ran short, the opportunity to feel clean was welcomed. Many went years without a hot bath as fuel was always in short supply.

RAF aircrew were given the best of what was at hand and, apart from the thought in the minds of Blenheim crews that they might next day be sent on a low-level shipping strike, life on Malta between September and November 1941 was tolerable, although mail from the UK was spasmodic and entertainments few and far between. Leave was not given but, in any case, there was nowhere to go. After one of the cinemas

* 'The Gut' was out-of-bounds to officers.

was hit, with nearly 100 casualties, even this entertainment palled.

For Blenheim pilots, most operations involved flying at 50ft and the exhilaration of flashing over the ground or sea at such a low level made their tasks more endurable. Even when being shot at, there was the thrill of the chase as the pilot ducked and weaved, skidded and turned with heart in mouth. For the air gunners, there was the delight of firing his guns at everything which moved at almost point blank range but the navigators had a poor time. They shared the common danger without any of the compensating features. During attacks, they simply had to sit still and take it. One used to take with him on operations the Army tin hat which all in Malta acquired as protection from shrapnel and, when the aircraft was under fire, he would sit on it! He regarded it as necessary to protect his essentials. Also the navigators, as a 'breed' tended to be older and more seriously inclined. They had been selected for their brains rather than for their youthful enthusiasm and high spirits. Navigators, also, were more likely to be married with family responsibilities and it is little wonder that a few of them reached a point where they were reluctant to continue. They, in particular, were constantly counting each operation, as thirty was the accepted yardmark after which an operational rest was deemed necessary.

After the members of 107 Squadron had all arrived, the sad remains of 105 were allowed to fly to Egypt but Sgt pilot Broom, the 'new boy' who had lately been forcibly incorporated into the unit, found himself posted to the newly arrived 107 Squadron. The 'few weeks' in Malta, which had earlier been mentioned, was turning out to be months rather than weeks. During September, no less than eight Blenheims had been lost and Hugh Pughe, as ever, needed replacements. A pilot such as Ivor, blessed with the ability to survive and one who appeared to be quite unconcerned, was far too precious a man to be allowed to leave the island. Before the month of September was out, Ivor and his crew had completed two Ops with 107; both being low-level strikes on motorised convoys near Beurat on the Tripolitania coastal road in North Africa.

October began with a low-level attack on a chemical works at Catanzara, Sicily, followed by a shipping sweep. Although no merchant ships were sighted, the formation did come upon three destroyers in Zuara harbour. These were not attacked as they were after cargo-carrying vessels. Another shipping sweep around the Gulf of Sirte, also with none sighted, and two more strafing and bombing attacks against transport on the North African coast road followed and deemed 'great fun for the pilot and gunner.' On the second of these on 9 October they attacked a bus that virtually disintegrated in a cloud of smoke after being hit.

Sadly, it was not all one way traffic as, on the same day, two of the four Blenheims that set out on a shipping strike were lost and one of those who failed to return was the 107 Squadron CO, the South African, Wing Commander 'Bunny' Harte. After a brief hiatus, Wing Commander Barnes took command and, to replace losses, it was known that fifteen more Blenheims from 18 Squadron would soon be arriving. It was their turn next to enter the 'lion's den', which Malta had become.

Ivor Broom's twenty-sixth operation on 11 October was his first experience of actually attacking ships. He was one of a formation of six Blenheims which found an enemy convoy in the Gulf of Sirte. Between them, they hit and set on fire a 3,000-4,000 ton merchantman and hit one of the escorting destroyers. However, the cost was the usual high price and two of the six failed to return. This was about the average with 1 in 3 lost.

Much has been written about these low-level strikes against Axis shipping *en route* to Tripoli and their heavily armed escort vessels. Ron Gillman, in his book *Shiphunters**, has described it brilliantly. Ron was another transit Blenheim pilot whom AOC Hugh Pughe Lloyd had shanghaied. Like Ivor he was a Sgt pilot who imagined that he would be flying on to Egypt. As had been the case with Ivor Broom, Hugh Pughe had, with his uncanny judgment, picked himself not just a winner but also a survivor. Before the war was to end Ron Gillman had

---

* Published by John Murray 1976.

been awarded a DFC and a DFM. Post war, he became a senior BEA Captain and test pilot flying more than 100 different types of aircraft. Like Ivor, Ron was to find himself in 107 Squadron.

Less well known than Ron's classic accounts of these low-level attacks is one from WOP/AG Eric Chandler DFM. He describes one attack as under:

It was soon made very clear that, despite hugging the sea, we had been sighted. Black puffs of smoke could be observed and after an interval, which seemed like ages, the sea both ahead and to each side of us started to erupt, as heavy shells hit the water. The formation, still closely following its leader, were turning first to the left, then to the right, slightly rising and falling. It was fascinating to see how the ships' gunners were constantly changing their direction of fire to follow our direction of flight.

At this stage the leading 'vic' of three turned to port while we turned to starboard. Out of the corner of my eye I saw the leading aircraft of the other 'vic', start to smoke from one engine, then the other. A sharp jolt to our own machine not only indicated that we also had been hit but threw me violently against the side of my turret. An unbelievable pain paralysed my right arm. I ducked down to check the arm, quite expecting to find it had been blown off! As I did so, a snaking line of Bofors tracer played across the aircraft, passing through the perspex cover of my turret. This brought me to life with a vengeance and a determination to fight back.

I was amazed to find that we appeared to be flying just below deck level between two destroyers. Everyone on board these vessels were firing weapons of one kind or another and I at once opened up with my two Brownings in reply. Climbing suddenly, we clawed our way up and along the deck of the larger of the merchantmen, releasing our four eleven second delayed bombs as we struggled to clear the superstructure and funnels. Expecting we would then dive away and make for the open sea, I was horrified to find that we were still climbing and making a very clear target for the ships' gunners.

The reason for this was that our pilot had been wounded by a shell, which had torn away the calf of his right leg almost severing the leg from the knee downwards. To add to this, a machine-gun bullet had hit him between the legs. Our observer rushed back to his aid, pushing the control column forward to stop our rate of climb before we stalled. At last out of range we had a quick conference as a tourniquet was applied to the pilot's leg and it was decided to make for the nearest friendly landfall — Malta. We would try to make it before the pilot bled to death or the engines, which were now making very unhealthy noises, packed up.

It was at this point that my radio exploded into my lap and I observed a CR42 curving in for a second attack. I took my time lining up my sights, allowing the necessary deflection, and opened fire at almost the precise moment that he recommenced firing at us. At once his nose went up, then he seemed to slide down, tail first, then turning over, slid into the sea below.

Almost an hour later we were back over Malta. Wheels down, we motored straight in, cutting the engines as we touched the ground. One tyre must have been damaged for we started to swerve at once, ending in a ground spin. Getting out quickly I shouted for help then, scrambling onto the wing, I commenced pulling up and out our wounded pilot; while the observer pushed up from the cockpit.

Help arrived and I recall seeing Atkinson, Doc Monroe and Hugh Pughe Lloyd. We must have looked an awful sight. The observer was covered in blood, the pilot also very bloody but looking as white as a sheet, while I was thick with sweat, dust and dirt. The pilot was awarded the DSO — in my view it should have been a VC. He recovered but never flew operationally again.

Another first hand account comes from yet another Blenheim pilot who also was hijacked, by the aggressive AOC of Malta, to join 107 Squadron. This was a young Australian, F/O Williamson. The AOC was at that time almost desperate for officers who could fly Blenheims as virtually every commissioned pilot of the Blenheim unit had been lost on operations. When F/O Len Williamson arrived with a brand new Blenheim, he stood no chance of proceeding further. And, as before, Hugh Pughe Lloyd had found himself, with his unerring eye, another winner. Len survived and went on to become a highly decorated Air Commodore in the RAAF. Len kept a diary of events in Malta and has written down a full description of all his Malta operations. An extract follows:

Briefed to fly at 1130 with Sergeant Ray Noseda as leader. Very overcast with occasional showers and I was finding it hard to keep my eyes open as I'd been up late the night before. When nearing the coast, spotted a 'plane high up but it didn't pay any attention to us; we closed up just the same. Noseda and I broke off from the main body and I fell in about a hundred yards behind. He pulled up over the sand dunes and as he did so disturbed a flock of ducks which flew into the air straight in front of my 'plane. No time to dodge and the next thing I knew we'd smashed into them. The impact was so great that the nose of the navigator's section was stove in and the heavy bodies of the dead ducks were forced into the aircraft. Arthur was hit in the face by one and just fell forward; blood, guts and feathers filled the cockpit and were kept moving by the fierce slipstream entering the nose.

The kite was very hard to control at this stage, especially as I couldn't see for the blood on the windscreen. The right wing dropped and it was all I could do to keep the kite from diving into the palm trees. Regained control — evidently there had been some obstruction in the right aileron.

Managed to keep Noseda in sight as most of the feathers and mess had blown to the rear. Couldn't get any sense out of Arthur as he was still dazed by the blow he'd received. Aircraft felt OK except for the drag created by the hole in the front so I kept on after the leader. Passed over some Arabs standing by a well and a camel nearby and I kept wondering if I'd be in closer contact with them in the very near future. Suddenly we spotted a train over to the right. 'L' immediately turned into it, attacked but overshot. I was too late to release the first time so came around again and, releasing my bombs early, let them roll along the sand into the train which had now stopped, blowing up the middle.

The occupants began pouring out and ran in all directions. Steep turned and came back firing the front gun into their midst. Too low to take good aim so sprayed with tracer. Dropped the other bombs and could see them bouncing towards the train, however, they bounded a trifle too high and went over the top and into a group of buildings on the side of the line where a lot of passengers had taken shelter and up they went. Noseda had scored more hits on the train and half of it was on its side and the remainder burning. 'L' set course for home and I opened up to catch him. Noticed some smoke to the east where our other 'planes had spotted a convoy to the north of us.

Tallyho came through and a line of bullets swept across the bow. Opened up to 9 boost and threw the old kite around as well as I could but the added drag made us sluggish, a CR42 was stuck dead on our tail and the bullets were whistling around us. I ducked instinctively as one explosive bullet hit the top of the cockpit and the little pieces of metal from it spattered Arthur's hand. Harry put a few bursts into him with no result but we were taking more than we gave out. Caught up with Noseda and formated. The CR2 made several attacks but our combined fire wasn't to his liking and after ten minutes he broke off.

Arthur held up his hand to show me and he was a sorry sight with a face caked with dry blood. Harry came through on the intercom to say that oil was running out of the port engine — it certainly was and the wing was one lake of it. Climbed to 5,000ft in case the engine cut out.

The wireless had been put out of action by some bullets and the IFF aerial broken when we clocked the ducks. The weather was too thick up high and I had to keep close to the leader. It was raining when we came over Malta. I fired a Verey and did a rapid low circuit and landed. As we taxied in, Arthur sat on top looking like a butcher's shop with a dead duck in each hand. There were five of the ducks which were comparatively whole and Harry and Arthur took them to their mess that night and had them cooked!*

Finally Ron Gillman's wireless operation/air gunner, Ron Weeks, has also contributed an account of what it was like to fly from Malta on anti-shipping operations. He writes:

We set course to attack two MV2 escorted by a destroyer … the destroyer opened up accurate fire from 3 miles range … the sea was churned up by machine-gun fire and AA … No. 4, 'floppy' (Sgt W A Hopkinson), went in and must have been hit because he hit the mast and blew up. We, in 5, had no time to swerve and had to fly through the flames of No. 4. No. 6 came after us and 'Grif had an explosive shell through the turret which knocked his tin hat over his eyes and went out the other side. He was jolly lucky. One MV sustained a direct hit from 'Gilly' and was left low in the water.

Ron Gillman, in his book, refers to a loss rate on low-level strikes as nine out of ten but this alarming rate refers to a pilot's total time while in Malta. How many shipping strikes a pilot made was, like so many other things in the life of an RAF crew member, largely a matter of luck.

As a general rule, a crew went on operations one day and was stood down the next. This made him available for the next sortie. That sortie depended entirely upon the military situation of the day and might, or might not, be a shipping strike. It follows therefore that, with good luck, a crew might complete the entire thirty operations without ever being on a shipping strike. Losses on other operations were almost trivial by comparison. It also could result that a pilot, after being assigned a number of shipping strikes, might never sight an enemy ship

* NB. The accounts of Eric Chandler and Len Williamson are taken from the author's book *Faith, Hope& Malta GC* published by Newton Publications 1992. The foreword is by none other than Air Marshal Sir Ivor Broom KCB, CBE, DSO, DFC and two bars, AFC.

to attack. Again Dame Fortune held all the aces.

Including sorties flown from both UK and Malta, Ivor by the end of October 1941 had flown thirty-one operational flights.

Ivor's luck held in other respects, too. On the one sortie which found ships to attack, he had been assigned to fly on the right of the leader. Another pilot approached him with a request. 'Would he be prepared to swap places?' It transpired that this other pilot always found it more difficult to format on the leader's left. Ivor didn't mind on which side he flew and so readily agreed. The leader and the other pilot now flying in the position originally allocated to Ivor, were both shot down and killed. Ivor was the only survivor but he brought back the news that they had left the merchant ship on fire.

As stated before the ratio of losses on shipping strikes which found ships to attack was about 1 in 3 on average. This was about the same cruel loss of life which had occasioned Winston Churchill to question whether 'Butch' Stevenson was asking too much from his 2 Group crews. However, it has to be remembered that the PM had emphasised that such terrible losses might be justified 'for attacks on Tripoli-bound convoys.'

In some respects A V-M Stevenson as AOC 2 Group and A V-M Lloyd as AOC Malta were similar. Lloyd, in fact, had been Stevenson's right-hand man at 2 Group before being promoted and posted to take charge in Malta. Both were aggressive minded and both were determined to stop enemy ships from reaching their destinations. Similarly they were both accused, by some, of being too demanding of the Blenheim crews under their commands. A few called Hugh Pughe Lloyd a butcher behind his back. However, there the similarities ended. The AOC Malta was one of those rare high commanders who could be found at any of the airfields within his bailiwick and because of this he got to know, by name and sight, a number of his fighter and bomber crews. He saw to it that everyone in the RAF knew him by sight and was always prepared to stop and chat with airmen of whatever rank. He was a flamboyant figure in a sky blue car with white wall tyres which everyone easily recognised. His pep talks at a time when Malta was under almost constant aerial bombardment and was fast becoming besieged, were music to the ears of his followers. Hugh Pughe disdained shelters and also denied himself sleep and he was just as liable to appear at Luqa to welcome back night bombers, as he was to send off Blenheims on day-time strikes.

After having completed the magic number of thirty operations, Ivor could have reminded his CO that he was due an operational rest as, by the end of October, his total stood at thirty-one. These now included a second effective shipping strike on 21 October when he took part in an attack in which two ships were claimed as sunk. For this trip, Ivor had a replacement navigator, a Sgt Stanier as Bill North was sick. The conditions in Malta were not conducive to healthy living nor were there adequate medical services if ill. It was not unusual for at least one crew member to have fallen foul of the 'Malta Dog'; a local form of dysentery and a first cousin to 'Gyppy Tum' and 'Delhi Belly.' Another common complaint was Sand Fly fever, a local form of malaria which left its victims with a splitting headache and high fever for several days. The food was also far from nourishing and many suffered nutritional deficiencies that resulted in boils or carbuncles.

It never seems to have occurred to Ivor to point out that he had completed his mandatory number of Blenheim operations and he simply carried on. Les Harrison, the WOP/AG appears to have done likewise. Crew loyalty was always high in the RAF, especially a crew driven by a good skipper. Bill North had, in all, missed three operations so, not until the crew had completed thirty-three operations could he record his personal quotient of thirty. When this figure was reached, he asked to be taken off operations. It was a difficult decision on his part and it must have been an embarrassment to ask a captain, who had completed three more to be let off. However, Ivor fully appreciated the situation and made it plain to his faithful navigator that there was no possible stigma about the request. As has been pointed out, the navigators of the Blenheims suffered all the anxieties but none of the joys of operating at low level.

November was a memorable month for Ivor Broom. By then he had become known as an outstanding Malta-based Blenheim captain, having safely survived six weeks of active operations without a scratch. After carrying out two, rare, high level attacks on Sicilian targets from 8,000–9,000ft, Ivor found himself appointed leader of the next few low-level strikes. Len Williamson was yet to be hi-jacked and the squadron was bereft of officers! Some idea of the situation can be gleaned from this report from Eric Atkins.

Eric was a Blenheim pilot who had arrived in Malta, flying a Blenheim while leading a flock of Hurricanes which had been flown off the aircraft carrier HMS *Ark Royal*. Eric's job had been to depart from Gibraltar, locate the *Ark Royal* when she was about half way to Malta and then navigate and lead the Hurricanes as they flew off her deck, all the way to Malta. He successfully completed this arduous task and thirty-four Hurricanes from 'The Ark' and the carrier HMS *Argus*, duly arrived in Malta. His next task was to fly back to Gibraltar and lead another bunch of Hurricanes to Malta, via the *Ark Royal*. However, the German submarine *U81*, commanded by *Leutnant* Guggenberger sank 'The Ark' on its way back to Gibraltar, leaving Eric high and dry in Malta. Eric tried to signal his squadron in England but before he received a reply, he received a terse message: 'Sgt Broom wants your crew and aircraft.' Eric's first reaction was: 'Who the Hell is Sgt Broom and what gives him the right to sequester my aircraft!' As Eric has written: 'We soon learned that Sgt Broom was something of a legend in Malta. All officers of his squadron had been killed and he seemed to be in charge.'

This improbable situation was resolved by AOC H P Lloyd in his usual decisive fashion. He sent for Ivor on 9 November, by when he had already been the leader of two anti-shipping sweeps and a low-level attack on an MT filling station near Tripoli, and announced that he was henceforth no longer Sgt Broom but was now Pilot Officer Ivor Gordon Broom. 'The paper work will catch up in due course. You just trot along to Gieves and see what they can supply you with.' Gieves, like every store in Malta, was short of many things but at a cost of

£5 Ivor was able to purchase an officer's forage hat and some Pilot Officer's braid to attach to the epaulettes of his battle dress serge. Apparently, smooth Barathea cloth as worn by officers was one of the items in short supply. P/O I G Broom henceforth went about Malta 'improperly dressed' in sergeants' serge and officers' tabs but as the sight was not too unusual, it caused no comment.

Hugh Pughe Lloyd had, just as Ivor's headmaster had done several years before, and F/Lt Mills more recently, given Ivor Broom a big nudge forwards. It was a major turning point in his life.

To complete the story: Eric Atkins did briefly join 107 Squadron and, like so many others whom A V-M Lloyd had shanghaied, he also turned out to be both a winner and a survivor. By war's end Eric was an officer with DFC and bar and, in recent years, became the founder of the Mosquito Aircrew Association. And who is that Association's President? Air Marshal Sir Ivor Broom!

As an officer, Ivor had to leave his brother sergeants at Marsaxlokk and move into the officers' mess at Luqa. The mess buildings had been demolished and the officers' 'lounge' was a big flapping tent. However, some newly constructed barrack blocks still stood and Ivor was assigned a room. It was one which two officers shared. The other occupant was a Canadian ground radar specialist. F/O Albert ('Al') Glazer who cheerfully greeted his new companion with 'You're the third new room mate I've had this week. I hope you will last longer than the other two!'

Both Ivor Broom and Al Glazer survived Luqa. In 1992, thanks to both of them belonging to the George Cross Island Association, they were able to make contact again after a lapse of over fifty years.

Al Glazer was another Malta hero. Due to his poor eyesight he could never aspire to being accepted for aircrew duties but he flew so often in radar equipped Wellingtons and Beaufighters, about 500 hours in all, mainly on operations, that he was awarded the DFC.

In her hours of travail, Malta, from unexpected sources,

saw man after man rise to unprecedented heights, including the great Warburton*. The supply seemed limitless but much was owed to Hugh Pughe Lloyd who had an eye for spotting winners and who encouraged the RAF and FAA in Malta to do things in their own way.

---

* P/O Adrian Warburton flew into Malta as a navigator as he had put up too many 'blacks' as a pilot. He left three years later as a W/Cdr with DSO & bar, DFC & two bars and an American DFC!

CHAPTER SIX

Pilot Officer Broom

Pilot Officer I G Broom had no trouble in finding a navigator to replace Bill North. In Malta aircraft were often damaged beyond repair by bombing and when this occurred, it left a crew without an aircraft. Moreover it was next to impossible for surplus aircrew to get themselves off the beleaguered island. The only ways off were either by submarine or in a transit aircraft. The former occasionally had to go to Alexandria and it was also possible to cram a few extra bodies into the fuselage of Wellingtons en route to the Middle East. Such rare 'seats' were usually filled by VIPs, although, in the case of the Wellingtons, 'seats', as such, were totally lacking except for the ELSAN toilet one!

Initially Ivor flew with a Sgt George Hutchinson as his navigator but, for his last few weeks in Malta, he flew with Sgt Curry. Sgt Hutchinson was the proud possessor of the rare George Medal. This bravery award was one which, with the parallel George Cross for officers, had been conceived by King George VI and went to those who had performed feats of outstanding bravery; not in the face of the enemy. It was as rare and almost as prestigious as the Victoria Cross. With so many bombs falling upon Malta, several of these outstanding awards were given; for dragging aircrew out of burning aircraft; for dealing with the hundreds of unexploded bombs which fell; for rescuing casualties from bombed buildings and for similar acts of unselfish heroism. As is widely known, King George personally decided that a unique George Cross should be given to the island of Malta and its inhabitants and to this day the island, now an independent nation, is proud to call itself 'Malta GC.'

Although Les Harrison carried on with Ivor until his total of operational flights amounted to thirty-eight; ie. eight more than was necessary, he then decided that 'enough was enough' and, as before with the case of Bill North, Ivor made it easy for Les to come to this difficult decision. A successful aircrew is a closely knit unit, especially if all three happened to be of the same rank. To tell a skipper that he wanted out was embarrassing but with crews constantly going out and not coming back, a man almost had to be super-human not to regard a legitimate way out as, literally, a life-saver.

One day before Les had sought operational relief, he was walking the 2 to 3 miles into Valletta with Bill North, when AOC Hugh Pughe Lloyd passed in his car. As was his habit, the AOC offered the Sgts a lift as A V-M Lloyd seldom missed an opportunity to chat with men in order to obtain information at grass roots level. He had in his briefcase a signal from London which showed that the work being done by the Blenheims was not going unnoticed. The signal was shown to Les and Bill and provides yet another example of the personal touch that endeared the AOC to so many of the men under him.

During this encounter Hugh Pughe Lloyd noticed that Les was not wearing his RAF cap and, when enquiring as to its whereabouts, he was informed that it had become lost (many personal items of clothes were frequently being lost in demolished barracks and some men were not averse to making good their losses at the expense of others!). Les went on to explain that although he had applied to Stores for a new cap, he had been told that they replaced caps only if a used one was handed in. Fishing out a piece of paper from his briefcase the AOC wrote and signed an order to Stores to supply Sgt Harrison with a new cap. 'Will that do the trick?' he enquired. Les looked doubtful 'I don't know, sir. They're a pretty queer lot in Stores!'

In truth some who looked after Stores were a 'pretty queer lot.' At another place later in the war, a WOP/AG went to Stores to replace a pair of flying boots as a cannon shell had wrecked his pair. The Warrant Officer in charge, a man who had been in the RAF for well over a score of years, informed the applicant that flying clothing was only issued out on Tuesdays and Fridays. This was reported back to the Squadron Leader who personally decided to tackle the Stores Keeper. The Warrant Officer was firmly ordered to issue flying clothing, if required immediately, on every day of the week, whereupon the 'old salt' was heard to grumble half aloud, 'It's always the flying crews who upset things. If it wasn't for them we could run a decent war!'

By the time that Sgt Broom had received his 'shot gun' commission S/Ldr Barnes was promoted to Acting Wing Commander and given temporary command of 107 Squadron. He was 'Tour Expired' and, as Ivor now recollects, he never flew with the unit. By then Ivor Broom and Ron Gillman had become the two most experienced pilots of the unit and the two were pretty much 'birds of the same feather.' Both were of the same young age (20 or 21). Both had become superb flyers, and had been hijacked by Hugh Pughe Lloyd to lead formation attacks. It was therefore no surprise that an immediate DFM was soon awarded to Ron who had led several successful low-level shipping attacks. Ivor had, however, been Ron's leader for the shipping attack mentioned in the citation of Gillman's immediate DFM.

Wing Commander Barnes' appointment was only a stop-gap one until another Blenheim officer could be flown out from the UK. A Canadian, Wing Commander Dunlevie, replaced Barnes but he also was 'Tour Expired' and was lame from a damaged leg. He had no need ever to fly but did, on a few occasions, take part in operations.

Ivor took all this in his stride. He was more than content to leave the paper work to the experienced Regular senior officers who knew how best to cope with such Administrative matters. Ivor was happy to continue to lead the squadron during operations.

A change of operations came when on 12 November P/O Broom took part in a search for four Swordfish of 830 Squadron which had all mysteriously disappeared from a night operation. Nothing was found and it later transpired that the Swordfish had been led totally astray by a new CO who had 'navigated' them 200 miles away from where they should have been! This, perhaps, was an example to show that senior officers new to the local environment and without previous knowledge of what the local requirements were, should not attempt to take the lead. It was better for an experienced young Sgt pilot to lead a formation than to ask a newly appointed CO to do so.

Another new element now began to dominate the operations of 107 and 18 Squadrons. So many enemy supply ships destined for Tripoli had been sunk by surface ships, submarines and aircraft operating from Malta that the enemy had ceased to try to run supplies direct to that port. During October and November 1941, over seventy-five percent of the supplies destined for Rommel and his armies had failed to reach North Africa. Malta held the key.

To counter this threat, the enemy decided to change the shipping route. Instead of the short direct route, more or less due south from Palermo or Naples to Tripoli, the Axis supplies which Rommel needed to receive in order to fight the war in the Desert, were being routed *via* the Strait of Messina, then due east until within sight of the Greek coast or Greek islands of Corfu and Cephalonia; thence southwards to Benghazi. Although Benghazi itself was not capable of handling other than small ships, the main supplies could, from there, be sailed close to the shore, along the coast to Tripoli. By keeping their supply ships away from Malta by several hundred miles, the enemy entirely negated the efforts of the night torpedo Swordfish and Albacores and made it many times more difficult for the Blenheims and Naval forces in Malta to reach their still well defended convoys. It was, however, a victory for Malta as the Axis' dwindling number of available ships were being forced to take two or three times as long to reach their final destination.

The Blenheims could just reach the new shipping targets off the Greek coast but it required a long over-water flight and very exact navigation. Ivor Broom now led shipping sweeps and strikes to places such as Zante, an island off Peloponnisos. On 17 November, when leading a formation to Zante, he successfully set on fire a 4,000-ton merchant ship of a small convoy. These flights of nearly 900 miles in all, depended both upon accurate navigation and first rate intelligence as Malta never had petrol to spare for anything other than reliable information of enemy movements. On many days, therefore, the Blenheims would be stood down.

Another way of getting at supplies destined for the *Afrika Korps* — and this also depended upon excellent Intelligence — was to attack the railway marshalling yards in Sicily where supplies were being accumulated. P/O Broom also led these raids although, during the latter part of his stay in Malta, he appears to have been kept back for those operations where the chances of finding a suitable target were high. The more vague 'shipping sweeps' were left to others. Broom was now being reserved for action when something special was being attempted.

One such special operation — and Hugh Pughe Lloyd was always on the look-out for something new to keep the enemy off balance — was to launch a pre-dawn attack upon an Italian harbour where Intelligence, or Malta's own excellent PR 69 Squadron, had informed him that ships loaded for Africa could be found. Daily photographs which 69 Squadron, brilliantly led by Flying Officer Warburton, brought back enabled the planners to deduce when the ships would have been fully laden. Only then would an attack be planned. To launch a 'first light' attack on a harbour required a night take-off. Although Ivor Broom's night flying hours, since first enrolling in the RAF, came to only three and a half hours as first pilot; largely acquired several months previously on Oxfords or at his Blenheim OTU, he was selected to lead a low-level night raid of two Blenheims on Trapani, a port on the north-west tip of Sicily. It was about 150 miles from Malta but the plan was to fly further west so as to approach from a surprise over sea direction.

It was suggested to Ivor that, as he had not flown from Malta at night, and indeed had not flown at all at night for some time (apart from having once to land soon after sunset after a long flight from a Greek island), he might first carry out a brief 'Circuit and Bump' practice prior to the operation. His new WOP/AG, Sgt Curry, had other ideas. 'Not ruddy likely,' he exclaimed. 'Let's do the Op between the circuit and the bump!'

The flight went smoothly and, by approaching in darkness

from over the sea, surprise was achieved and a 5,000-ton ship was hit and set on fire. This operation nearly doubled the number of night hours of P/O Broom.

His forty-third operation is memorable for Ivor. It was to attack shipping which was known to be at anchor in Argostoli harbour in the island of Cephalonia, off the west coast of Greece. It was shipping which was being formed up for a convoy dash to Benghazi and included at least one tanker as oil was always uppermost in the requirements of *General* Rommel and his Axis armies. The raid has been made memorable by Ron Gillman who devotes a whole chapter to it in his book *The Shiphunters* but Ivor Broom, who led it, remembers it now for quite another reason.

Six aircraft, three each from 18 and 107 Squadrons, took part. Ivor and his navigator played a leading role by bringing the formation to Cephalonia in such a manner that the Blenheims approached at low level from the north. By this ploy, he avoided many of the gun positions which had been placed to defend the harbour from an expected attack from the open end of the inlet. The formation, after flashing over the north coast, followed a road leading up to a saddle between hills on either side. It was a tight fit and the wing men only just scraped through. Once over the saddle, the inlet could clearly be seen and the six Blenheims swept down with all eyes straining for a sight of the ships at anchor around the harbour of Argostoli. After releasing their bombs at mast height, the pilots had the difficult task of escaping as, by then, they were being fired on by a number of guns and destroyers in the harbour. To get away fast, Ivor led his followers out to sea by turning smartly to starboard and climbing up over the hills which lay to the west of Argostoli. It was a stiff climb and, by then at full throttle and using the max engine boost of 9lb, they just managed it*. It was all done so swiftly that there was no time to assess results. On attacks, it was left to the gunners

---

* During 1993 at the ceremony to dedicate the Battle of Britain memorial on the cliffs near Dover, Ivor ran into a former Blenheim navigator whom he had not seen since Malta. As they chatted about those times, Fred Deeks, who had also taken part in the Argostoli raid, remarked: 'I never thought that we were going to clear those hills after the attack.' 'Me neither,' confessed Ivor.

in the most rear aircraft to see what had been achieved and, if possible, they also took photographs.

Sadly only four of the six attackers emerged from the withering fire and the two which were lost were the rearward couple. In view of this, no claim of ships hit or damaged could be made. Two more Blenheim crews had been lost and, perhaps, nothing positive had been achieved. There the matter rested for many years.

After his retirement from the RAF, Air Marshal Sir Ivor Broom became a successful businessman and consultant. He was doing business in London with a wealthy Greek, Makis Panas, who inquired if he had ever bombed Greece during the war. Ivor at first said 'No.' However, after thinking about it, he had to confess that he had misinformed the gentleman.

'I'm wrong, I did once bomb some ships in a harbour off a Greek island.'

'Would the island be Cephalonia, by chance?'

'Yes, that was it. I bombed shipping in Argostoli harbour. It was a memorable raid.'

'Could it have been a week or so before Christmas?'

'Yes. That was the time, just before Christmas 1941.'

'Then I was there. I was a schoolboy and your 'planes came right over our school at such low level that it seemed that they must hit it. We all flung ourselves upon the ground and the aircraft went directly over us with a tremendous roar. I distinctly remember looking straight up at one aircraft. It was only inches over my head: so it seemed.'

Makis Panas went on to inform Ivor that the event is commemorated in the Argostoli museum but with few details. Later Ivor arranged to follow this up and sent the museum additional information, pictures and details which are now on display.

Ivor's Greek friend, for his part, has advised that the Blenheims sank two ships, one of which was a tanker. Moreover, he subsequently sent Ivor a postcard on which he had marked, with crosses, the positions of where the ships sank. When the snow came in January, their masts could still be clearly seen sticking out against the white background.

Makis also advised that one Blenheim hit a ship's mast, crashed into the sea with all killed. The other pancaked on the water and the crew became POWs.

He went on to tell him that when the Italians decided to surrender, having ceased to be Hitler's ally, they had a crack Alpine regiment guarding Cephalonia for the Axis. This unit refused to hand over to the Germans who had come to take their place but as Italy had, overnight, changed sides they were in a difficult predicament. The Germans who had come to take charge, herded the Italian officers into a field and shot them. Meanwhile all the Italian non-officers had been loaded on to a ship for 'repatriating to Italy' but when the ship was far from the coast, it was scuttled and all the prisoners were drowned.

It did not pay to be an ally of Hitler's during the Second World War, as the Russians had earlier found out.

Another new element was about to befall the Blenheim crews in Malta for the successes, which ships and 'planes from Malta continued to inflict against Rommel's essential supply lines, left Hitler and the German High command with a need to take drastic action. Either Malta had to be taken by invasion or otherwise rendered useless. The plans for the former — their Operation *Herkules* — were laid and thousands of men and equipment were prepared. However, Hitler instead set about neutralising Malta by an intensive bombing campaign. Accordingly he moved the entire *Luftflotte II* from the Eastern Front, where it was facing Moscow, to Sicily and began a ruthless and remorseless bombing campaign against the RAF's airfields and the Royal Navy's harbours in Malta.

Although P/O Ivor Broom carried out two more operations from Malta; his thirtieth and thirty-first from that battered isle, the writing was on the wall. Blenheims would soon be unable to operate from Luqa as their losses in the air would increase to beyond a point where they were acceptable. The last Blenheim squadron, number 21, to fly itself from 2 Group in the UK to Malta was virtually wiped out within a month. Non-stop raids day and night and with Me 109s often patrolling over Luqa in broad daylight and then strafing the place at low level, made operations impossible.

However, by then, on 12 January 1942, having barely been able to fly at all during the previous three weeks, P/O Broom with the DFC which he had recently been awarded, flew Blenheim 29745, which had been patched up for him, to the comparative safety of Helwan, 15 miles south of Cairo. With him were his former crew mates Sgts Bill North and Les Harrison (both having been trying for many weeks to find a way off Malta), Sgt Webber and Sgt Ron Gillman DFM: all five cramming into the aircraft.

A boy had arrived but a man was leaving. The 'few weeks until 107 can get themselves operational', had turned into several months. Apart from having been given the chance by Hugh Pughe Lloyd to develop his qualities of leadership, Malta had improved Ivor's skills and these were often put to the test by having to cope with a number of unexpected experiences. A pilot with nothing but 'Average' assessments in his log book, would soon be rated 'Above Average' and then be given the highest accolade of all: 'Exceptional.'

Perhaps the most unusual outcome of Ivor Broom's long period under fire in Malta was that it seems not to have touched him, mentally or physically. The rain of bombs, the food shortages, the lack of leave or entertainment left a mark upon nearly all and an all-male society tends to become coarse. The innocent became cynics. Many men became giants while others degenerated to pygmies. Several who, like Ivor, had never before touched alcohol, now took every chance to indulge in whatever potion was available. The Gut — the street of low dives and prostitutes — was where many an airman went when desperate to get away from it all: to seek relief somehow, somewhere, with someone. A good thrashing, in one sense or another, even with the resulting hangover, made it possible to carry on and temporarily to wash away the ever-nagging fear that Malta was going to be the last place on this earth that the crew member would see. Nothing of this seems to have crossed Ivor's mind nor was he ever weighed down by the additional responsibilities which were placed upon his young shoulders. As Al Glazer, his room mate in the Officers' quarters, has confirmed. 'Ivor was a quiet chap. He kept largely to himself and simply carried on doing whatever had to be done and doing it cheerfully without ever finding a need for alcohol. The main difference between him and my other room mates was that he survived! He often accompanied me on the journeys I had to take (Al Glazer, as the number one radio and radar expert on the island, had been provided with a camouflaged MG car) but I cannot now remember what we talked about.'

Hugh Pughe Lloyd had given Ivor Gordon Broom a big nudge forward. Malta made its own rules and survived as a result. Many who had shot to fame there never fitted comfortably into the more regular Air Force. What would the future hold for newly-commissioned P/O Broom?

CHAPTER SEVEN

A Long Way Back to 13 OTU

How lucky Ivor Broom had been in Malta can be gauged from the fact that, by the time he came to fly himself to Cairo, his was one of only three of the original crews not missing or killed.

The slaughter of Blenheims which had commenced in France, continued during the period when Hitler had crowded his Channel ports with invasion barges, and which later evoked comment from Winston Churchill during the period when 'Black' Stevenson had been in charge of 2 Group, had been repeated in Malta. It was a 1930s aircraft in a 1940s European war.

During his period in Malta — September 1941 to January 1942 — not only had Ivor Broom blossomed into full manhood (and commissioned status) but the scale and nature of the Second World War had also undergone enormous changes. During December, while Sgt I G Broom had been carrying out shipping sweeps along the Palermo-Tripoli shipping route, Japan, having first made a pact with Hitler's Germany, launched a surprise attack upon the main Pacific US naval base at Pearl Harbor, in the Hawaiian Islands. This had brought the United States into the now-global conflict. Japan had become desperate for oil, minerals, rubber and other such supplies which she needed in order to continue her conquest of China. Only by first eliminating the USA fleet from the Pacific and capturing the British naval base of Singapore, could she hope to be able to help herself to the many natural resources of Malaya, the Philippines and the Dutch East Indies. The principal antagonists thereafter were Germany, Japan and Italy on the Axis side and the USA, USSR, Britain and the Commonwealth on the Allies side.

It might almost be said that P/O Ivor Broom left Malta as a 'Big fish in a little pool' to enter into a wider world at war where he would be a very insignificant fish in a pool of ocean-wide dimensions.

Although it had taken Ivor Broom only three days to reach Malta from the UK, it was to take him the best part of three months to complete the return journey. But first he had the opportunity to enjoy a period of leave in the Egyptian capital.

Flying crews appearing in their own aircraft from Malta, gave the Middle East HQ in Cairo quite a problem. Generally they arrived totally unexpectedly and, especially in the cases of those who had in the first place been hijacked in Malta, it was difficult for the large Air HQ in Cairo to determine who they were, what they had become and what to do with them. 'Tour Expired' crews could not be used operationally and Air HQ must have regretted that crews from Malta never seemed to be returned to the UK the way that they had arrived there. A flight first to Gibraltar and thence back to Portreath was never attempted. With all these unaccounted for aircrew around it was often a puzzle to determine whether the person who had arrived was genuine or not. Also it was hard for Air HQ, which ran the RAF in the Middle East on very Regular lines, to appreciate that the P/O, Acting F/ Lt (or even Acting S/Ldr) was the same person who, according to their books, was a Sgt pilot who had failed to arrive in the Cairo area a few months earlier!

Cairo in wartime, even when Rommel was on the advance into Egypt, was as big a contrast to Malta as was possible. Whereas Malta was short of almost every commodity, Cairo was overflowing with the good things of life. Apart from the enormous numbers of men and women in Allied uniforms, the war seemed a million miles away despite its actual closeness. By some undeclared pact, the huge city was never bombed unlike Malta which, by war's end, had been subjected to 3,340 air alerts: moreover virtually every raid had been directed at either the three airfields or the harbours in Valletta and Sliema.

In Cairo there was super abundance of everything that Malta, under siege, lacked: food, drinks, cigarettes, soap, toothpaste, clothes, shoes, petrol, entertainment and every creature comfort was available in apparently unlimited quantities. At Groppi's well-known tea rooms and ice-cream parlour, enormous and exotic ice-cream sundaes — about a foot high — could be bought for a few 'ackers.' There were night clubs and half a dozen plush dance halls with live orchestras playing for the crowded tea dancers. A collection of local lovelies and a smattering of WAAF, WRNS and ATS girls whirled away the afternoons, much fortified by rich 'sticky' cakes, in the arms of their uniformed partners. Service clubs proliferated and the well-known Continental and Shepherds Hotels were crowded nightly. Madame Badhia was among the best known of popular 'belly dancers.'

Cairo was a dusty crowded city, overflowing with peoples of many different tongues: Greek, Armenians, Syrians, Arabs, French, British (German and Italian, too, but they were keeping a low profile while awaiting Rommel's arrival), as well as a variety of Egyptians. Nominally it was a kingdom with a bloated dissolute King Farouk at the head, supported by a Court of fabulously wealthy *Pashas* of equal bulk. All wore the red *fez* as well as expensive silk suits but, at the other end of the scale, there were millions of desperately poor *fellahs* who somehow eked out an existence during their short, overworked life in the streets; in the doorways of which many lived and slept.

In between these two extremes of riches and poverty, were thousands of RAF, Army and a few Navy personnel on a period of short leave away from the fighting in the desert. They were there to spend money as, while in action, there was no outlet for their pay. Their short stays in Cairo gave them unlimited opportunities to have a splurge and tens of thousands of locals were doing all they could to help the money go even faster! Royal Navy personnel seemed to prefer Alexandria as their HQ was in that large city and could provide equal opportunity for drink, food, games and frolics. These included the well-known brothel, Mary's House.

Mixed up within these ever-bustling, ever-dusty and noisy cities were an army of street beggars, vocal shoe-shine boys from about five years of age upwards, sellers of 'filthy pictures; you look Captain', guides: 'I take you pyramids' or 'I take you nice place: big girls?', street traders selling everything from peanuts to 'my own nice sister; very clean,' and scores of battered buses with as many people clinging on to the outsides as there were crammed inside. These and the donkey carts, mules, camels and equally battered cars, not forgetting the Rolls-Royces of the *Pashas*, caused great traffic jams with many sounding their horns or beating on the sides of their cars. There were pavement cafes, each with their own *gully-gully* man who performed 'impossible' conjuring tricks while the customers would have to beat off the street traders who were endeavouring to tempt them with prawns and such from their unofficial menus.

As well as the inevitable bars into which to lure the free spending servicemen, there were a number of open air and other cinemas showing films in English with much of the lower part of the screen taken up with sub-titles in several languages as well as Arabic. A local police force, aided by the British Military police, vaguely kept some kind of control in line with what few laws there seemed to be. Most men wore long white garments but the women were shrouded in black. A mixture of strange unfamiliar smells permeated everything. Flies and dust were everywhere.

Aircrew were generally kept in vast transit camps, such as the one at Almaza, until someone could decide what next to do with them. Naturally all wanted most to be returned to the UK but, with Britain on the retreat in Malaya, the Services in India were being boosted in an attempt to stop the rampant Japanese from sweeping into that 'jewel' of the British Empire. Blenheims were much in demand in Malaya and India and Ivor Broom, as a Blenheim pilot, was of obvious use there. Happily the fact that he was definitely well over the 'Tour Expired' limit saved him from being sent further east.

In Transit Camps, Movements were not known till noon. This meant that the morning had to be spent in the Camp with nothing better to do than to sun bake, sweat and swat at the billions of flies which buzzed incessantly around. Everyone was dressed in khaki shorts and bush shirts and slept in rows of tents but, after midday, individuals not assigned a posting were free to do whatever they fancied provided they were back in camp by a late hour.

However, none of the privations of an RAF Transit Camp were to affect P/O Ivor Broom. On arrival in Egypt, he found himself treated as a VIP! But to this day, Ivor has no idea why he was so treated along with several other 107 Squadron officers who were similarly accommodated. At one time, when Lt General Dobbie was obviously played out as Governor of Malta, Tedder even did his best to get A V-M Lloyd appointed in his place. Hugh Pughe's vigorous efforts to fight the war in his own way never seem to have annoyed Tedder, who backed him all the way.

For whatever reason, the recently-commissioned Ivor Broom, still wearing the rough cloth of aircrew battledress, found himself ensconced in the luxurious Continental Hotel. It stood in a key position almost overlooking the Nile and, pre-war, was the most serious rival to the world-famous Shepherds Hotel. Then wealthy British and American tourists or businessmen filled its elegant palm court lounges (complete with orchestra) and luxurious rooms. Its restaurants had international chefs and every guest was expected to wear evening dress for dinner.

Ivor can recall one immediate reaction. Len Williamson, his Australian friend, had been equally favoured and when, immediately after arrival, the smart waiters appeared with the dinner *hors d'oeuvre* trolley, Len and he practically devoured the man's entire supply. After months of seeing little other than bully beef, M & V stew and rough Maltese bread, (Hob), such goodies as were on display were too good to let pass. With almost everyone in Malta suffering from loss of weight, individuals did not realise how famished they had become until away from the place. Many had lost stones in weight.

If destined for the UK, there were two ways of getting there from Cairo. Most men were sent home around Africa by ship and a procession of giant ocean liners: the *New Mauritania*, the *New Amsterdam*, the *Georgic*, the *Ile de France* and others, with thousands of British Army and some RAF personnel crammed on board, plied regularly between Port Tewfiq in Egypt and the South African port of Durban. After having been greeted with song by the famous 'Lady in White' who sang as the ships docked, they entered another overcrowded Transit Camp, while waiting for a vessel bound for Cape Town and eventually for the UK. It all could take months.

The much more popular route home, and one which was normally used mainly for VIPs, was to be flown home *via* a circuitous route. Ivor again struck lucky. After two weeks in the luxurious Continental with time enough to visit the pyramids and the Sphinx — both monuments totally unprotected with servicemen clambering all over them while beating off attempts by persistent dusky traders to sell them almost everything and camel owners who tried to persuade them to ride on their mangy beasts — Ivor's posting came through with unexpected swiftness. Moreover he was given a seat in a BOAC Empire Flying Boat which, after a short stop at Wadi Halfa, deposited him at Khartoum. Here he left *Ceres* (G-AETX, Capt Shepherd) and after two or three days in another extremely hot, noisy and crowded city, he boarded a Pan-Am DC-3 (N-18117, Capt Brann) for an interesting flight west across the width of central Africa.

In order to get aircraft to Egypt and beyond (without having to risk them being purloined by Hugh Pughe Lloyd), the British had created a series of airfields between Lagos and Khartoum. Hurricanes and the like would be taken to Lagos by ship and, after being assembled and flight checked, they would be ferried in short stages; all flying being only by day and often with another aircraft to navigate and lead them, stage by stage, all the way to Khartoum. Ivor was now doing this in reverse. First to El Obeid in Sudan then, the next day, to El Fasher. The following day to El Geneina: both in the huge Sudan, then a longer leg overflying French Equatorial Africa (now Chad) to Maiduguri, Nigeria where Ivor remembers sleeping in the open under a mosquito net, then Kano to end at Lagos. He had left Cairo on 27 January and arrived in Lagos in 2 February 1942.

At Lagos, there was the inevitable Transit Camp and further delays until someone discovered who he was and put him on the waiting list for a passage home to the UK. He finally ended up on a ship which first went to Freetown in the British Colony of Sierra Leone. The ship sat in harbour for a week and then became part of a very slow convoy heading for Britain.

As the convoy could only proceed at 7 knots, it was by no means certain that he would ever reach Britain! The U-boat menace was almost at its peak and convoys heading for the UK were being mercilessly destroyed. Britain and her Allies lacked adequate numbers of escort carriers, destroyers, sloops, frigates and corvettes with which to defend them. The sea voyage from Freetown to Liverpool took twenty-three days and with Ivor's fellow passengers being largely British civil servants of various West African colonies going home on leave, he found himself the only service officer on board. In this capacity, the ship's Captain asked him to arrange for the passengers to form a duty U-boat watch. Ivor at first asked for volunteers but found little enthusiasm among the civil servants who had personally not been touched by the war and who may even have paid for their passage home. He was still aged only twenty-one and was hardly in a position to order these mature citizens to comply. But, using common sense, and not a little cunning, Ivor put up a notice that men were required for the task and asking all who did not wish to volunteer to sign their names in a space below! Not one name appeared, so Ivor was able to arrange the additional watches. This was very necessary as, in spite of its miserable speed, the sole escort for the twenty or so ships which comprised the convoy was a solitary armed merchant vessel with very limited armament. It might, with much good luck, have warded off a U-boat should it have been sighted but it would have been totally useless against the fast modern battlecruisers, the *Scharnhorst* and *Gneisenau*: both of which at that time were known to have slipped out of Brest and were 'somewhere at sea' looking for convoys to massacre.

From start to finish, good fortune had stayed with P/O I G Broom since leaving Malta: first a luxury hotel, then a privileged flight in a comfortable flying boat, then, among the VIPs, his flight across Africa and finally the long slow journey home without even a U-boat scare.

On arrival in Britain, Ivor reported straight to the Air

Ministry. One of his immediate concerns was to get himself a correct officer's uniform as he was still in sergeant's serge. After some discussion he was given £25 with which to equip himself as an officer and a gentleman. However, a fresh snag arose. Throughout the war, Britons, in order to buy clothes, had to produce clothing coupons which were severely rationed. When Ivor asked for some of these, he was informed that RAF Regulations decreed that the station which had commissioned him was responsible for issuing the clothing coupons. Apart from the fact that Malta had no system of clothing coupons and had precious few clothes to offer anyone, it was clearly impossible for Luqa to do this. After much argument Ivor eventually found someone in authority to use a little common sense and to provide the necessary. The argument had taken place on a bitterly cold day and Ivor, who wanted a greatcoat among other items, refused to leave the Ministry without clothes coupons.

Ivor also learned that the DFC for which he had been recommended by A V-M H P Lloyd, had come through and he was able also to have this prestigious ribbon sewn on to his smart new officer's tunics.

After a spell of well-earned leave, and the usual delay before Postings could catch up with him, Ivor found himself back with 13 OTU at Bicester. He had left there as a Sergeant pilot pupil on 8 July 1941. Now, nine months later, he was returning as an officer instructor with the ribbon of the DFC sewn on to the smooth cloth of his officer's tunic, which, at last, he had been able to buy in the UK.

It had been a staggering nine months and a period that completely changed the life of Ivor Broom. Soon there was to be another event which also did much to shape the future for the twenty-one-year-old former Civil Service clerk from the Rhondda valley.

CHAPTER EIGHT

Ivor Instructs

It was normal for a pilot who had satisfactorily completed a Tour of Operations to be 'rested' by taking on instructor's duties at an Operational Training Unit (OTU). That way, the experience gained 'in the field' could be passed on to others about to enter the fray for the first time. This was to be the fate for the next year or more for P/O I G Broom DFC.

For the first few years of the war, when the priority was to produce operational pilots by the most expedient method, a 'Tour Expired' pilot simply went straight to an appropriate OTU and began instructing. The fact that he had survived a Tour was then deemed sufficient evidence that he was a fit person to instruct others! However, by spring 1942, a more rational method had evolved. 'Tour Expired' pilots were now being given a short course on how to instruct before being let loose upon the relatively raw recruits. As a result, P/O Broom found himself posted to the Central Flying School at Upavon where he attended, for the best part of a month, No. 7 Flying Instructor's School. Here he again flew Airspeed Oxfords and carried out a comprehensive course of nearly fifty hours flying; some being at night. The school generally sharpened up his flying and concentrated upon the correct techniques of how to teach others to cope with emergencies such as: flapless landings, flying and landing twin-engined aircraft on only one engine, (not easy with an Oxford), cross-wind landings, emergency and glide approach landings and other fine points of piloting. At the end of this he emerged with a certificate asserting that he was an 'Average' multi-engined Flying Instructor. It was a good system as not every, even good, pilot has the necessary natural ability to become, overnight, an effective instructor. This course brought his total flying hours up to 436.

Within a few days of departing from Upavon, the newly

qualified instructor found himself back at Bicester with No. 13 OTU. Here he had to teach the operational pilots of the future how best to fly the Blenheims in which they would soon be required to operate in the desert and, especially, in the Far East: India and Malaya. The type was still being produced in large numbers although operations from both the UK and Malta had ceased on account of being deemed too punishing. At Bicester Ivor became a 'bombing' instructor and most of the exercises were designated either High- or Low-level bombing practices. However, the High-level exercises were in effect only Medium bombing practices as they took place at about 5,000-8,000ft.

The Low-level exercises were indeed low as it had, by then, been well established that the best hope for survival was to attack ships below deck height. All exercises were of short duration and in June, for example, Ivor flew a total of thirty-five hours but had carried out forty-seven flights: one of these being a 'one-off' Air Sea Rescue search for a fallen comrade in the North Sea and this had lasted nearly three hours.

Being detailed to fly as low as possible came as a shock to the pupils who for the most part were youngsters and, like Ivor himself in 1940, had volunteered to join never having flown before. Throughout their various training courses, it had been drummed into them that under no circumstances should they indulge in low flying. If caught doing so — and the temptation to 'beat up' friends and to show off their recently won skills was considerable — they were liable to be severely punished; even to being dismissed from the Service. Now, they were being ordered to fly low.

A few of the pupils were more senior as they had been roped in at the commencement of hostilities to instruct and had been unable to get free of this necessary chore. However, by 1942, some were now being released for operational duties and were being processed for such via the OTUs. One such, a man much senior in rank to P/O Broom, was so horrified by Ivor's demonstration of how low flying should be carried out, that he reported Ivor to the Chief Instructor for his 'near suicidal demonstration' and refused to fly again with him! Probably he had, in Canada, where he had come from, been in a position of authority to discipline low-flying pupils and it was now an anathema for him to have to do it himself. He declared that there was no way that he would ever fly so dangerously. Sadly he must have adhered to this belief as, shortly after leaving the OTU, he was killed in action.

Malta had been a truly traumatic experience and, in a way, carrying out this skilled and demanding form of instruction, may have enabled Ivor to unwind in a progressive manner. For some who were given less exacting tasks, life after Malta fell woefully flat and caused adjustment problems.

After a few months of this useful instructing; months when he was able to hone his own flying to a peak not before attainable (teaching others to fly invariably much improved the technique of the instructors), Ivor's life entered into a new realm when he married the girl he had left behind.

Before even leaving the tax office at Ipswich and joining the RAF, the young tax clerk had met Jessica in Ipswich both having attended the same Baptist Church there. An affinity had sprung up and, during the separation, the two had kept in touch via letters. During a week's leave, towards the end of July 1942, the young couple were married with the simple ceremony taking place in the Burlington Baptist Church where they had first met. As the Minister was away serving in the Army, Ivor and Jess were united by his wife who had taken over the running of the Church, lady Chaplains being quite normal in that Christian sect. Two people who shared Christian beliefs made this a lasting marriage of mutual benefit to both. Many young RAF pilots married in haste in wartime and such marriages did not always last, especially with the enforced separations and the temptations on offer both overseas and later in the UK when the country began to fill up with free-spending Canadian and American troops who had arrived in their hundreds of thousands prior to the great cross-Channel invasion.

Thereafter the team of Ivor and Jess established themselves as a delightful duo during the rest of Ivor's long and distinguished RAF career; and continue to do so in their many useful activities since his retirement. The good fortune which had watched over the young pilot when operating with 114, 105 and 107 Squadrons was continuing but, in this case, Ivor's own sound judgment obviously played a major part in this life-long operation.

Life at No. 13 OTU proceeded in a smooth uneventful way for just over a year without it being marred by any accident or incident involving Ivor. A welcomed alteration was when Pilot Officer Broom became Flying Officer Broom. Pilot Officers were paid only 14/6d (just over 70p in current British money) per day and although a F/O's pay was not great (18/2d per day) every little helped. Pre-war RAF officers were not encouraged to marry until at least aged thirty and, as a consequence, no marriage allowances were paid to junior officers. However, as a wartime concession, these rules had been relaxed and a small marriage allowance was paid to all officers' wives. But junior officers, whether married or not, were far from being well paid.

The flying weather was often not conducive to the exercises to be completed and on many days, especially during the winter months, F/O Broom and his fellow instructors were grounded. However, on the suitable days they flew as many as five or more sorties with various pupils. Some were as brief as twenty-five minutes.

It was with welcomed relief that Ivor, now mentally removed from the dramatic days of Malta, was posted in May 1943, still as an instructor, to join 1655 MTU. This stood for Mosquito Training Unit at nearby Finmere. Ivor could not have chosen better himself as this aircraft type had rapidly caught the imagination of both the public and the RAF alike. In many respects it could claim to be Britain's most outstanding aircraft of the Second World War.

The de Havilland Mosquito, which rapidly earned itself the name of 'The Wooden Wonder', was unique. At a time when, for many years, the latest aircraft of both sides had been largely built from aluminium alloys, the de Havilland firm, with chief designer R E Bishop well to the fore, came up with a military design which was revolutionary in two important aspects. Firstly, the wings, tail surfaces and fuselage were constructed entirely of laminated wood held together by strong adhesives and secondly the aircraft would be totally unarmed and would depend upon its speed and height for survival in war. It could be used as a bomber with a maximum speed of over 400mph and could easily attain a height of 30,000ft. This speed meant that even the fastest of the enemy's day fighter aircraft would have difficulty in overhauling it. Also cruising at 300mph at great height, it presented a small, fast, difficult to hit target for the best of the enemy's big AA guns. No Luftwaffe night fighter of the time could hope to outpace a Mosquito.

At first these revolutionary concepts did not evoke enthusiasm among the RAF hierarchy. However, the design found one champion in Air Marshal Sir Wilfred Freeman, Air Member for Research & Development, and, after much discussion, a small order for fifty was placed. These were intended for long-range (another asset of the design), photographic reconnaissance duties. It speaks much for Air Marshal Freeman's powers of persuasion that the order was placed on 1 March 1940, which was nearly nine months before even the prototype first flew on 25 November.

It was always to the project's great advantage that the 'Mossie' (as all came to call her), was intended to be powered by two Rolls-Royce Merlin engines as this engine, ever since first appearing in the early Hurricanes, had proved itself to be reliable, easy to produce and a design which was capable of being modified to deliver more and more power. The original Merlins were rated at just over 1,000hp. By the time that the Mossie came to flow from the factories in numbers, all the early 'bugs' had been removed from the Merlin engines and the power had been increased to just under 1,500hp; with promise of even more to come. Moreover, enhanced supercharging enabled the later Merlins to compete with anything that the Germans had up to heights of 30,000ft. By the time that the Mosquito was in great demand, Merlins were being produced in large numbers in several British factories and in a giant Packard plant in the USA.

Initial flight tests of the Mosquito showed up well and before long, it was the type everyone was demanding. The Photographic Reconnaissance Unit (PRU) was in Coastal Command and later this Command also used the Mosquito for U-boat hunting in the North Sea armed with powerful solid head rockets which could blast clean through any U-boat caught near the surface. In Bomber Command, it came to be the type most in demand as it could carry one of the largest bombs then made — the 4,000lb one known as a 'Cookie' — and was found to sustain far fewer losses than any other bomber type used. Its range of 1,470 miles in still air enabled it to operate to Berlin and back without difficulty. Also the fact that it required only two crew, to the six or seven normally carried by the four-engined, heavily defended types, made it all the more attractive proposition. By war's end, Mossies had dropped 26,867 tons of bombs on Berlin alone and had done so for a loss rate of only 0.63 percent: a mere fraction of the heavy losses of the Lancasters, Wellingtons and Halifaxes. Most Bomber Command variants were powered by the Mark 72/73 Merlins with 1,680hp and two-stage superchargers. Some later also had pressurised cabins.

Fighter Command welcomed the Mosquito as the long-range day fighter that they had long wanted. Armed with four 20mm cannon and another four .303 machine guns it packed a formidable punch. As a night fighter it was supreme and, fitted with a late Mark AI (airborne radar), it steadily began to replace the formidable Beaufighters, having a much superior range which enabled it to roam over Germany at night seeking out Luftwaffe night fighters to overhaul and kill. 100 Group could never get enough of these deadly night destroyers. Part of its range came from the 100 gallon drop tanks which, after late 1944, became almost a standard fitting and which did little to detract from the high performance.

Group Captain John Cunningham DSO & two bars, DFC, the distinguished night fighter pilot and test pilot, has asserted:

The Mosquito, without doubt, was the most versatile and useful aircraft of the Second World War.

A few Mosquitoes were also used both by BOAC and by RAF Transport Command as unique 'Transport Aircraft.' They carried one passenger lying prone in the bomb bay area. As such they operated a VVIP service between Stockholm in neutral Sweden and Scotland. One such VVIP was the Danish physicist Neil Bors, the atom bomb nuclear scientist. The 'civil' Mosquitoes also brought to Britain valuable ball bearings made in Sweden.

These versatile aircraft were built at Hatfield, Portsmouth, Leavesden, Luton and in Canada, where 1,034 were made. The 212 built in Australia were used in the Pacific war. In all 7,781 were produced. The Canadian ones used the Packard built Merlin engines but they were only significantly different in that they could not carry the 'Cookie.' Instead, they carried four 500lb bombs in the bomb bay. In Bomber Command they were known as the Type XX and XXV, whereas the UK built ones were Type XVI.

So few were the losses in Bomber Command that one Mosquito successfully completed 213 sorties over Germany.

F/O I G Broom DFC, who had miraculously survived a baptism of fire in Blenheims and had, almost uniquely, completed a Tour of forty-five Ops in this most vulnerable type, was more than ready to move to Finmere. He was eager to get his hands on the highly esteemed 'Wooden Wonder.' Yet, life being what it is, this was to be so very nearly the end of his career and the end of his life.

CHAPTER NINE

Ivor has his Ups and Downs

Flying Officer I G Broom's first task at No. 1655 MTU was to learn to fly the Mosquito as it was on this type that he was expected to teach others. He found that one of the drawbacks of now being no longer a 'sprog' officer but one who displayed the DFC ribbon on his tunic was that it was assumed by others that he needed little instruction. After less than two hours dual instruction and two short solo flights, he found himself with his first pupils! However, even the briefest of introductions was enough to convince the new MTU instructor that the Mossie was all that it was cracked up to be. By then the few vices it had displayed were well known and documented; for example, it was known that it was highly inadvisable to open up both engines fiercely for take-off as the torque from the two powerful engines would then induce a pronounced swing. The throttles had to be advanced progressively with one lagging behind the other to counter the swing by asymmetrical thrust.

Another mild snag about the aircraft, was that it was not too easy to get into, or when in, to exit from. The two-man crew for take-off sat side by side in cramped conditions and they had to sit on their parachutes further encumbered by 'Mae West' life jackets. The navigator, earlier called an observer, also had to lug aboard his navigation bag containing up to about 20lb of equipment. While it might have been a bit awkward to exit the aircraft in a hurry, the fact that one seldom had recourse to do so more than compensated for this slight deficiency.

All who flew the Mossies rapidly came to love its fine handling and outstanding performance. For the first time since he had joined the RAF and had been asked to fly twin-engined aircraft, now two years back in time, Ivor found himself in an aircraft which made light of flying with one engine stopped and its propeller in the low drag feathered position. In many respects, its performance on one engine was superior to that of the Blenheim with both engines functioning. This was comforting to know because, if the Merlin had a weakness, it was that it relied upon engine cooling, not on air flowing past the cylinders as happened on Oxfords and Blenheims, but upon an internal glycol system. If this system were to be punctured or worse, it was only a matter of time before the cylinder head temperature gauge would rise rapidly into the red zone and the engine would have to be stopped before it caught fire or seized.

Within a few days of joining 1655 MTU, F/O Broom was showing his pupils how to operate the mighty Mossie and within a week or so he was confidently demonstrating one-engined landings, flapless landings and the other emergency drills. Each course included night flying but here again, the aircraft presented no great difficulty.

Ivor had not flown at night since his one night take-off in a Blenheim at Malta eighteen months earlier and had not then landed at night — the more difficult task — since many months before that. Nevertheless, after two quick dual circuits at night with a fellow instructor followed by two solo circuits and landings (totalling, in all, one hour), he then took up his first student; all in the same night!

The demonstration of how well the aircraft climbed away with only one engine operating was particularly impressive. A pilot could get away with this even if the engine failed at a very critical moment of the flight as, for example, during the take-off. The MTU used Mark III Mosquitoes, an early fighter version, and Mark IVs, the early bomber version. Later versions had engines up to 1,600hp and an operational ceiling of 37,000ft.

Not for the first time in his operational career, was the potential within Ivor Broom detected by a senior officer who was to give him, perhaps quite unknown to him, a further nudge in the right direction. This was S/Ldr Roy Ralston who, when Ivor joined the MTU, was the CO of the unit. Roy Ralston has written:

I was the CO of 1655 Mosquito Training Unit and had applied for three instructor pilots. However, two left a lot to be desired and when, a couple of months later, it was decided that we should move to Marham we took Ivor along with us.*

As will be seen later, this was not the only occasion when Roy did his best to promote the career of his friend Ivor.

It is significant that even before F/O Broom came to the notice of Roy Ralston as a person of marked ability, he had already, at the Blenheim OTU, been rated an 'Above Average' instructor. Roy Ralston appears to have kept more than a fatherly eye upon the young lad from the Welsh valleys and was soon to confirm this advanced assessment of Ivor as a pilot and instructor.

One of the advantages of not being on Bomber Command operations was that those who were married were encouraged to live out of camp with their wives and received an appropriate extra allowance for doing so. Ivor and Jess, while at Bicester, had been living in rooms near the camp and had again found themselves very satisfactory quarters. Little has been written about the difficulties which the young RAF wives had to overcome in the Second World War. In most cases, to be near their 'man', they had to find what accommodation they could, usually in totally strange surroundings: far removed from friends, family and familiar scenes. The procedure was that the young couple looked around a likely town or village, preferably one with a good bus service, and knocked on doors to enquire if the householder would rent them a couple of rooms: one up, the bedroom, and one down for privacy. Fortunately the RAF had received good publicity and the public were generally extremely kind. But it was an acid test for both wife and landlady as it meant that the one kitchen and bathroom had to be shared. Wives also had to live with the constant knot of anxiety about their loved ones as training accidents were not infrequent. Flying was not the safe mode of transport that

* Roy Ralston was himself a splendid pilot. He was once described by Air Chief Marshal Sir Wallace Kyle as 'the most brilliant low-level bomber pilot of the Second World War.'

it now is and, in wartime, corners had to be cut. Also fuel, coal and paraffin were all severely rationed and, with central heating virtually unknown, houses were apt to be cold and damp. Rooms generally included a fireplace but with nothing to put in it, this only added to the draughts.

Many a wife had problems with gas geysers. These were the normal method of heating the bath water but it required a technique of turning on the gas at a precise moment and then holding a lighted match in the appropriate slot. Quite a few minor explosions resulted, trying the patience of their owners. Hot water bottles were a 'must' — especially if a husband was away on night duty! Gas and electric fires were at times available in the bedroom and it was the custom to hang socks and underwear near these last thing at night before turning them off, in the hope that they might be less cold and damp for the following morning.

Bed socks were not unknown!

Two women sharing a kitchen and both having to draw their meagre weekly rations, such as one egg, a tiny modicum of lard, margarine or butter, an ounce or two of meat and tea was a test for the most kindly of landladies. It speaks wonders for Ivor and Jess that they kept in touch with the first person whom they dumped themselves on (for about £2 per week), for the next fifty years of their married life.

At the various places where pilots could live out, the same procedures had to be followed, but each station had a billeting officer whose services helped. On the whole the amazing good will which permeated almost every aspect of British life throughout the war years, resulted in most difficulties being resolved but many young wives spent long weary hours waiting and wondering in silence in an alien house in an alien town. And for some, their life seemed to come to an abrupt halt when the telegram boy on his bicycle knocked on the door with his dreaded message or when the squadron adjutant or Flight Commander called with the grim news, 'Missing…' Anyone who has had to break such news to a slip of a young wife, can never forget the experience. It aged even the most carefree.

Within a month or so after joining 1655 MTU, the unit

moved to Marham. Along with Jess, Ivor again set forth in search of local accommodation. In the village there were only a few modern looking buildings and one, called The School House, looked promising. It was aptly named as it was occupied by a Mr Kirkup, a local schoolmaster, and his wife. After a short chat, this kindly couple agreed to let the Brooms have a couple of rooms. As they had also done when looking for accommodation near Bicester, Ivor and Jess had struck lucky and they were soon on friendly terms with their 'landlords.' Moreover the Brooms and the Kirkups kept in touch post-war for dozens of years until the deaths of the latter. Clearly both Ivor, and in these cases especially Jess, had the gifts of adjusting their habits to fit in well, and to make friends with strangers under the unusual conditions and restraints of wartime Britain.

An amusing outcome of this fortunate arrangement was that when Ivor advised the Marham Adjutant of his address, he retorted: 'This can't be correct.' It came out that the Adjutant himself had previously called there only to be advised that the Kirkups did not take in lodgers! It was, of course, to Ivor and Jess's advantage that, unlike the Adjutant, Ivor's tunic displayed the RAF pilot's wings and the ribbon of the DFC. As has been mentioned before, youthful RAF pilots had caught the imagination of the public who were more inclined to be helpful to them than to more elderly 'wingless wonders' in Air Force blue.

The move to Marham was part of the continuing expansion of the RAF which by 1944 was still creating new units and by then had reached a strength of over one million personnel. This led to constant comings and goings of personnel in the Messes where the aircrews lived and ate. In a way this effectively masked the losses which were inevitable in war and which persisted throughout in training, as well as when on operations against the enemy. By war's end, technical and flying training had accounted for over 11,000 lives. This was more in numbers than were lost by either Fighter Command (7,436) or Coastal Command (9,145) although far less than the 58,375 lost in Bomber Command. Ivor himself could recall at least four losses which had occurred during his period as an instructor at 13 OTU at Bicester. In one of these two aircraft had collided and only one of the six aircrew involved had survived.

Although everyone who flew could remember many casualties, nearly all aircrew were imbued, as Ivor most certainly was, with the firm belief that it was *not* going to happen to *him*. Even the vernacular of the day was in this vein. The expression commonly used was that 'Poor old so-and-so got himself killed …', thus almost implying that, in some undefined way, it was the chap's own fault. Truly has it been said that 'We believe what we want to believe!'

It was at Marham in August 1943 that Ivor Broom's luck almost ran out. He was completing a night detail with a Canadian pupil when, about one mile from touch down, one engine failed and automatically feathered its own propeller. By then the landing flaps had been extended and the wheels had been lowered.

Not even a Mosquito could manage on one engine in this maximum drag configuration near the ground and with only a minimum speed on the dial. However, Ivor, after telling the pupil: 'I've got control' had the situation in hand. As the abrupt failure of one engine has caused the aircraft to drift away from the lines of flares delineating the runway ahead, Ivor decided that the safest course of action (and this had to be decided in a matter of seconds) would be to raise the wheels and to make a controlled belly landing on the airfield to one side of the runway.

Unfortunately the pupil panicked as he saw that the aircraft was about to land away from the lighted flare path. Without warning he grabbed the throttles and opened up the good engine to full power. As could have been predicted by any experienced pilot, the result was calamitous. The nose reared up and the Mosquito with full power on one side and none on the other, cartwheeled over.

The Canadian was killed instantly but Ivor escaped with a broken back. Roy Ralston who was near the flare path saw the accident and said afterwards that he thought that the aircraft was about to make a level crash landing when it suddenly climbed, turned upside down and ploughed in.

One of the advantages of being a person who never smoked nor touched alcohol, and who kept himself fit by taking part in sport when available, is that such healthy bodies heal well.

Within eight weeks of the accident Ivor was sufficiently mobile and, while on a visit to Jess's parents at Ipswich, was flown, by Roy Ralston, back to Marham. It would be another eight weeks before he could satisfy the RAF doctors that he was fit enough to resume flying but at least he could rejoin his comrades.

The practical way that the RAF dealt with smashed up aircrew during the Second World War had been partially responsible for Ivor being able to return to Marham so swiftly. Such men were not treated as invalids; as Ivor soon found out.

First he had been sent to the RAF hospital at Ely. He had been badly injured and was encased in plaster from neck to thigh. However, he learned to his surprise that men with broken limbs and also encased in plaster were being allowed home during weekends. He was even more surprised to discover upon inquiry that he also could do so if he felt up to it and if he could manage to get himself to wherever it was. He jumped at the chance although it required much manipulating due to his inability to walk more than a few paces or to sit down. Somehow he got himself to Ely station and in the train was embarrassed when kindly persons offered him a seat which he then had to refuse while explaining why. At Kings Lynn, Jess had to persuade the local bus which only ran on Thursdays and Saturdays to divert from its normal route to pick up Ivor at the station. Similar stratagems had to be devised to get Ivor back to Ely hospital. Due to his back, Ivor had to sleep on boards in the hospital but used the floor at the Kirkups where Jess was still lodging.

Ivor was soon posted to Loughborough which had become a rehabilitation centre for RAF victims such as he. There the RAF had enlisted the skills of a number of leading sportsmen. One Sergeant instructor was Raich Carter, the famous Derby County and England inside forward. Another was Dan Maskell of tennis fame who introduced the plastered (literally for the first time in his life!) Ivor to the game of squash by standing in the middle of the court and placing the ball so that Ivor could just reach it. Patients were not pampered. Every effort was made to return them to a natural life as speedily as possible. Ivor was even invited to find himself accommodation locally but since he could not walk any great distance he knocked at the door of the bungalow opposite the College entrance and again was lucky as the elderly lady agreed to provide temporary short term living quarters for Ivor and Jess. It would have been hard to turn away a wounded, decorated, young-faced, smiling pilot accompanied by a charming young bride. Ivor, by then, had also learned to emphasise to some who were nervous about admitting the 'wild young men of the RAF' into their homes, that neither Jess nor he smoked or drank.

Although still encased in plaster, Ivor considered that he could still be of some use to 1655 MTU. At his own request, upon his return, he gave lectures to the trainees. This was to have an important spin-off at a later time as it brought him into contact with the Chief Ground Instructor, a certain Flight Lieutenant with the same surname as himself. This was Tommy Broom (no relation), who was a trained and expert navigator.

Whilst back at Marham Ivor could not walk far as he was in plaster from neck to thigh. He could however, with assistance, sit on a bicycle but the plaster prevented him from operating the pedals. Every morning, therefore, Jess would accompany him and the bicycle to the top of the hill between the village and the airfield. Friends, such as Tommy Broom and George Forbes, would be there to meet him, help him onto the bicycle and then, with one on either side, push him around the camp during the day. After work they would escort him to the top of the hill and then give him a push down with the fervent hope that he would negotiate safely the T-junction at the bottom.

After about a month of this, Ivor had to return to Loughborough to have the plaster removed and undergo more rehabilitation exercises. The day it was removed he was pushed into a swimming pool. As this phase lasted another month, Ivor with Jess again went around locally knocking on doors in efforts to find some kindly soul who would rent them temporary rooms. As before they soon struck lucky.

One of the most remarkable characteristics of Ivor Broom was, and still largely is, his ability to join in a party and be as lively as anyone on just orange juice. Although, to be strictly accurate, he has in recent years come to appreciate an occasional glass of white wine while still avoiding beer and spirits. Unlike some who refrain from 'the demon drink', Ivor is no kill-joy. If there is a party going he is eager to enter into the fun and thinks none the less of those who do indulge.

Ivor's back healed with remarkably few complications and by 29 November, after being quickly checked out by his Flight Commander Johnny Greenleaf, he was deemed fit to resume flying. It was only about four months after the accident which had so very nearly put paid to all hopes that the young man held of making a career for himself as a pilot in the RAF. Next day it was business as usual with three flights teaching newcomers how best to fly the 'Wooden Wonder.' What had seemed a disaster turned out to be only a hiccup. Nor was Ivor tinged with the slightest blame for the unfortunate death of the pupil. Sadly, losses during training had to be accepted as one of the prices to be paid by a country on a full war footing.

Life for Ivor and Jess continued in this useful, but not too dangerous, fashion for some months. There were always problems caused by the ever more strict rationing of petrol, clothes, food, sweets, coal (central heating was practically unknown and all rooms had to be heated by stoves or open fires), paraffin and admonishments about never having a bath with more than five inches of water! Generally, the people adhered to such official restrictions, just as they had earlier given to the Government all their aluminium pots, pans and iron railings around their gardens, in response to the cry for metals with which to build more tanks, ships and 'planes. The British people were one hundred percent behind Winston Churchill and, inspired by his famous wartime addresses over the radio ('wireless'), they braced themselves and responded with every personal sacrifice.

Then three things happened: 1655 moved to Warboys, an

airfield near Huntingdon; Jess was preparing herself for their first child and Ivor, in the remarkably safe and reliable Mosquito, suffered a second bad accident.

This came about shortly after 1655 MTU had moved from Marham to nearby Warboys airfield as runways were being laid at Marham. However, a few Mossies on which work had to be completed remained at Marham. When one of these was ready for collection, Ivor agreed to go to Marham and fly it to Warboys. He also agreed to bring back to Warboys a Sgt Brown who had been working on it. He seldom missed an opportunity to cement further the good relations between ground and aircrews.

Soon after take-off from the bumpy grass airfield and after the wheels had been raised, the rudder pedals and control column started juddering madly. Ivor looked over his shoulder and to his horror saw what he thought was the tailplane flapping about in the slipstream. If this became detached, a disastrous swoop-up and uncontrolled plunge earthwards was inevitable. Already the aircraft was virtually uncontrollable. He swiftly decided — and there was no time for anything other than an immediate decision between life and death — that the safest thing would be to try to land, wheels up, straight ahead in the fortunately flat East Anglian countryside.

By reducing power the Mosquito was brought down to earth in some semblance of control. It was, however, a nasty crash and the aircraft was a complete write-off but Ivor and his passenger were able to climb out and walk away unhurt. No attempt had been made to lower the wheels.

The Accident Inquiry was quick to discover the cause of the 'prang.' It had been raining for days and the aircraft had been standing in the open. This had caused some rain to seep through the edges of the cover which protected the compartment in the aircraft in which the two-man dinghy was stowed. The dinghy itself was fitted with an automatic immersion switch so that when a Mosquito crashed on water, the dinghy would automatically inflate and pop out of its compartment ready for immediate use. The bumpy take-off from the grass airfield had caused the rain which had seeped into the compartment to activate the automatic immersion switch. The dinghy had then popped out and wrapped itself around the tail 'plane and elevators, rending them practically immovable. It was this that Ivor had seen flapping about in the slipstream.

As a result of the findings of the Accident Inquiry, the aircraft was modified to ensure that in future no rain water could enter this compartment.

This was the second time that Ivor had survived a Mosquito accident and had lived to tell the investigators the facts thereby enabling modifications to be made to future Mosquitoes and ensure that such accidents were unlikely to recur under similar circumstances. After the first horrendous crash, steps had been taken to modify the Mosquito's automatic propeller feathering device.

After Ivor had resumed his normal role as a flying instructor, the time soon arrived when it was the turn of both Tommy Broom, the CGI, and himself to return to operations again. Tommy was quite a few years older than Ivor and had joined the RAF several years before the war as an armourer, later transferring to become a gunner/observer and then a full-time navigator. Like Ivor, Tommy had worked his way through the ranks, had later been commissioned and by hard work and ability reached the rank of Flight Lieutenant and his position of Chief Ground Instructor at the OTU.

The opportunity for both to return to operations came when Don Bennett, the youthful Acting Air Vice-Marshal and AOC of 8 Group, let it be known to Roy Ralston that he was in the process of adding another Mosquito squadron to his Command and that he was on the look out for the right kind of aircrew. Bennett's 8 Group was a hand-picked élite group and the young AOC was doing all that he could to ensure that only the best pilots and navigators were allowed to form his squadrons.

Roy Ralston then had the idea of putting the two Brooms together and of suggesting to Don Bennett that they joined the new squadron as an experienced operational crew. However, he first arranged for them to fly a couple of short trips together: an SBA practice bad weather approach and an Air Test. The two Brooms seemed to hit it off well whereupon he put the idea before the AOC.

Tommy Broom then suggested to Wing Commander Hamish Mahaddie, a staff officer in 8 Group HQ, that since he and his new pilot had scarcely flown together, it might be a good idea if, before going on Ops over Germany, they could fly on a practice night cross-country over the UK. He was aware that Ivor had never flown any night Ops and knew that this is what they would have to do when in a Pathfinder squadron. However, Hamish retorted that Tommy and Ivor could carry out all the practice they needed over Germany! 'Go East for your training, young man.'

Bennett, as usual, acted with almost breathless speed. The two Brooms flew their brief air test on the 23 May 1944, were posted to join the new 571 Squadron on the 24th, flew a Mosquito of this unit on 25th and by the night of 26th they were over Germany, coned by enemy searchlights, being shot at by AA guns, prior to dropping a 4,000lb bomb on Ludwigshafen!

Roy Ralston's final 'nudge' in Ivor's favour was to give him an 'Exceptional' rating as a pilot; an accolade which was rarely given.

Ivor had much enjoyed his time with 1655 MTU. One of his Station Commanders had been Group Captain 'Digger' Kyle and a well-remembered incident was when a cookhouse airman was up on a serious charge of purloining and selling food on the black market. It looked like a cut-and-dried case with the food displayed on a table throughout the trial. However, the Adjutant appointed to defend the accused knew more about the law than did most and somehow got the accused off on a technicality. The Group Captain was furious and all but 'blew his top' when the adjutant pointed out that since the man had been found 'Not Guilty', then all the goodies which had been found with him and which had been on display, must now be returned to him!

Tommy Broom also remembers an occasion when the same Station Commander came into the Mess and found a party in full swing. With an almost sarcastic tone he inquired: 'What's the excuse for the party this time?'

'It's F/Lt Forbes, Sir. He has just become a father for the first time.'

'That's different and the next round will be on me. What are you all drinking?'

'Seven pints, Sir … and,' as one man they all pointed to Ivor, 'and a lemonade for HIM.' Ivor didn't mind in the slightest. He was pleased in a way that his friends always included him in their drinking sprees. He could generate the same party spirit on his soft drinks as they all did on their more potent brews.

It had been over two years since Ivor Broom, now an experienced Flight Lieutenant, last flew on operations. Many changes had since taken place and the test would be to see how well he coped.

CHAPTER TEN

571 Squadron

Ivor Broom had long been champing at the bit. He had fully recovered from his broken back and neither this bad accident or the second one had dampened his enthusiasm to fly. If anything he was, perhaps, more conscious of its inherent dangers and, therefore a better pilot for this knowledge. It had been over two years since he had last operated against the enemy and, with his DFC ribbon on his battledress tunic, it seemed almost absurdly overlong. More than once he applied to be posted to an operational squadron.

By then, April 1944, massive changes had taken place in the structure of the RAF which, along with the other Services, was preparing for the greatest invasion in history. No. 2 Group which formerly had operated the medium daylight bombers, had by then spawned a similar medium bomber force. Many of its personnel had been swallowed up in a new formation, called 2nd TAF (Tactical Air Force), a name devised by Air Chief Marshal Sir Arthur Tedder. The TAF was part of the reconstruction which the RAF was having to undergo in order to be more fully integrated with its sister Services. All three would be part of the Allied Expeditionary Force which would have to cross the Channel in order to retake Europe from the Nazi Germans and TAF was the RAF's part of the new Army/Air Force. Not too surprisingly, Basil Embry, that most pugnacious of all RAF leaders, had risen swiftly and was now an Air Vice-Marshal and AOC of 2nd TAF.

Another who had risen even more swiftly than Basil Embry was the amazing Australian Donald Bennett. Pre-war he had been a rising star of Imperial Airways: one of their youngest captains and one who had hit the headlines when carrying out record breaking and development flights. As a pilot-cum-navigator he was supreme with a world wide reputation. This had been partially gained from his comprehensive book *The Complete Navigator* on aerial navigation and was recognised as THE book on this subject. Part of it had been written on his honeymoon — it seemed nothing could deter Don Bennett from advancing the frontiers of aviation.

When war was declared Bennett was in the uniform of an Imperial Airways Captain; then that of a BOAC* Captain. However, in quick time he began to make a name for himself when, in late 1940, he pioneered self-delivery of RAF aircraft manufactured in USA by leading a flight of six Hudson medium bombers across the Atlantic from Gander in Newfoundland to Ireland and Scotland. This was a startling feat as, pre-war, only a handful of land 'planes had ever crossed this ocean and virtually none had dared to attempt the 1,850 mile crossing in winter. This set the pattern for others and, by war's end over 10,000 aircraft ranging from big bombers to twin-engined fighters had successfully been flown to the UK from America.

Don Bennett, now an RAF officer, landed in Bomber Command and again immediately began to make an impact. By 1943 he had shot up to the rank of Acting Air Vice-Marshal and was appointed the AOC of a new élite 8 Group which was to lead the way and accurately mark the targets which the rest of the Bomber Command would then bomb. This Group became known as the Pathfinder Force and, through their endeavours, bombing accuracy became many times more accurate.

Bennett was unique as no other RAF reserve officer has previously risen so far or ever would. No other AOC was capable of flying himself to any bomber station, taking off in whatever aircraft it operated and flying every type usually better than others who had been trained on them. It is not known how many raids the AOC personally flew over Germany nor in what types but the stories are legion. When a person becomes a legend in his own lifetime, then the tales proliferate.

The 'Great Don' had been among the first to appreciate the Mosquito and had made sure that many of the first deliveries were sent to his Pathfinder squadrons of 8 Group. In his opinion

---

* On 1 April 1940, Imperial Airways and all other British civil air operators, were amalgamated by Government decree into a new British Overseas Airways Corporation (BOAC) which then flew alongside the RAF but not on military operations, although on war work.

the Mosquito was a war-winning machine.

8 Group was expanding, and as well as the Mosquito squadrons which marked targets for the Main Force, A V-M Bennett was forming several squadrons of Mosquitoes which he named the Light Night Striking Force (LNSF). They would carry out a number of functions but their regular tasks would be to fly along with the Main Force but at a higher altitude to carry out diversionary raids. The LNSF would bomb targets adjacent to the main one, tactics that would lure the deadly Luftwaffe night fighters away from the heavy bombers. Nor was it particularly dangerous as the Mosquito had the legs of the Ju 88s and Me 110s which constituted the majority of the enemy night fighters. To lead the German defences further astray, the LNSF would also drop supplies of 'window', the metal foil strips which cluttered up the screens of the ground radar. Another important task for the LNSF was to operate in weather conditions unsuitable for the 'Heavies.' This kept the pressure on the enemy defences which now rarely had a quiet night.

As had earlier been the case with the Blenheims of 2 Group, the LNSF carried out an occasional daring spectacular raid attended by massive publicity.

Most of the 8 Group pilots were hand picked. Bennett, like many men of genius, could not tolerate fools gladly and, at times, seemed unable to comprehend that not everyone had his many talents. He could be fiercely intolerant of anyone who fell below the high standards which he personally set and which he expected from others in his Command.

The Pathfinder squadron which the two Brooms had so abruptly joined was No. 571. It was based at Oakington in Cambridgeshire and had been formed a few weeks earlier. Under Wing Commander Mike Birkin DSO, DFC, its Commanding Officer, they had carried out their first operation on 12 April when he had led a couple of aircraft on a high-level night bombing of Osnabrück. Although there were other Mosquitoes operating in daylight, virtually all operations by the LNSF were carried out at night: hence the name of the force.

It is not known what had prompted Roy Ralston to pair the two Brooms together but it did not take 571 Squadron long to realise that they had been sent a top-notch crew. It helped that they were posted to 'B' Flight and that this was commanded by S/Ldr Johnny Greenleaf. He had also been a Flight Commander with 1655 MTU and therefore knew their respective worths.

Although F/Lt I G Broom's total number of hours were now close to one thousand, he had still carried out only thirty three hours at night as first pilot but, as 571 operated almost entirely at night, this total was rapidly to increase. Even after only one week with 571 Squadron, he had increased it by nearly one third as, after the initial Ludwigshafen attack, Tommy and he completed two more operations before May gave way to June. On both these occasions they were also coned and held for some anxious minutes by batteries of German searchlights. However, it was beginning to dawn on them that, with their speed and height, they were almost immune from the normal German night fighters. Also the aircraft was equipped with a device which carried the name of 'Boozer' (very inappropriately for Ivor). This showed a light in the cockpit to warn the crew that they were being monitored by German radar. It glowed red at first but became brighter when in greater peril.*

As the German heavy AA guns were radar directed it made sense, when seeing a bright red Boozer light, to start to jink smartly and to change height as such moves threw into disarray the pre-calculations of the hostile gunners below.

Five more bombing raids followed during the first ten days of June and on each the Mossies, in their widened bomb bays, carried the 4000lb 'Cookie' as the big bomb was called. These five included the first that the Brooms had flown over Berlin. Some crews felt an extra anxiety when sent over Berlin as the city was ringed with AA but Ivor's only comments in his log book were 'Wizard trip' and 'Very good trip.' His confidence in the Mosquito was almost unbounded. He knew that even if hit and losing one engine, the aircraft was capable of getting

---

* A white light alongside the red one glowed whenever the radar of an enemy night fighter triggered it but, in a Mosquito, this was a rare occurrence.

them back on the other one.

By then Tommy and he had acquired a personal aircraft, Mosquito MM 118, and their ground crew had embellished it with a painting of two crossed broomsticks; adding a caption 'The Flying Brooms.'

The two Brooms soon were 'at home' flying at 25,000ft and more over Germany. They had known each other, albeit less closely, for a number of years as they had both been at 13 OTU, Bicester and at 1655 MTU. They had both also been involved in low-level attacks on Cologne but, in Tommy's case, this had led to disaster. His aircraft had crash-landed in Holland but, after a number of hair-raising escapades, and thanks to the heroism of the Dutch and Belgian people, he had managed to get all the way back across the Pyrenees into Spain and then back to the UK in six weeks.

Searchlights were a perpetual annoyance and on one occasion when over Berlin, they held the Mosquito for a long fourteen minutes. To avoid this exposure (and blinding light inside the aircraft), Ivor twisted and turned, dived and rose in attempts to escape their glare. When all was done and he asked Tommy for a course back to base, all Tommy could reply was: 'Fly west with a dash of north while I sort myself out!'

As well as bombing the main cities of Germany, several of the operations were directed against specific synthetic oil plants and these may well, indirectly, have saved many a Mosquito from subsequent disaster. This was because the Germans had it within their grasp to produce a night fighter which could account for Mosquitoes with as much ease as the Ju 88s and Me 110s were accounting for the Heavies of Main Force Bomber Command. This was the Heinkel 219.

Fortunately for the Mosquitoes of the LNSF, the He 219 was never produced in numbers. The Luftwaffe commanders, *Reichsmarschal* Göring and his aides had decided to pin their faith upon the latest Junkers night fighter. This Ju 388, like all variants of the 88, was an excellent machine but was still unable to catch up with a Mosquito going at full speed. This also applied to the latest night-fighting versions of the Me 110: the Me 210 and Me 410. But the He 219 was quite a different threat. It possessed ample speed, height and the capability to overhaul any Mossie, even one going flat out. It was armed with a menacing combination of machine guns, 20mm and 30mm cannon and could blast Mosquitoes out of the sky without difficulty. It also carried advanced Marks of 'Lichtenstein' radar which could seek and find RAF bombers even on the darkest of nights.

A few had been produced for trial evaluation and in one of these on the night of 11/12 June 1943, *Oberstleutnant* Werner Streib, during a single sortie, shot down five British bombers. However, upon returning, the landing flaps failed and he crashed. He was not hurt but his radar operator on the Lichtenstein SN 2 set broke both legs.

This was seized upon by Göring and Milch as a good reason to continue with the Ju 388 contracts at the expense of the He 219 competitor. As a result, no large He 219 contract was ever placed and during the first four months of 1944 when German production of night fighters reached a peak with over 2,000 Junkers and Messerschmitt models being built, only sixty-six He 219s were made.

It may have counted against the Heinkel firm that their four engined design, the He 177, for which quite large orders were placed, had failed miserably and had killed so many aircrews that, within the Luftwaffe, it had become dubbed as 'The Widow Maker.'

Perhaps the most cogent reason for not proceeding at full pace with the He 219 — the only night fighter on either side to have been designed specifically for night fighting — was that, to attain its speed of nearly 450mph, it required a special brand of fuel. This could well have been why the Mosquitoes were directed at the synthetic fuel plants at Wanne Eickel, Homburg, Duisburg, Kamen and elsewhere. They might have been instrumental in adding another nail in the coffin of the He 219; although it is most unlikely that anyone in the squadrons, even their commanding officers, knew anything about either the He 219 or its need for very special fuel. Intelligence reports, rightly, did not filter down to anyone who was liable to be shot down and interrogated by the enemy.

Germany also produced two other night fighters which could have threatened the Mosquitoes. One was their Wooden Wonder, the Ta 154, a product of Professor Tank who had designed the Fw 190. This had much the same high performance as did the He 219. In this case, it was not proceeded with because the Germans never managed to produce the required special adhesives to hold it together. Late in the war, the Luftwaffe was given a number of the jet-powered Me 262s but this day fighter was seldom modified for night fighting although a few known as Me 262B-1 a were produced for a trial. However, the war was all but over by then.

Although the Luftwaffe chiefs could be criticised for not pressing forward with the He 219 which could perhaps have destroyed hundreds of Mosquitoes, it has to be remembered that they were concentrating upon the Ju 88 and Me 110 night fighters which were shooting down the RAF Heavies in their thousands. When fitted with the 70° upward firing cannons, their *Schräge Musik* (Slanting Music) weapon, the Lancasters and Halifaxes seldom knew what had hit them until far too late. The German night fighter group NJG/1 alone claimed no less than 2,173 destroyed, mainly Lancasters.

Mosquito operations were of such short duration, almost always less than four and a half hours and often less than three, that crews were expected to operate two nights in a row before being stood down for the third. However, weather conditions were apt, on occasions, to prohibit all operations by 8 Group. After six weeks of Ops, the crews were usually granted six days leave.

By then Jess had given birth to a fine boy and the couple had rented a house in Ipswich, where her parents lived. Jess had in fact moved to Ipswich prior to the birth of the boy and she was there when Ivor had his second accident with 1655 MTU. This gave her father an anxious couple of days because just before the birth he called Ivor at Warboys only to be told that he had taken off but had not returned. He called again later that day and also the next, a Sunday, only to be told the same story. Not knowing what flying duties Ivor was carrying out, he feared the worst and was in a quandary what to tell his daughter when visiting her later that afternoon.

All that had happened was that Ivor had flown back to Marham to attend a Saturday night closing-down party and did not return until next morning. Meanwhile, Jess's parents had to live with the fear that their son-in-law was 'Missing' on operations at the very time when their daughter was giving birth: as duly did happen on the Sunday.

When Ivor returned to Warboys on the Sunday for lunch, a waitress asked if he knew that he was a father. He at once telephoned the hospital and advised Jess he would visit her as soon as his duties would allow, on Tuesday. He had not been informed that his father-in-law had been asking for him so did not communicate with him.

On the Sunday, when her parents saw Jess and were about to break the sad news that her husband was 'Missing' — that most dreaded of wartime words — Jess mentioned that she had just had a call from Ivor!

The final chapter of this 'drama that never was' is that when Ivor did visit Ipswich on the Tuesday, acquaintances he met all warmly wrung his hand and said how very pleased they were to see him so fit and well. His hand was pumped enthusiastically rather to his bewilderment but the explanation eventually emerged that the news had got around that he had, in the language of the day, 'Gone for a Burton.' Jess even received one letter of condolence.

All this had happened some months before Ivor Broom had returned to operations upon being posted to join 571 Squadron. Once back on Ops, no member of Bomber Command crew was allowed to live off station. It was not thought fair for a young wife to be living adjacent to her husband at a time when on almost every night whenever flying was taking place, the BBC broadcast next morning would begin — after extolling the damage done — with an announcement that 'twenty or more (and in one case ninety-seven after the raid on Nürnberg) of our bombers have failed to return.'

Although the ratio of losses incurred by the Heavies of Main Force and those by the Mosquitoes of Pathfinder Force bore little resemblance, the statistics were not generally known

New Inn Council School circa 1930. Young Ivor is the fourth boy from the left, front row. A fellow pupil, Trevor Evans, also served in the RAF becoming a Warrant Officer and was awarded the AFM (third from left, second row) (*Ted Jenkins*)

'B' Flight, No. 3 Squadron, Initial Training Wing, Aberystwyth, September 1940. By coincidence Sir Ivor is again fourth from the left in the front row

Blenheim V-RT V6391 of 114 Squadron over Knapsack Power Station, Cologne on 12 August 1941;
Pilot - Sgt Ivor Broom, Observer - Sgt Bill North, WOP/AG - Sgt Les Harrison

Bill North, Ivor Broom and Les Harrison, 1941

The two Brooms known as 'The Flying Brooms' in front of their Mosquito of 571 Squadron, August 1944

'Q' Queenie of 128 Squadron being bombed up with a 4,000lb bomb at Wyton, November 1944

163 Squadron, March 1945

Celebrating VE day in front of the officers' mess at RAF Wyton. Note the Russian officers on the extreme right and Ivor sitting on top of the lorry's cabin

No. 28 Spitfire Squadron pose for the camera

57 Squadron, Cottesmore, 1953

S/Ldr Ivor Broom leads 28 Squadron in immaculate formation over Malaya (*RAF Official*)

Canberras of 57 Squadron flying from Cottesmore in October 1953 (*RAF Official*)

Above: HRH The Crown Prince of Iraq being briefed by Flying Officer Paddy Brook prior to taking a flight with S/Ldr Broom (*RAF Official*)

Left: A proud CO accompanies HM King Hussein after inspecting 57 Squadron at Amman (*RAF Official*)

Photograph taken shortly after record-breaking Ottawa-London flight showing from left to right: S/Ldr Bob Seymour, S/Ldr Dougie Bower and S/Ldr Ivor Broom

W/Cdr Dickie Arscott, OC 213 Squadron, shows HRH Princess Margaret around the static display with G/Capt. Broom and Air Marshal Sir Ronald Lees (C-in-C RAF Germany) following behind. (*RAF Official*)

Meeting the Royal Family at the Central Flying School, June 1969. The wheelchair and plastercasts being the result of a crash in a Folland Gnat two weeks earlier. (*RAF Official*)

The joy of flying a Red Arrows Gnat at the Central Flying School, 1969

Air Vice-Marshal Ivor Broom

Broomsticks Guard of Honour by Officers of RAF Coltishall after formal 'Dining Out' in 1972 on leaving No. 11 Group

Proud husband, father and grandfather celebrates his 70th birthday with his family

Sir Ivor and Lady Broom leaving St Clements Danes after the service to dedicate the statue of Air Chief Marshal Lord Dowding in front of the Church, 1992

to young wives. All they knew was that their men were 'bomber boys' and that they went nightly over Germany carrying large and deadly bombs and that 100 or more aircrew would go out and not return.

On every raid, as well as carrying the big bomb (although when attacking oil plants the load would be four 500lb bombs) the Mosquitoes of 571 Squadron also carried a supply of 'window' which was launched via a chute. The bag of 'window' was between the navigator's legs and he had to drop this first as until he had done so, he was unable to get down in the nose of the aircraft to the Mark XIV bombsight which was used for accurate bomb aiming.

Tommy soon established himself as an accurate bomb aimer but on one occasion he was too accurate. Other Mossies of 130, 105 and 109 Squadrons using both OBOE and H2S*, did the actual target marking for Main Force and the LNSF. The Heavies and LNSF bomber Mosquitoes then bombed on the target markers. Whenever possible Ground Target Indicators (GTIs) were dropped. These were coloured flares which burned bright. A back-up system used, when the ground was obscured, was that the Pathfinders then dropped cloud markers at which to bomb. On one clear night, Tommy dropped so accurately on the Ground Target Indicator that he hit and obliterated it. He even brought back photographs to prove his deadly marksmanship!

It is an indication of the different risks involved that, whereas the Mosquitoes always hoped for a clear night so that they could bomb more accurately, the Heavies prayed for a cloudy night as these conditions made it more difficult for the enemy night fighters, searchlights and AA guns.

Mosquito crews in the LNSF were obliged to carry out fifty operational trips (and by then aborted trips did not count towards the number) before being able to ask for an operational rest period. With the crews operating, in theory, about twenty times each month, it did not take too long for a Tour of Ops to be completed. However, leave, weather, occasional sickness

* OBOE was the most accurate of all navigation aids and H2S radar 'painted' a pattern of the ground below and around the aircraft.

etc inevitably stretched the period beyond the theoretical seventy-five day total duration. The Heavies, by contrast, had to complete a Tour of thirty Ops but, sadly, a great number never achieved that sought-after number. By war's end, no less than 58,375 aircrew from Bomber Command had been lost and tens of thousands had become Prisoners of War. Remarkably few were crews of Mosquito aircraft.

For navigation over Germany, the principal aid was LORAN, an electronic system which the enemy seemed unable to jam. In the cramped cockpit, it required the navigator to almost twist around as the set was almost behind his seat. GEE was simpler to operate but was of little use after crossing the coast, due to enemy jamming.

Crews were given precise times and heights for bombing. Upper air wind vectors were partially a matter of guesswork by the Met Office and tricks had to be learned how to speed up and slow down if discovering that, due to unforecast winds, the aircraft was ahead or behind schedule. Another difficulty to be overcome was that the Germans had become experts at making dummy targets. Whole cities were faked and attracted a lot of bombs. Dummy airfields were numerous and attempts were made to produce fake target markers which meant that attention had to be paid to ensure that the bombs were dropped upon the correct coloured markers (changed each night), as briefed.

Much has been made about the validity of the attacks upon the cities of Germany but little seems to have been written about the enormous expenditure in man hours, machinery and uniformed men who manned the German defences in order to try to defeat the attackers. Until June 1944, it was still the Russians who were having to face the main might of the German armies and, until the Allies also landed in France, much of RAF planning was intended to tie-up large numbers of German forces at home in an attempt to relieve the pressure on Russia.

It was also fairly obvious that there could hardly be any town in Germany that was not participating in the war effort. Whereas, here at home, in towns like Stratford and Edinburgh, never renowned for heavy industry, there was scarcely a garage, clothing factory, mill or store in either place that was not working flat out on some war work or other. Any large conurbation in Germany hitherto untouched, was an obvious place into which to move machines from those towns that had been razed to the ground.

Berlin became a favoured target and the Flying Brooms flew more sorties to the enemy's capital than anywhere else. But scarcely any big German city went untouched by them: Hanover, Hamburg and Homburg, Kiel, Gelsenkirchen, Osnabrück, Metz, Stuttgart, Cologne and others where the enemy defences seldom seemed to trouble them unless they had to abort due to the weather.

The last days of July 1944 were ones that the crew remembered well. On the 26th they bombed Hamburg but Ivor had problems fighting against severe turbulence and saw much lightning. It had been a rough ride. However, conditions on the 29th were far worse and, when over the North Sea, Ivor and Tommy found themselves enveloped at about 25,000ft within the stormy folds of a vicious cumulo nimbus (thunderstorm cloud). The Mosquito was tossed about as if chaff and, when eventually they did emerge from the cloud's entrails, they had lost some 10,000ft of height and were heading in the opposite direction! Ivor then called it a day. The wonder is that the aircraft did not break up and it speaks well both for the manufacturer and for Ivor who managed to keep some semblance of control without overstraining the airframe. His next log book entry is to record that Tommy and he practised an 'Abandonment of aircraft' drill!

Many notable events happened to Ivor G Broom during the months of August. It was in August 1940 that he first reported to the RAF. It was on 12 August 1941 that he took part in the memorable Knapsack raid. On 10 August 1943 he crashed and broke his back. Now again on 9 August 1944 he was to take part in another spectacular low level event: his first attempt to do so over Germany in the dead of night.

The two flying Brooms, in their MM 118 with its crossed broomsticks, were among the ten crews of 571 Squadron which were detailed to drop mines into the Dortmund-Ems Canal. As the canal is only 125ft wide, the only way to ensure accuracy was for the Mosquitoes to drop their mines at extremely low levels while almost skimming over the smooth water. It was also decided that the operation would be carried out at night. This in itself was no simple task.

The Royal Navy supplied the mines, known to them as Mark IVs. Each resembled a torpedo being ten feet in length, cylindrical in shape with an eighteen inch diameter and they weighed 1,500lb — which caused no difficulties for the Mosquitoes. The big problem was to get the aircraft over the canal under ideal conditions at the desired place and precise time.

Although the Bomber Command crews were unaware of it, the attack had been planned with the Battle of the Atlantic much in mind. By then, August 1944, the U-boat threat had largely been temporarily eliminated. Thanks to the Allied Navies being supplied with an increased number of escort carriers, destroyers, frigates, sloops and corvettes, and with massive assistance of little-known RAF Coastal Command, the Type VII and Type IX U-boats which, during 1941 and 1942 had threatened to win the war for Germany, had at last been defeated. The turning point had come during the spring months of 1943 when Coastal Command, which had not sunk a single U-boat until well into 1941, sank eighty-seven of the 122 destroyed in a four-month period. Thereafter aircraft continued to sink more than did the surface ships. The long range B-24 Liberators, enhanced radar, more effective depth charges, better tactics and the Leigh Light for night attacks had all contributed to the success of aircraft both from Coastal Command and from escort carriers which now accompanied many convoys.

However, *Admiral* Karl Dönitz, promoted from commander of all U-boats to overall command of all German naval forces, was a brilliant and wily leader. Neither he, nor Winston Churchill, ever deviated from the belief that, after 1942, only the U-boats could provide an Axis victory. New U-boats were ordered and were being built. From

Intelligence reports, the Allies knew that the new designs would not only be equipped with the snorkel, which would allow the diesel engines to work with the U-boat largely submerged, but they might also be powered by revolutionary Wankel engines which would give them a faster, more deadly surface speed, a very much faster underwater capability and would enable them again to become a major problem.

The first counter to this grim Intelligence was to bomb the yards at Wilhelmshaven, Bremen and other ports where U-boats were traditionally built. Some attacks by the US 8th Air Force, using B-17s and B-24s in daylight, were particularly effective. Dönitz replied by pre-fabricating the U-boats and bringing the massive parts to the Baltic ports for a swift final assembly inside vast bombproof sheds which had roofs of reinforced concrete up to seven metres thick. The pre-fabricated parts were so large that they could not be transported to the ports except by using Germany's many waterways. A key section was built in Dortmund and could only reach the coast via the Dortmund-Ems Canal. This is why the canal had already been attacked by large numbers of Lancaster bombers. At considerable cost, they had managed to close this vital waterway for a matter of a month or so*. It had since been repaired but this time an attempt would be made to close it using just a dozen Mosquitoes; ten of which were from 571 Squadron.

Some of the crews which had been detailed for this special operation had not before, as had Ivor Broom, operated at 50ft or so. They were therefore given practice flights of descending rapidly from 26,000ft to 50ft over a similar waterway. Fortunately the Fens could supply canals and straight sections of rivers, such as the Old Bedford and Delph rivers, for realistic practices. For a few days, the Mosquitoes came hurtling down to flash along these. As can be imagined, the local population and farmers were quick to complain. Livestock panicked and stampeded. The peace of the countryside was being rudely disrupted!

* A still earlier attack had been made against the canal by eight Lancasters of Bomber Command's most élite squadron, the Dambusting 617 Squadron. Not only had it failed but more than half the raiders failed to return.

For such an important mission, CO W/Cdr Mike Birkin, typically, put himself down to operate: also S/Ldr Norman Mackie the CO of A Flight. 571 Squadron under Birkin was one which prospered from being led from the front. Another key squadron officer was S/Ldr Ashley, the unit's navigation chief. Much of the burden for working out how best to get the ten Mosquitoes to the precise spot at an exact time fell upon him.

The timing had to be exact as it was recognised that the only sure way of being able to detect the water of the canal, even though a straight 7 mile section had been chosen, was for the crews to attack on a night when the water would be reflecting the light of a moon shining more or less in line with the 7 mile straight. The moon had to be directly ahead or behind the attacker and in line with the chosen stretch. Only a few days of the month would be right. Moreover, the night would have to be relatively clear of cloud or else the moonlight would be absent.

The plan was for the Mosquitoes to fly at a normal 25,000-26,000ft in the direction of Osnabrück as if intending to bomb that city but, at a predetermined point, to descend rapidly at a controlled speed so as to arrive over the canal within a short space of time. Other pathfinding Mosquitoes were brought in to help. One would mark with a green target-cloud marker the point over which the attackers should start to descend and, much nearer the target, a red Ground Target Indicator, known as the 'Red Spot', would be dropped. By then the aircraft would have slowed down by lowering flaps and opening bomb doors. The Red Spot was just 5 miles from the canal and the attackers would then fly a track of 045 degrees for about ninety seconds before arriving over the SE end of the 7 mile stretch. Hopefully the crews would then catch a glimpse of the water in the canal, reflected in the moonlight.

As can be imagined, everything depended upon a reasonably clear night and for a night or two, within the small 'window' of days when the moon would be co-operating, the met forecasters predicted too much cloud and the operation had to be put back till the next night. Even when the go-ahead was given for the 9 August 1944, the forecast was far from perfect. Clouds were expected, but by that time it was a case of now or never for that moonlight month.

As was usual for such a special operation, a spoof diversion was arranged. This was for other Mosquitoes to accompany the minelayers *en route* to Osnabrück but to carry on and bomb that town, while the dozen attackers swept swiftly down from over the green marker towards the Red Spot. The Red Spot was dropped to explode on the ground and, to make sure that it could be seen, would be dropped several times at two minute intervals.

The weather did cause problems but the green marker was dropped dead on time between 0247–0251 hours, and in the right place but it had to be dropped on top of a 10,000ft cloud layer. After passing over this, the attackers had to descend, while reducing speed from 260 knots to 200 knots, on track and hope that they would emerge with sufficient visibility below the cloud to avoid flying into high ground and still be able to pick up the burning Red Spot.

In most cases, all went well but at least one aircraft, not from 571 Squadron, never caught sight of the green marker and a few didn't detect the Red Spot. All those who missed this vital clue flew around a while in the hope of being able to pick up the canal waters in the moonlight and at least one did so and was then able to 'garden' effectively.

Throughout Bomber (and Coastal) Command, mines carried in bomb bays were always referred to as 'cucumbers', on account of their long thin shape and mine laying was therefore called 'gardening.' Bomber Command often 'gardened' and thereby sank several U-boats in the Baltic as well as damaging the *Gneisenau*, one of the big battlecruisers, towards the end of her infamous dash through the English Channel.

The two Brooms had an almost copy-book trip. They easily picked up the green marker and thanks, no doubt, to Tommy's excellent navigation, broke cloud with the Red Spot just where it was expected to be. Thereafter it was fairly easy to 'garden' in the correct section of the canal without encountering much opposition, as a measure of surprise had been achieved. The entry in F/Lt Broom's log book was typically succinct: 'Operation 71. Mine-laying in Dortmund-Ems canal from 150 feet.'

Although 150 feet is mentioned, there clearly were times when the aircraft was below this height while flying along the canal. This is because to this day, Ivor Broom had the clearest recollection of the operation for an unusual reason.

While flying along the canal, he suddenly got a quick glimpse of one of the crewmen of one of the barges. As his aircraft passed by at a very low altitude, this man, startled by the noise, had popped out to see what was happening outside. With the light streaming from his open door, Ivor caught a distinct, but fleeting, glimpse of his head!

There can be few people serving with the Pathfinder Group of Bomber Command who came almost face to face with one of his German enemies over Germany... and lived to fly again.

It is thought seven, or possibly eight, of the Mosquitoes successfully dropped their mines and all was accomplished without loss. One aircraft experienced engine trouble and had to jettison the mine. Another definitely failed to locate the canal. This compares well with the previous Lancaster attack when a large number of aircraft, each with half a dozen or more aircrew on board, had attacked and had suffered losses. Yet this small number of Mossies had managed to close this vital waterway without loss, except only the one aircraft which had crashed on take-off.

It was learned later that they had successfully closed the canal, while Germans swept for mines, for about six weeks. This being approximately the same length of time that the canal had been closed after the big Lancaster attack. Don Bennett's calculation that a Mosquito was worth about seven Lancasters was perhaps close to the mark?

As had happened almost exactly three years before when on 12 August 1941 Ivor had been involved in the Knapsack raid, the Press were again brought in to tell the world about this spectacular raid. It drove another nail into the coffin of a Germany which, by then, was in full retreat on all Russian fronts and had just been badly mauled in the Falaise gap, leaving the way wide open for the British and American armies to start streaming across France towards the Rhine and the heart of Germany's industrial power base.

By failing to get a single one of her super new U-boats operational before the surrender in May 1945, Germany had lost her last chance of winning the war.

For their part in this well-planned operation, both Ivor and Tommy Broom were awarded immediate decorations. For F/Lt I G Broom, it was a bar to the DFC which he had gained from his Malta period and for F/Lt T J Broom, it was the DFC. Tommy's navigation was always first class and even on this mission, although not the first to take-off, Tommy was able to guide Ivor to be the first to arrive back.

As was expected, AOC Air Vice-Marshal Don Bennett was there in person to greet the returning heroes and to debrief the crews in his own forceful direct manner. Although 8 Group had a number of aircraft of different types and had a number of functions to perform, there was very little that Don Bennett did not know about it at first hand: and, of equal importance, there were very few men in the Group who did not know his slight figure by sight.

Although the Allies were now firmly entrenched in France and were streaming rapidly in vast numbers towards the Rhine, the German night fighter defences of the Fatherland, which must by then have been employing the best part of a million men, were far from weakening.

Five days after the much-publicised Dortmund–Ems Canal raid, Ivor records in his log book, after again dropping a 'cookie' on Berlin, 'Strong opposition all the way.' Two days later, after a literally flying visit to his family at Ipswich, worse was to happen. Their aircraft, MM 118, was so badly hit by flak during another raid on Berlin at 27,000ft that although Ivor and Tommy brought it back to Oakington, it was classified as 'Cat AC', or beyond repair on unit and it never flew on operations again. It must have been a terrifying experience but all Ivor wrote in his personal log book was: 'Operation 74. Berlin. 1 x 4,000lb from 27,000ft. Aircraft Cat AC — flak.'

Thereafter the two Brooms seldom flew in the same Mosquito. However, their period with 571 Squadron was drawing to a close.

After adding Mannheim and Düsseldorf (there and back in three hours) to the list of cities which the pair had attacked, F/Lt I G Broom DFC & bar, along with F/Lt T J Broom DFC were posted to help form 128 Squadron at Wyton. Together they had completed thirty-three operations with 571 Squadron and eleven of these had been to drop 'cookies' on Berlin. With 128 Squadron still part of the LNSF of 8 Group, they would again be operating Mosquitoes at night and flying together. The only difference of any significance was that, henceforth F/Lt T Broom would be sitting alongside S/Ldr I Broom as Ivor had been promoted and had been put in charge of 'A' Flight of 128 Squadron.

As before, when he had departed from 1655 MTU, Ivor had left a unit with the highest accolade of all as Wing Commander Mike Birkin had sent him on his way with the rating of 'An Exceptional Mosquito pilot.'

This was no more than Ivor deserved but the test would be to see how the still young man, who had never attended an RAF administration course and who, pre-war, had only 'flown a desk' as a junior clerk in an Income Tax office, would shape up to a position of command in an RAF operational squadron with his country at war.

CHAPTER ELEVEN

128 Squadron

The position of a Flight Commander in an operational squadron of the RAF did not in itself require a great amount of administrative knowledge or office work. However, it was an important stepping stone as the Flight Commanders of 'A' and 'B' Flights ranked as second and third within the squadron with only the Wing Commander, the CO of the unit, ahead of them. Nonetheless it was where an officer first cut his teeth in disciplinary and man-management matters.

The fact that Ivor was not a Regular and had been too busy flying aircraft to bother his head overmuch with RAF codes of behaviour was not, in 8 Group, the drawback that it might have been in other Groups as A V-M D Bennett, AOC of the Group, had also not been dressed in Air Force blue prior to the war.

The promotion from Flight Lieutenant to Squadron Leader, or even to Acting Squadron Leader as was usually the case in wartime, was of greater significance. Provided an officer committed no serious offence, promotion during the Second World War from Pilot Officer, through Flying Officer to Flight Lieutenant was automatic after about two years had lapsed since first becoming an officer. Thereafter it went by merit and many an officer never rose beyond Flight Lieutenant. Squadron Leaders also personally mixed with higher ranks and were apt to be called to Group HQ for conferences. Their potential and worth were for the first time under scrutiny by those near the top of the hierarchy.

In other respects Flight Commanders carried on as normal and took their turn at operations without special privileges. Another important issue was that pay leaped up to about 30 shillings per day (£1.50 in 1993 money).

The first flight made for 128 Squadron by Ivor, with Tommy beside him as usual, was the customary brief test flight which was made shortly before every full operation. This checked that the aircraft was in a fit state for the nightly task. Although Tommy usually accompanied Ivor on these, he had no navigation function to perform and, on occasions, pilots such as Ivor would take instead a man or girl from maintenance or Flying Control. This helped to cement the bond between those who flew the aircraft and those who looked after them. It is also significant that by 1944, many of the fitters and riggers who serviced the aircraft and who manned the Flying Control tower were WAAFs (Women's Auxiliary Air Force) and their numbers were by then close to the total strength of the pre-war RAF.

Although Ivor and Tommy first operated with 128 Squadron in a Mosquito Type XX, a Canadian machine which like others built there did not have the widened bomb bay so could not carry the 4000lb bomb, it was not long before they laid personal claim to a machine, a Type XVI, PL 401, but it never reached the stage where it flew with crossed broomsticks adorning its sides.

The most memorable raid carried out by the new Flight Commander and his namesake, was the one upon Essen in October 1944. They were part of the 1,050 aircraft which plastered the city that night: Bomber Command's biggest bomb load dropped. Their contribution was the usual supply of 'window' and another 'cookie.' Don Bennett was often around to see them off or to greet them back having established himself in married quarters at Wyton to find out for himself at first hand what his squadrons were doing. He had already singled out Ivor as a pilot upon whose judgment he could rely and had asked him, before he had departed, to 'hang around a bit' after releasing his 'cookie', to try to assess the success of this enormous attack. On Ivor's return, he reported to his AOC that the bombing had been 'a bit scattered' and Don at once picked up the Red Scramble phone and advised Air Marshal 'Bomber' Harris of what Ivor had said, using his exact words. This great raid had taken place on the night of the 23 October. A few nights earlier the two Brooms had dropped four 500lb bombs on Hanover from 25,000ft and Ivor has written in his log book, a most appropriate comment: 'Bang on!' … four bangs actually.

With vast armies now advancing at a pace on both her fronts, the position of Germany was hopeless. The Romanian oil fields, Germany's only source of natural oil, were about to be over-run. This at best only supplied about fifteen percent of her requirements and the bombing of the plants which turned coal into oil, by the B-17 and B-24 aircraft of the 8th US Air Force, had by then further compounded Germany's plight. The 'Big Week' in February 1944, when the Luftwaffe rose up to defend the attacks by US Fortresses and Liberators upon the aircraft manufacturing factories, had cost the Germans dear. During February and March they had lost over 1,000 experienced pilots and, by late 1944, lacked the fuel with which to train replacements in anything other than an inadequate manner. On one daylight raid alone the Luftwaffe had lost 120 fighters to the P-47 Thunderbolts and P-51 Mustangs of the 8th USAF which had accompanied their big daylight bombers. By August there were only 100 serviceable day fighters to put up against attacks when some single raids by American bombers were escorted by over 1,000 of their P-47s and P-51s. What few fighters remained were being used to defend the German heartland against the remorseless nightly attacks by Bomber Command with Me 109s and Fw 190s, nominally day fighters, being used: with appalling losses of pilots not trained in night or instrument flying.

Hitler, however, raged on with broadcasts which foretold of war-winning terror weapons coming into production and which he assured his followers would soon turn the tide. The V 1 flying bomb, the so-called 'Doodle Bug', did for a while cause tremendous damage to the towns of south east England but did little to affect the Allies' by now overwhelming military might. These successes were short lived as ways of destroying Doodle Bugs with fast, low-flying aircraft and massed ranks of AA guns on the cliffs overlooking the Straits of Dover, not to mention the clusters of balloons to the south of London, all took their toll. Moreover, as the Allies swept across France to the Pas de Calais, the launching sites were rapidly over-run*.

These fast advances also meant that airfields were being

captured nearer and nearer to German soil making it possible for much of Bomber Command to join their American brothers in daylight as well as night attacks. Generally the fear of the Luftwaffe was waning and Ivor was among those who attacked Limburg at night on 13 December 1944 from only 14,000ft.

November and December 1944 saw the first high level daylight formation raids by 8 Group Mosquitoes on the Ruhr. The first two targets were Duisburg and Hamborn. In both cases Ivor, flying as usual with Tommy, was appointed formation leader. By then their fame had spread. It was widely recognised that they were a team which could accurately find any target and then bomb it with precision.

The Duisburg raid was both significant and memorable. By sending a large formation of unarmed Mosquitoes in broad daylight to attack a target in the Ruhr, it showed open contempt for the Luftwaffe. Another matter of significance was that, by appointing S/Ldr Ivor Broom to lead the raid, it showed that the AOC and other senior officers of the Group clearly had an eye on him as a man to be noted. It was further significant that a specific target had been singled out, the Benzol production plant in the city, and this was duly hit and damaged. The target had been selected as part of the overall bombing strategy of the Allies. The plan to deprive Germany of her oil supplies was being carried out by certain elements of RAF Bomber Command as well as by the huge formations of American daylight bombers. Post-war critics of Air Marshal 'Bomber' Harris are apt to forget this.

The raid was memorable for Ivor Broom for personal reasons as, for once, he fell foul of his determined AOC. As the formation leader, he was privy to the full details of the attack. Upon examining this he noted that the speed at which the Mosquitoes were supposed to fly to Duisburg was a good deal less than they were capable of maintaining at the prescribed height of 26,500ft and was too slow for formation flying in comfort. This seemed an obvious error as unarmed

---

* With their launching sites captured by the Allies, the V1 flying bombs were then crudely attached to He 111 bombers for low-level air-launching over the North Sea. They caused little further damage to England but many losses among brave German pilots.

Mosquitoes literally lived or died by their speed. Accordingly Ivor increased the speed by a big margin and, when briefing the crews, gave them the amended speed to fly. The formation therefore flew to Ivor's orders and not to Group's instructions.

Upon the return of the crews from a very successful operation and almost before he could rid himself of his flying gear, Ivor, in front of the other crews, was violently assailed by Don Bennett. 'Why did you not fly at the speed which I had laid down? the angry AOC demanded.

Ivor's logical explanations were thrust aside and scant praise was given for a job well and truly done.

But how did the Air Marshal know that the Mosquito speeds had been so increased? It transpired that The Great Don had decided to see for himself how his LNSF operated in daylight and, unknown to the others, had followed them flying a Beaufighter. The 'Beau', while an excellent aircraft, was a lot slower than the Mosquito and the AOC had soon fallen far behind. He therefore saw nothing of the attack and, from his point of view, had wasted a journey.

The conclusion to be drawn is that the original inadequate speeds had been set so as to enable the AOC to keep up with the Mosquitoes. However, this seems to have ignored the point that whereas the Beaufighter was the most powerfully armed of all Allied fighters, with its four cannons and six machine guns, the Mossies which were used by the LNSF were totally unarmed! When, about two weeks later, another large Mosquito daylight raid was planned also led by S/Ldr Ivor Broom, 8 Group HQ laid down the higher speed which Ivor had used when leading the earlier raid on Duisburg.

By late 1944 the number of Mosquitoes had steadily grown. Although the LNSF was only a small part of 8 Group nevertheless, for an attack on Nürnburg, seventy-five Mossies were used and, for one raid on Berlin, as many as ninety-one. However by then huge formations of Lancasters had joined in the daylight raids, escorted by Spitfires flying from captured airfields.

Bad weather and accidents were as much a deterrent as were the enemy. The records of 571 Squadron show that from nearly 1,000 attackers of Berlin alone over a period of about one year only three Mosquitoes were believed lost to enemy night fighters (two for sure to He 219s), four to enemy AA but another seven to weather and accidents. There were also three unaccounted losses which may have been due to weather, malfunction or enemy defences. Yet Berlin trips were regarded as the most hazardous and were as long in distance as any.

Towards the end of the year Tommy and Ivor were detailed to take part in another well-publicised spectacular one-off Mosquito raid. As 1944 closed, the German Army made one last desperate counter-attack. In a well-kept secret, they managed to assemble four Panzer divisions in the same Ardennes forest area from which they had mounted their lightning *Blitzkrieg* attack upon France in 1940. They were aided by atrocious weather, which had prevented the Allied Air Forces from detecting this build-up and they also maintained complete radio silence. This secret force burst out upon the unsuspecting Americans in that part of the Western Front and initially made much ground. By then the Allied Air Forces had long since ceased to camouflage their airfields and aircraft. Because so few airfields had been attacked, they now lined up aircraft in almost pre-war fashion. Accordingly, when the surprise attack came, the Luftwaffe in support, using 'planes brought from as far afield as Vienna and Prague and increased to about 750 aircraft by draining the training units of their men and machines, at first caused havoc. On the opening days they destroyed 151 Allied 'planes on the ground and damaged another 111.

For a few days, it almost looked as if the Germans had won a great victory but, before long, the attackers ran out of steam and the Allies, who had thousands of 'planes to make good all losses, were driving the enemy back to beyond whence they had advanced.

One reason why the attack failed was that the Allies had for many months, both before D-Day and thereafter, been following the bombing policy advocated by Professor Zuckerman. This was to isolate all German troops by concentrated attacks upon both road and rail links. Every major rail line, road and rail bridge etc had been plastered. The Germans also had to contend with low-flying Typhoon 'tank-busters' and other aircraft which patrolled, unmolested by the Luftwaffe, in daylight and beat up anything which moved. Enemy supplies and troop movements could only take place, with any safety, at night when Mosquitoes and other aircraft of the TAF also searched around for road and rail 'custom.'

The south German rail system had attracted little attention as the main thrusts had been nearer Paris and the Channel. Now, with the initial success of the Ardennes attack much in mind, it was essential to halt all road and rail services in that area. 8 Group had been given the task of blocking every rail link leading to the Ardennes fighting area. As this was mountainous country and the rail lines included many tunnels, 8 Group decided to block the lot.

Nine aircraft from 128 Squadron were available to attack nine different tunnels and, as could be expected, the two Brooms would fly one of these. The attack was planned to take place on New Year's Eve, with the actual bombing to be carried out at first light on 1 January 1945. Other squadrons probably had similar assignments as everything that could be thrown into this last big battle in Europe, was being used.

Ivor himself briefed the six 128 Squadron crews and for once he decided that radio silence could be broken in the target area and each crew, if successful, was instructed to transmit his call sign and simply say 'Happy New Year.' The tunnel assigned to Ivor and Tommy was one near Kaiserslautern on the rail link between Mannheim and Saarbrücken.

To attack such a target required a special skill and practice. It was decided that the best chance of getting a large bomb into a tunnel was to fly at the tunnel at almost nought feet and toss the bomb into its yawning mouth; much as Ivor had before tossed bombs at Italian convoys destined for Tripoli. A couple of practice flights were arranged as not all had done anything like this before.

The first that Tommy Broom knew about the timing of the actual attack was when on New Year's Eve, with a pint in his hand, Ivor tapped him on the back (it was about 9 pm) with a

'That's your lot for the night. We start at about 6 am tomorrow so off you go to bed and get some sleep before the early call.' With that he departed to bed but Tommy has admitted that although he did get to bed earlier than usual — and unusually early for New Year's Eve — he did manage to sink another couple of pints first!

Tommy had long before undertaken the not-too-arduous task of drinking for both Brooms. If, by accident, when ordering another round in a pub or the Mess, a pint was ordered for Ivor, Tommy duly dealt with it. He also defended his pilot against those who tried to press drinks upon him 'He does not want it … He does not like it. He does not need it but if you will insist upon buying him a drink, go ahead. I'll drink it for him.'

Pints did not affect Tommy Broom's navigation and he led Ivor to his Kaiserslautern tunnel with his usual deadly accuracy. Ivor had decided to attack from the Mannheim end so as to be flying towards France after the attack. Fortunately the line was not electrified but it still contained its share of telegraph poles and signals; obstacles which had to be avoided during the low-level run-in towards the gaping mouth of the tunnel. As luck would have it, the Brooms arrived just as a train entered the tunnel with clear white smoke from the engine rising up in the sharp winter's morning air. The bombing went in copybook fashion with the 'cookie' bounding into the tunnel as Ivor pulled hard back on the stick to clear the rising ground immediately ahead. The bomb had an eleven seconds delay fuse but the Brooms were still near enough to see black smoke from the bomb burst obliterate the former white smoke.

As no AA fire or enemy aircraft seemed to be about, Ivor circled back and was pleased to note that the white smoke had been entirely replaced by the black of the bursting bomb. This was now pouring out of the tunnel's mouth.

The aircraft had been fitted with an F24 RAF camera with mirror attachment which automatically took pictures behind the aircraft as the bomb was released.

Ivor was also delighted to be greeted with a 'Happy New Year' from five other attackers. It was only when he returned, low level all the way without opposition, that he learned that the sixth aircraft had crashed in darkness during the take-off.

Later that day, Don Bennett rang to congratulate Ivor and to ask him to have dinner with him that night as he wanted to show him the pictures that the cameras had taken. This put Ivor in a difficult position as he had already agreed to attend a dance in the Mess and had arranged for Jess, then living in Ipswich where Ivor had rented a house for his wife and son, to come to Wyton for the dance.

An invitation to dine with the AOC was practically a command and Ivor eventually managed to arrange it so that both Jess and he would first dine with the AOC but would leave early so as to be able to attend the Mess dance. As Jess, who was only just aged twenty-one, has said, it was a rather frightening experience as hitherto she had not even spoken to anyone of higher rank than Wing Commander but it all went well as Don Bennett's wife Ly (pronounced 'Lee'), a former Swiss beauty, was a charming hostess and one who even managed to get the conversation occasionally away from the war which the AOC was determined to win: single-handed if needs be.

The photographs had been interpreted by the experts and confirmed that Ivor's bomb had indeed caused the black smoke which had overpowered the white smoke from the train. There was also Ivor's personal assurance that, although he had circled around a while after the attack, the train had not emerged from the other end of the tunnel. Bennett also pointed out two small dots in the background of the prints. 'What are those?' asked Ivor. Don Bennett informed him that the photographic interpreters put them down as two Fw 190s! Ignorance is at times better than bliss.

In attacking tunnels, the Mosquitoes were again going where the big Lancasters of the famed 617 Squadron had previously been. A small force of these, led by Leonard Cheshire VC, had earlier attacked the Samur tunnel in June 1944. They had used the 'Tallboy' bombs of 12,000lb weight: each capable of removing 5,000 tons of earth and able to penetrate to enormous depths. This tunnel was so heavily blocked that by war's end even hard-working Germans had not got the line working again.

As before, when playing a leading role in a spectacular and successful attack requiring great daring, flying skill and accuracy of navigation, both Brooms were immediately given gallantry awards. Ivor Broom received a second bar to his DFC and Tommy a bar to his DFC. Not many pilots received three DFCs and fewer still navigators a DFC and bar.

The Ardennes attack fizzled out and the Luftwaffe lost in all 270 aircraft. It was as *General* 'Dolfo' Galland, the famous Luftwaffe pilot and leader has, post-war, asserted: 'The Luftwaffe received its final death blow at the Ardennes offensive.'

The 151 Allied aircraft destroyed on the ground on the opening day of the Ardennes offensive were soon replaced, as by then the British and American Air forces in Europe had over 10,000 available. Also, unlike the enemy, Allied pilots were being trained in vast numbers. There was such a surplus that some 10,000 potential new ones were transferred to the other Services. In addition, with unlimited petrol supplies in the USA and Canada, training was now much more concentrated and carefully undertaken while that of the enemy was being truncated below a rational level.

Before January 1945 was out, the two fighting Brooms, now with five DFCs between them, would cease to serve 128 Squadron at Wyton. They spent part of that month on a well-deserved vacation and only completed one more operation. This was when they bombed Berlin for the sixteenth time and left their usual 4,000lb 'calling card.'

This final Op was one which so nearly ended in disaster as the weather for their return turned really nasty. A cold winter's drizzle had set in with the cloud base of only 300ft and with visibility of less than half a mile. With no sophisticated electronic landing aid, as has since been developed, this posed big problems. It was on such a night as this that, after about six Mosquitoes had crashed trying to land in such conditions, the remaining crews still in difficulties, were ordered to bail out. The navigator of one successfully landed in a field but the fog was so enveloping that he failed to find a way out of it! Finally he gave up the struggle, wrapped himself in the silk of his 'chute and 'went to bed' and was still sound asleep on the ground when discovered by locals in the morning.

However, thanks to Ivor's skill and cool head as a pilot and Tommy's assistance, they managed to get down at Wyton without damage. Tommy had become an expert at interpreting the electronic pulses of the 'Gee' navigation set and he had noticed that one of the grid lines of the Gee chart coincided with the runway at Wyton. This, and practice at making a Standard Beam Approach* (SBA) let down, enabled the pair to survive but Ivor in his log book has written: 'Shaky do!!' In all their Mosquito had been airborne for five hours and ten minutes and was just about completely out of petrol. It was the kind of natural risk that the night operators in wartime had to accept and why so many casualties (on both sides) occurred NOT due to enemy action. It is why also during all their training, the pilots had been detailed to carry out so few night-flying practices. It was too dangerous an undertaking, except under the most favourable conditions, for beginners to attempt until really familiar with their aircraft.

It was better for aircrews to abandon their aircraft and to take to their parachutes rather than attempt to land in such marginal conditions. By 1945 Mossies were being produced in large numbers by the skilled carpenters and cabinet makers in a number of UK factories. Replacement aircraft were rapidly available whereas it took the best part of a year to replace a lost crew.

Not only were replacement Mossies available at almost instant request but additional squadrons of this all-purpose machine were being formed at almost the proverbial 'drop of a hat': as Ivor and Tommy were about to find out. Their days with 128 Squadron came to an end with almost alarming suddenness. Roy Ralston, now in 8 Group HQ, had again done the prompting but this time it was Don Bennett himself who

---

* During a SBA approach, the pilot was guided towards the centre of the runway by hearing dot and/or dashes in his head set. If on one side of the centre line, he would hear dots: if on the other he would hear dashes, but when correctly lined up the two would merge into a continuous note.

was to give S/Ldr I G Broom, DFC & two bars, a further nudge upwards. He may have been miffed by Ivor's actions of changing the speed for the Duisburg raid but he knew a good man when he saw one and he knew how to get the best out of them.

CHAPTER TWELVE

163 Squadron

A lthough A V-M Don Bennett lived with Ly in the married quarters of RAF Wyton, his Group HQ was at Huntingdon and one afternoon late in January 1945, S/Ldr Ivor Broom was ordered to report to him there. He recalls the actual time of the appointment. It was 4pm.

The AOC wasted neither time nor words.

You are now an Acting Wing Commander and you will form a new Mosquito squadron tomorrow and will operate tomorrow night. It will be at Wyton so you should have no movement difficulties. It will be No 163 Squadron.

It was all over within a few minutes. The Great Don did not believe in wasting time.

Ivor left the office almost in a daze but had managed to extract a little more information. The new unit would occupy an empty hangar where formerly an 8 Group Lancaster squadron had been based. Wing Commander Broom was advised that some maintenance men would be arriving next morning and also a few Mossies — 'That should be enough to get you started right away.'

Fortunately Wyton was a well-built pre-war RAF station with giant solidly-constructed hangars with a built-in range of squadron offices along one side. The hangar with its massive doors could easily accommodate a large number of Mosquitoes.

Along with Tommy Broom, Ivor duly went to his 163 Squadron HQ early next morning. At first the two stood horribly alone when they realised they constituted 163 Squadron. However, things began to look up when about 250 maintenance men duly trooped in. This was the good news as men to service the aircraft were essential. The bad news was that they had all come from a Wellington OTU which was being closed down as that venerable wartime bomber was, at last, being phased out and not one man had ever serviced a Mosquito before.

Things definitely improved later on in the day when six Mosquitoes, drawn from different operational squadrons within the Group, flew in. They were all experienced crews and Ivor appointed two senior aircraft captains to be his Flight Commanders. One was already a Squadron Leader and the other was given this acting rank. With Group's consent Tommy Broom DFC & bar, was also upgraded to Squadron Leader. He was put in charge of all the navigators and made the Squadron Navigation Officer. Bennett was right, No. 163 Squadron could have operated that night.

Fortunately for Ivor, who wanted a moment to get his breath back, the weather that night was not suitable for operations. As a result, a whole forty-eight hours was to lapse between Bennett's talk with Ivor and the Squadron's first operation.*

One blessing, especially for a CO who had never attended any RAF officer's course, was to discover that a Squadron Adjutant known to him soon appeared. This was 'Dizzy' Davies, a former solicitor and the man who had been the Adjutant at 1655 MTU when Ivor had been instructing there. This was the same officer who, with his superior legal knowledge, had successfully defended the cookhouse man against the charge of stealing and selling rationed food; to the fury of G/Capt Kyle.

A good adjutant with the kind of brain to easily interpret the Services 'King's Rules and Regulations', was a priceless asset. Much of the 'bumph' that inevitably accumulated as the RAF had grown in size, could safely be left for him to deal with. This delighted Ivor because, almost in anticipation of the distant day when he might be given a command, the new CO had absorbed two fundamental ideas which he would, for the rest of his RAF career, always put into practice. From AOC Malta, Hugh Pughe Lloyd, he had learned the respect that a senior commander earned from all under him, by taking the

---

* The RAF had a wartime unofficial motto of: 'If the job is very difficult it will be done *at once* but if 'impossible' it might take a little time!'

time and trouble personally to visit airfields and get to know by name and personality the men (and women) who worked there. AOCs who sat in remote offices and gave orders by phone, never gained this respect. Hugh Pughe Lloyd never treated men of inferior rank as inferior persons.

From Don Bennett, not the same open-hearted man as was Lloyd, Ivor had learned the respect that a commander gained by being able to demonstrate that he personally could, and did, operate every type of aircraft which he expected others to fly. Don Bennett was also prepared to risk his own neck and share the common dangers of his crews by operating alongside them: as no other AOC in Bomber Command, excepting Basil Embry, attempted to do or was capable of doing. No AOC in the RAF was more highly regarded for his skills than The Great Don and this more than made up for his lack of personal warmth. His abilities inspired others. Wing Commander Mike Birkin, Ivor's CO of 571 Squadron, also flew his normal quota of operations and made a point of flying the more dangerous ones. Ivor had noted that this also had enhanced his reputation within the Squadron. All in all, these were good examples which he intended to follow while leaving the tedious office work to Adjutant Dizzy Davies and his staff.

If there was a manual on how to manage an operational squadron of the RAF in wartime, then W/Cdr Broom had not read it. Consequently he set about running 163 Squadron in the way that he thought a squadron ought to be run. He was guided solely by his experiences of having been in a number of squadrons; and in a number of ranks from Sergeant pilot upwards to Flight Commander. The one principle which seems to have guided him throughout was that a squadron should work as a team. The differences in ranks and status need not separate the men. Consequently he initiated a daily 2pm aircrew conference where all were invited to put in their oar, make suggestions, air any grievances and generally 'chew the fat' as well as reporting upon the previous night's operations and discussing those about to be flown. These daily sessions also considered the problems which the groundcrews might be facing: such mundane matters as their cups of tea, transport and matters which might make their lot more pleasant. The groundcrews were a wonderfully loyal and devoted collection of men drawn from dozens of peacetime occupations. They regarded the aircraft they serviced as 'their' aircraft and the crews who flew them as 'their' crews but at the same time, on some stations, they were subject to severe disciplinary actions as ordained by a few senior peacetime Regular NCOs who had learned the rigours of strict discipline in quite different circumstances.

To make the lot of the groundcrews of 163 Squadron more amenable, the new CO soon started a football team where groundcrews and aircrews mixed freely. Ivor himself was not skilled in this form of football but sportingly played for the team in the most exposed position of all — in goal! It was one of the ways in which he broke down the barriers between the commissioned officers and the humble 'erks.' Another was that he arranged a Mess dance for the men with beer selling at 2 pence per pint! The difference in price coming from Mess funds. Again, he and other aircrew members attended and a good time was had by all. For men who hitherto had never had occasion to speak to officers before except on most formal occasions, all this helped to bind the Squadron into one happy band of warriors. As can be imagined, the airmen responded by putting their backs into their work as never before. Nor did discipline suffer.

Frank Lilley was one of the early crew men to arrive. He was a Sergeant navigator. 'The difference was amazing. In my previous squadron I had been regarded as just a number. Now I was one of a team.' He had never before even spoken to a senior officer. Frank also stresses the part that Tommy Broom played. 'He was a bit older than the rest of us and did wonders to create the right atmosphere. He was looked upon as almost a revered 'father figure.' Tommy also acted as the eyes and ears of 163 Squadron when, as was inescapable, Ivor was away at Group or was having to cope with the administrative matters much aided by Dizzy Davies. Tommy, having worked his way upwards from lowly rank, knew all the dodges that the 'old lags' were liable to try upon a young naive CO and was able to protect him, as occasions required. In Frank Lilley's words: 'Tommy was almost a father figure to his CO as well.'

Another great boost to 163 Squadron were the medal ribbons which both Tommy and Ivor wore. Men are always proud to follow a recognised hero and to respect courage. To have a CO with the DFC & two bars was a great rarity and an inspiration to others. The fact that neither of the Brooms were prepared to rest on their laurels, added to their reputations. Within days of 163 getting off the ground, the flying Brooms were on operations again in a Canadian-built Mosquito XXV. This was similar to Type XX except for a slightly different Mark of RR Merlin engines. The Squadron also noted that not only were its CO and navigation leader taking a normal quota of the operational trips but that they generally elected to fly on Berlin raids. The one on 1 February, as Ivor noted in his log book, was 'The biggest Mossie raid so far.' From 25,000ft they dropped their four 500lb bombs as well as the usual 'window' chaff. In addition it was noted by others that the CO also duly carried out his quota of Link Training exercises. These synthetic but realistic practices, where flying problems were solved under make-believe conditions, were regarded by some very experienced pilots as an unnecessary chore: something which they did not need. The presence of the very experienced Wing Commander subjecting himself to this uncomfortable procedure, was yet another morale boost to the new squadron. 'If he still thinks that there is something to be learned from the Link Trainer, then perhaps it is not the 'bind' that I thought it was.'

No. 163 Squadron soon settled down, despite its odd start, without difficulties but a personal problem for the Wing Commander now arose. The Squadron's first raid on Berlin was to be his fiftieth in Mosquitoes and the edict was that after fifty raids, the crew had to be operationally rested. With the Allies now well across the Rhine and advancing on the Russian Front with equal speed, it was obvious to everyone, except to Adolf Hitler and his bemused followers, that the end of the war was in sight. Both Tommy and Ivor had come to the same conclusion and it seemed a pity to have to stop when so near the end. Ivor's predicament was that whereas he was ordering others to stop upon reaching their fifty, he was continuing. He sought the advice of the Senior Air Staff Officer (SASO) of the Group, Air Commodore Boyce, who advised that unless Ivor wished to declare himself as 'Tour Expired', he was not going to be asked about it. 'Just let me know when it is all over, how many you have done.'

The Brooms therefore carried on adding such towns as Magdeburg and Schleiszheim to their long list but mainly selecting raids on Berlin for their night sorties. The 'Big City' was now being bombed from a level of only 21,000ft although occasional night fighters were still being encountered and the searchlights were as numerous as ever.

The raids were not without danger as apart from sighting conventional night fighters, sightings of jet ones were also reported and these could easily overhaul the unarmed Mosquitoes. There were also the normal hazard of night flying to be faced. On 26 February, for example, the much-decorated pair had to abort their operation when one engine failed. Also the winter weather set its usual rain and low cloud problems.

A Mosquito had one advantage over most, if not all, RAF operational machines. The cockpit heater actually produced an adequate amount of heat! The crews did not, therefore, have to dress up as if attempting to climb Mount Everest and they flew in their normal RAF battledress although still encumbered by a parachute and a 'Mae West' life jacket. Many Mosquitoes were pressurised models and this meant that the oxygen masks and tubes could also be dispensed with. However, bearing in mind that the German AA was ever present (it could not be heard inside the aircraft but was evident both from occasional 'bumps' from near misses and could at times be seen as black puffs in the moonlight), it was considered safer to put up with the inconvenience of the oxygen apparatus rather than risk an explosive decompression which would follow after a rupture of the pressurised shell.

Following upon the success of the 2pm afternoon daily meeting, Ivor also started a voluntary 2pm Sunday Church Service. This was held in the Squadron crew rooms but, as its popularity grew, the Service moved into the station church. It may seem incongruous that men should meet for a Christian service in the afternoon and then help reduce a German town to rubble in the evening but all were convinced that this was a just war: a war against an excessively evil regime and, in another way, a fight to survive. Although then the appalling massacre of the Jews, Gipsies and whole Russian villages were not fully known — and were so horrible to be almost unbelievable — there was enough evidence available for all to realise that if Hitler and his Waffen SS troops were not wiped off the face of the earth, then Britain and its way of life was finished. Post-war studies have confirmed this in full and had Britain fallen to the Nazi warlords all able-bodied men in Britain between the ages of sixteen and sixty would have been deported to Europe for slave labour. It can be argued that the destruction of German cities might not have been the best way of removing this scourge from Europe but how better could Britain have aided the Russians whose resistance alone was almost all that stood between Hitler and total triumph during 1941-1942? How many more tanks, U-boats, guns etc would have been produced but for the millions employed on attempts to defend the Reich? As the raid on the Dortmund–Ems canal shows, the destruction of Germany's transport system was a major factor in helping to win the Battle of the Atlantic and who knows what factories lay in their cities.

During the war both the Luftwaffe and the German Navy were basically honourable Services but the atrocities committed by the German ground forces were almost beyond belief. Even in France at the village of Oradour, near Limoges, 455 local people were herded into a church which was then set ablaze: and all because some Resistance fighters had killed a German or two a few days after D-Day. Yet over 500 villages in Belorussia suffered this fate. There it was especially effective because the churches were built of wood and burnt better. The women were killed *en masse* in order to rid the world of a race which Hitler and Himmler regarded as 'impure' and therefore had to be eliminated.

One of the perks of a squadron commander — or indeed

of any senior officer at a wartime RAF station — was that he could claim first call upon the aircraft of the so-called Station Flight. Every airfield somehow had obtained one or more non-operational aircraft. Some were tiny Tiger Moths or Magisters. Others were the popular Oxfords or Ansons since half a dozen or more 'passengers' could be crammed into these. Some were Lysanders which were popular among those who wanted to visit friends or families far removed from RAF airfields since they could be landed in quite small fields. With his family at Ipswich, Ivor managed to find the time for a few short visits there either in an Oxford or a Percival Proctor. This was a type new to him but it gave him no problem. In a typical move, whenever Ivor flew to Ipswich or went there by car, he gave a lift to his engineer Warrant Officer, who also had his family there.

Ivor also took an opportunity to indulge in some local flying, with a F/Lt Willis, in a Lancaster bomber which happened to visit Wyton. This was to have useful repercussions later. Keen pilots were always eager to fly as many types as possible to add to their log book list. Once, earlier, Ivor and some others had accepted a local ride in a visiting US Air Force Flying Fortress: perhaps the extreme opposite of the Mosquito as a bomber. The B-17 bristled with guns and carried a crew of about ten in order to man the many gun positions. It was a four-engined aircraft to the Mosquitoes two yet the two bombers carried the same bomb load to Berlin!

Five of Wing Commander Broom's last six operations, before the war finished, were to Berlin; a point which others in the unit duly noted with respect. The men were aware that there was no need for Ivor to operate at all due to having completed his quota of fifty Pathfinder Operations. One of the last six was, for once, a very unusual operation. Tommy Broom did not sit alongside his namesake! It was the only time that Ivor had, operated without Tommy in Mosquitoes during a period spanning eleven months and one which had taken them through three different squadrons. It even went back to their final days at 1655 MTU when Roy Ralston had deliberately teamed them together to see if the combination gelled prior to recommending that Ivor and Tommy should be posted as a crew to 571 Squadron.

This one 'maverick' operation came about accidentally. Even when not operating himself, the Wing Commander would carry out the pre-flight briefing and would then drive down to where the aircraft were parked in order personally to see his crews off and to wish them well. It was all part of Ivor's excellent man-management tactics. He never missed an opportunity to emphasise that 163 Squadron ran as a joint team effort.

Usually Tommy went with him on these occasions but that night Tommy had a date with a WAAF and so Ivor had taken the station doctor with him. Good medical officers were always key people on every operational base and they could also be father figures. As F/O Neale was climbing up to board his Mosquito, he had the misfortune to slip and damage an ankle badly. He was in great pain and as the station doctor happened to be present, he examined it and declared Neale as unfit to operate. This meant that there would be an abort even before take-off and all keen squadron commanders were sensitive about aborts. They tried to have less than any other squadron as it could be construed as a measure of their efficiency or determination. Ivor sized up the situation in a flash. 'Give me your kit. I'll go in your place.'

As he had done the briefing, Ivor knew what route had been laid down, the time to bomb and the height from which to bomb. The navigator was a reasonably experienced Sgt Brown but he may have had a few qualms about having to navigate for his CO in place of the renowned S/Ldr Tommy Broom.

The trip went smoothly although one tale about it has been reported. However, since Ivor had by then also become somewhat of a living legend the tale might have grown in the telling.

The raid was to bomb Berlin and this, as ever, was the hottest area for AA fire. On the bomb run towards the target indicators which the OBOE-equipped Mosquitoes would have dropped about one minute earlier, the story goes that Sgt

Brown, down in the nose with eyes glued to the Mark XIV bomb sight, instructed his pilot with: 'Steady, right, steady, left, left, steady ... Dummy Run!' With the knowledge that Tommy Broom had the reputation for dropping bombs with almost incredible accuracy, the young Sergeant had decided that they were a fraction off target and instructed Ivor to go round again. This was definitely not the normal way of operating when over the most heavily-defended city in the world: one ringed with massive flak guns and wavering searchlights. However, Ivor duly obliged and did make another run over the target.

What is without any doubt is that Tommy Broom was furious that his skipper had, as he put it: 'sneaked in one more Mossie Op than his own total.' Again and again he begged his CO to give him an extra trip so that in numbers they would be back to equal again but Ivor was adamant that he would remain one ahead of his companion in arms. It still rankles today but only in the nicest of ways, as between two good friends who still never miss an opportunity to get together and talk about their days of yesteryear.

Another truly natural hazard of operations at height in the 1940s was that almost nothing was known about upper air jet streams. The meteorological knowledge of the day did not cater for upper winds of even 100mph and those who reported much stronger winds on the way back when the lighter aircraft might be taken up to over 30,000ft, were at first inclined to be disbelieved but it was soon evident that winds in the jet stream at 30,000ft or above could reach velocities of 160mph or more. This caused many a late arrival back at base with aircraft almost critically short of fuel. It was one of the many discoveries about aviation made during wartime which were to be put to good use in the post-war aviation boom which was, by March 1945, soon to follow.

A rather unnatural hazard which became of growing concern was that the air space over Germany at night began to include a hundred or more British night fighters of the secret 100 Group. These were there to hunt down the German Ju 88/ 188/388 and Me 110/410 night fighters. The German twin-engined machines were being shot down in large numbers thanks to our night fighters carrying electronic devices such as Serrate and Mandrel which enabled them to 'home' on to the radar, or other emissions, of the enemy aircraft.

Although the experienced night aces such as Wing Commanders Bob Braham and Branse Burbridge — who, respectively, became the most-decorated British fighter pilot of the Second World War and our top-scoring night fighter of the conflict* — were punctilious about positive identification before opening fire. Some of the newcomers on a first chase were occasionally guilty of firing at almost every twin-engined aircraft with a single tail which included both the Mosquito and Junkers night fighter. The 100 Group Mosquitoes mingled with the four-engined bombers of Main Force and flew at their altitudes in order to get on the scent of the Luftwaffe aces who had been so successful in shooting down the Lancasters and Halifaxes.

Wing Commander Ivor Broom flew his last operation in the Second World War on 18 April 1945; about two weeks before the final German surrender. It was his fifty-eighth for the Mosquitoes of the LNSF and his 103rd in all. A few days earlier he had bombed Berlin for the twenty-first time. It was an impressive record and in October 1945, with the conflict in Europe over, he was honoured with the prestigious Distinguished Service Order (DSO) award. The citation mentions his Berlin trips, his fortitude, courage and determination and gives credit to his high standard of devotion to duty.

By 7 May 1945, all German troops had surrendered and the evil Nazi regime had totally collapsed. The war in Europe was at last over and the general relief was beyond words.

By a happy coincidence some Russian Officers were visiting 163 Squadron and their photographs appear among

---

* Wing Commander J R D Braham was the only pilot in the Second World War to receive the DSO & two bars and the DFC & two bars. Nineteen of his confirmed victories were at night. Wing Commander B Burbridge DSO & bar, DFC & bar shot down twenty-one German twin-engined night fighters over Germany. This made him our top-scoring night fighter. 'Sticks' Gregory DSO, DFC & bar, DFM, and Bill Skelton DSO & bar, DFC & bar, were their respective AI (Airborne Interception, ie. radar) operators.

some taken during this euphoric period. As could have been expected many, both in the RAF and elsewhere, went wild on what became known as VE (Victory in Europe) night when vast quantities of alcohol were consumed, although Ivor, almost alone, joined in the celebrations while consuming only lemonade. One event recalled by a 163 Squadron navigator Robinson was that the DROs (Daily Routine Orders pinned up for the next day) went up in flames!

In their exuberance, a number of pilots beat up the airfield with forbidden high-speed low passes. This was seen by the SASO, Air Commodore Boyce, who sent for Ivor and ordered him to assemble all the aircrews. He then tore them off an almighty strip and grounded the Squadron for a week. Later in private he told Ivor that he was not really all that livid and 'not to take it to heart' and leaving it to Ivor to decide when to lift the ban which he had only imposed as he did not wish the brave young aircrew members to lose their lives unnecessarily 'just because the war in Europe was over.' Ivor lifted the ban after forty-eight hours.

Robinson also recalls, and Ivor confirms, that some prankster had borrowed a monkey from a pub with the object of introducing it to a forthcoming Officers' Mess party. He had been warned by its owner never to allow it to drink more than two glasses of port in an evening! For the party the beast was put on a perch. It so happened that Don Bennett came into the mess along with his young son who was naturally intrigued by the beast. However, the monkey, far from reciprocating, bit the youngster and later further blotted its copybook by falling into the bowl of punch much to the anguish of the punch drinkers.

The end of the war in Europe after over five and a half years posed a number of problems for those who had joined the RAF during it. None were in the RAF proper, only in the RAF Voluntary Reserve (RAFVR), and thought had now to be given as to what to do next.

In Bomber Command and, perhaps, especially among the hand-picked pilots whom Don Bennett had collected for his Pathfinder Force, there were three schools of thought. All were aware that the Government had given an undertaking that those who had responded to the call could have their pre-war job back, if they still wanted them. In the first place none then could foretell when and if Japan would also be totally defeated. The Americans had made great strides in the Pacific and had by 1945 recaptured almost every island ever taken by the Japanese during their initial successful rush towards Australia. But Japan itself had yet to be taken although bombing raids upon their mainland were now wreaking frightful damage.

Even assuming that the war might soon end — and no one except a handful knew about the atom bombs and could possibly imagine that Japan would surrender without even being invaded — few in Bomber Command wanted their pre-war jobs*. Some of the more elderly groundcrew might, and the likes of Adjutant Dizzy Davies, the former solicitor, but few of the aircrew felt this way. They were young and had come to manhood while serving the RAF and quite a few, with no thought to the more distant future, were keen to carry on doing to the Japanese what they were doing to the Germans. Pre-war they had been just existing in offices, factories, shops and schools. Now they had learned how to live dangerously but gloriously. They had learned to drink, chase the 'popsies' and command others. They had been rushed into manhood and experienced the joys of being part of a crew; sharing common dangers and triumphs. Compared with the mundane existence of their lives pre-war, this was IT.

Even the few who nursed secret qualms about the morality of bombing German cities — and they were very few — had no qualms whatsoever about being prepared to bomb the life out of as many of the 'nasty' Japanese as possible. The appalling atrocities committed by these fanatic sadists: their habit of working to death their half-starved prisoners and their custom of beheading with swords POWs almost at whim, all this had been well documented and publicised. The Japanese merited no sympathy and received none.

It was known that a bombing force, to be known as Tiger

---

* The Inland Revenue offered Ivor a post-war job as an Assistant Inspector of Taxes: rapid promotion from the junior rank held in 1940.

Force, was being assembled. Armed with Lancasters and based at an island such as Okinawa within range of Japan, they would soon be flying alongside their American brothers in arms. Hugh Pughe Lloyd, now Air Marshal Sir Hugh Lloyd would see to it that they carried on in the right spirit. He had been appointed to command Tiger Force.

The third choice for those who neither wished to return to their old jobs nor to bomb the Japanese in the Far East, was to train themselves for the civil aviation boom which surely would flourish as soon as conditions would allow: and in Europe that meant almost immediately.

This had many attractions for those pilots of Pathfinder Force. They had found their métier in flying aircraft and they were good at it. They had no worthwhile jobs to go back to and already they were working for Don Bennett. This last was important as it was known that the Great Don, who had left the RAF to win a by-election for Parliament, would soon be forming a new privately-funded airline to carry passengers and goods to the central and south American countries which had never been served by BOAC or its predecessors. This British Latin American Airways would initially fly converted Lancasters and York transports. With Don Bennett at its helm, its future looked bright. All in Pathfinder Force knew that they stood as good a chance as any of being selected by their former AOC. He had, in effect, already chosen them once.

To become civil commercial pilots, ex-RAF pilots would require to obtain both a commercial Civil Aviation B Licence (the A was for private pilots) and one of the more difficult to obtain Civil Air Navigation licences. This could be either a very difficult First Class one — known as a 'First N' — or the more normal 'Second N.'

The qualifications for the B Licence worried no one. It was largely a flying test plus some elementary knowledge of the aircraft systems: fuel, hydraulic, electrical, controls etc. These had always been required by the RAF and experienced pilots who had flown many types for years while in the RAF, could pass these tests without difficulty but even the lower 'Second N' required much classwork. It called for sound knowledge of international meteorology, swiftness and accuracy of plotting using a number of techniques including astro, compasses and magnetism, Civil Air Legislation, even tides* and an ability to send and receive by Morse code. It required many months of hard work but without a 'Second N' only the simplest and most lowly paid jobs in civil aviation were within reach.

Ivor was among those who was more than just interested in a future career in commercial aviation and, when the end of war left his 163 Squadron with no obvious challenges (immediately after the war in Europe ended, flying for 163 Squadron almost ceased), Ivor arranged for B Licence and Civil Air Navigation classes to be started in his Squadron.

He found the required instructors, lent a hand himself while also studying as a pupil. It was one of several ways by which he kept the idle Squadron up to scratch. He also arranged cross-country flights and other exercises while never missing an opportunity to arrange a sporting match or athletic occasion. The letdown after all the pressure to get as many aircraft over Germany at night on every possible occasion, was marked and it was a difficult task to try to keep 163 Squadron in good fighting shape when there was no enemy to fight and when domestic matters such as leave, home, demobilisation and future jobs were uppermost in the minds of all.

One outstanding effort was his 'Cook's Tours.' Somehow he, and some other Mosquito squadron COs, obtained a few Lancaster bombers (this type existed in huge numbers but now had little to do) and arranged to take groups of groundcrew on low-flying flights over the German towns which these airmen and women mechanics had, indirectly, helped to destroy. It was typical of the common touch which was a hallmark of everything that Ivor did in the RAF. Junior officers and 'erks' were never far from his mind. If he could find a way to make their life more fulfilling, he invariably tried to do so.

First Ivor himself had to learn to handle a big four-engined Lancaster. On the basis that he had once before been taken for

---

* Many civil aircraft were then flying-boats or float-planes and a knowledge of tide tables was essential for pilots of these.

a short flight in one as second pilot, he reckoned that he was both fit to fly one solo and to instruct others! Accordingly, he checked out himself and a few other pilots of 163 and, with about nine airmen crammed into each, they were soon flying low over the completely devastated cities of the Ruhr and beyond. Since most of the flying by the Squadron had been at high altitudes at night, it was almost as great an eye-opener for the pilots as it was for the 'customers' of the 'Cook's Tours.' Whole cities had been rendered almost derelict with block after block reduced to empty shells. It was an awesome reminder of the power of aerial bombing: a power which was soon to be given a new dimension by the dropping of the atom bombs upon Hiroshima and Nagasaki; swiftly followed by the complete capitulation of the once-proud and arrogant Japanese.

The number of hours which crews now flew was suddenly dramatically reduced. Ivor was as determined as any to keep in good practice but all he could manage during June 1945 — the month immediately after the collapse of Germany — was two hours on Oxfords when flying to visit his family in Ipswich, another two hours on the same type of navigation exercises: probably connected with his 'Second N' studies as another pilot flew the aircraft, two short Mosquito practice flights and one night navigation exercise in a Lancaster. In July, he flew, as first pilot, one 'Cook's Tour' of the Rhineland and one practice bombing with Tommy but he also flew a few navigation flights with other pilots.

With the war in Europe over, the politicians were quick to impose financial restrictions upon the UK-based RAF. Flying hours were cut to the bone. Yet with the war still raging in Japan and with the best part of a million men to be demobilised, the process of reducing the RAF to a satisfactory size had to be a slow and gradual one. Ivor's total hours for all of August and September came to a bare 3 hours 25 minutes flown on Air Tests of Proctors and Oxfords and one short bombing practice in a Mosquito.

By August Japan had also been defeated and the Second World War was over. It was already all too clear to most that the peacetime RAF was going to be something very different from the force which had achieved so much from September 1939 onwards. Its glory days were over. It would shrink to a much smaller force and those who were retained would henceforth carry out less flying. Few of the heroes of the RAFVR who, by war's end were largely carrying the load on operations against the enemy, would be required, especially those who had not attended administrative, or full officers', courses. Also ranks would have to be dropped. Most officers in positions of authority such as Ivor had an Acting rank above that which they held: and that lower one was not a full one. It was only what was termed a 'War Substantive Rank.' This was generally one rank above their true rank. A person in Ivor's shoes was, therefore only a Flight Lieutenant with a war substantive rank of Squadron Leader and an acting rank of a Wing Commander. The few who might be invited to stay in the RAF post-war, would have to adjust themselves — and their pay — to a much reduced status. Moreover, subsequent promotion would be a slow process; quite unlike that which had rapidly elevated Ivor and others to their present exalted positions.

Two events were now to shape the career of Ivor Broom. At Group HQ, the tremendous efforts which Ivor had made to sustain morale in 163 Squadron after the collapse of Germany had not gone unnoticed. This was needed in the days of peace: a leader who could keep a unit on its toes in spite of the severe limits imposed upon their flying and in spite of there being no enemy to oppose. Both Air Commodore Boyce and Wing Commander Ralston had come to the conclusion that Ivor Broom was made of the stuff that the RAF required in peacetime. Also he was an ace pilot who did not indulge in drinking sprees, was one who was happily married to the right sort of RAF lady and was an officer who obviously cared deeply for the airmen under him. This made him a very 'rare bird', as many wartime ace pilots were unmarried; some had married the wrong type in haste and others had become extroverts with some fairly wild habits which hardly confirmed with the RAF's standards of peacetime discipline! Also at about this time Ivor sat his Civil Aviation examination for a Second N licence and failed one subject.

Although in such matters it can never be shown positively or exactly what factors came into play, the outcome was that Ivor Broom was offered a permanent RAF Commission and was posted overseas where Don Bennett could not easily get in touch with him. At least two people aver that the posting was deliberately arranged to get him as far away as possible from the new airline which the Great Don had now taken over as Managing Director. His planned BLAA had been taken over by one of the newly-formed nationalised air corporations and was now British South American Airways. Practically every pilot in it was a former prominent Pathfinder pilot; known to Bennett from his period when AOC of 8 Group. Some had attended the civil aviation classes which Ivor had arranged.

CHAPTER THIRTEEN

Peace in the East

The die was cast. Ivor would not become one of Bennett's 'Boys', a pilot of the new British South American Airline, instead he would face up to a world at peace as a Regular RAF officer with a permanent commission as a Flight Lieutenant with seniority dated from 1 September 1945. He was among the first batch of thirty RAFVR to be so selected and it was an honour as hundreds would have been eligible and more than willing.

The rank of Flight Lieutenant was given to all those RAFVR who held acting ranks of Acting Squadron Leaders and above but who were still under the age of twenty-seven. If over this age, then these wartime leaders were enrolled in the RAF proper as Squadron Leaders but precious few were engaged at all.

For F/Lt I G Broom the bitter pill of having to drop down to the rank of Flight Lieutenant when even his war substantive rank had been Squadron Leader was sweetened. He was given a posting which allowed him to carry on as an Acting Wing Commander. It also took him out of heavily-rationed Britain, although, sadly, away from his wife and children. He was appointed Command Air Movements Officer at HQ Air Command South East Asia. The HQ was at Kandy in what then was the British island of Ceylon, now the independent country of Sri Lanka.

It was shortly after the final surrender of the Japanese in August 1945 that Ivor set forth for this appointment. First he travelled to Bombay in the pre-war luxury Atlantic liner the *New Mauritania*, which had once been the pride and joy of the Cunard Shipping Company. Now stripped of every luxury with bunks piled high in the cabins, it held 6,000 troops. Most were Army personnel but, because he was the senior RAF officer on board with the three broad stripes of a Wing Commander on his sleeves, he was made OC of the RAF contingent. As such he was responsible for their behaviour.

At Bombay, after waiting a week, he joined a train bound for Madras on the other side of that sub-continent. This time Ivor's rank made him the highest of all and he was appointed OC of the train! This too was overcrowded, as were most wartime trains with scant consideration for comfort. The space set aside for some army officers so disgusted those who boarded the train at Poona that they wanted to delay departure while voicing their protests. He resolved the Army's difficulties by broadcasting an announcement that the train would be leaving in five minutes whether the army officers were on board or not. It left. They were.

The journey across India with the stop at Poona took about thirty-six hours but on arrival at Madras no one seemed to know who he was or what next to do with him. This was typical of many wartime postings. Accordingly Ivor took himself to a nearby Fleet Air Arm airfield and looked around for an aircraft proceeding to Ceylon. A pilot with his Wings badge, medal ribbons and high rank was still much regarded, even though the war was over. Within a short time Sub Lt Davies was flying the new Air Command Movements Officer to Ratmalana in Ceylon.

By the time that Ivor Broom finally arrived at Kandy, having travelled in all for nearly a month, it was only to find out that the HQ of Air Command South East Asia was about to be moved to Singapore!

One of his major responsibilities was to arrange flights for aircraft of a VIP Flight. This included a specially-equipped Avro York transport 'plane which was used as a personal aircraft by Admiral Lord Louis Mountbatten: Lord Louis then being the Supreme Allied Commander South East Asia. As there was no immediate call for this aircraft, which was scheduled to move to Singapore, Ivor used it to fly himself and his staff to RAF Butterworth, the big military airfield in Malaya, opposite the island of Penang. From there they took a DC3 Dakota to Singapore. By the time that they arrived it was well after dark. They had flown for about ten hours in all.

Upon arrival they were taken in a lorry to an empty private

house and given camp beds for the night. By next day the house had been requisitioned and it remained an Officers' Mess well into 1946.

With no civil airlines yet started in an area the size of Europe the job was a demanding one. In effect Ivor was responsible for arranging flights for all air transport over a huge region from Ceylon, Burma, Malaya, Hong Kong, Singapore, Vietnam, Thailand, Sumatra, Java and beyond. Everyone wanted to travel. Servicemen wanted to get home, VIPs had to get to conferences, businessmen, both British and Chinese, wanted to get in on the ground floor and start trading again. Goods had to be brought in.

Ivor first had to prepare priority criteria for himself and others to follow. Having done this, he set up Air Priority Boards to decide who should take up the very limited number of seats available. He then established Air Booking Centres in the principal cities: Kandy, Rangoon, Singapore, Kuala Lumpur, Saigon, Batavia, Hong Kong etc, to handle local seats and problems.

With everyone wanting to travel, he was subject to almost every form of blandishment. Though he was not personally offered a bribe, it can well be imagined that those down the line were so tempted.

For his own transport on inspection visits to the far flung places where the booking centres were established, he used one of the small Beech Expeditor aircraft. He had not flown at all for over three months but found the Beech a pleasant and handy personal transport. For the longer flights he went in Yorks, DC3s and Sunderland flying boats of 209 and 233 Squadrons. He had chosen not to try to join Don Bennett's new airline but was now a kind of 'General Manager' of one covering an even greater area.

A big shock for Ivor came, when on a visit to an outstation in the Dutch colony of Sumatra, he found himself being marshalled to his parking area at the airport by a Japanese soldier with a rifle slung over his shoulder!

As was happening all over the area, local nationalists were taking the opportunity to overthrow their European Colonial masters. In the area where he had landed the Dutch were being threatened and, lacking sufficient security troops to maintain order, they had released some Japanese POWs to help guard vital installations such as the airport.

When summoned home for a conference, the 'General Manager' put himself on to a Lancastrian which took him as far as Malta where he was given a seat in a DC3 to the UK. It involved 40.10 hours of flying. For the return he used the BOAC flying-boat service which made pleasant night stops and took a leisurely three to four days and 47.30 hours flying. It was a mode of flying which is now but a memory for most but, although the standards of comfort were high, the hours in the air were long as speeds were slow by modern jet standards.

The Lancastrians were hastily converted Lancaster bombers. In spite of their four big thirsty Merlin engines, they carried only nine passengers. However they had both an impressive range and speed for aircraft of the time. Commercially they were definitely not viable and when offered for trial for BOAC, the captain who checked it out could only report that it was useless as a commercial airliner but added with dry humour that 'It might with a few modifications make a good bomber!'

An unusual assignment in October 1946 was to arrange transport around China for a big British Trade Mission led by Sir Leslie Boyce, the Lord Mayor designate of London. The Mission was looking for post-war orders. The party were travelling in two RAF aircraft — a York and a Lancastrian — and apparently the transport arrangements since leaving London had not gone smoothly. The AOC, Air Marshal Sir George Pirie, gave a reception for the Mission in Singapore and Ivor was invited. Sir George introduced Ivor to Sir Leslie and looking Ivor straight in the eye said 'You know all about China, don't you?' It was as much command as question and defied a denial. Whereupon Ivor, who had never set a foot in China, found himself nominated to join the Mission as a China aviation expert!

Their first flight was from Singapore to Hong Kong in an Avro York but the airport was then so small and difficult to get at, it was decided to land first at nearby Canton in China and from there complete the journey in a smaller DC3. Upon arrival at Canton, the York was met by a posse of heavily-armed soldiers which would not allow them to disembark. Political upheaval was already dividing China and those at Canton were not going to play ball with those at Shanghai who had arranged the visit of the trade mission. Ivor eventually managed to arrange for the party to board the DC3 awaiting to take them to Hong Kong. The China expert at work!

The Mission then flew to a number of important centres in China. Generally they were greeted with great esteem and many a long banquet was given to the distinguished foreigners. Many toasts had to be drunk and although Ivor managed to avoid these fierce drinking sprees, the excess of rich foods after many years of spartan British rationed food, made him ill. They were at Tsiang Tao, but a US Navy hospital ship was nearby and Ivor was taken there for treatment. The internal disorders were not too serious but while there Ivor mentioned that one of his eyes was sore and was bothering him. The eye was examined and it was discovered that he had an ulcer in the corner of the cornea. This called for immediate treatment which an American surgeon successfully completed with no subsequent worries or after effects. Had he not been in hospital, Ivor would not have bothered too much about the eye especially as he was not personally doing any of the flying. However, the American surgeon informed him that if he had not acted at once, Ivor would probably have lost the sight of the eye within two or three days.

During October and November 1946, by when he had successfully managed his Far East civil and military 'airlines' for over a year, three events happened which were to change the pattern of his life. The job was down-graded to a Squadron Leader's position. Airlines were beginning to take over and the urgent need to fly thousands back to the UK for demobilisation was largely accomplished. To compensate him for his drop in rank and pay, Ivor Broom, still a basic Flight Lieutenant, was given command of a Spitfire squadron based at Kuala Lumpur. This also carried a Squadron Leader's rank.

He was therefore able to remain an Acting Squadron Leader. The third most welcome piece of news was to learn, after having been flown back to Hong Kong by the Americans on 5 November following his eye operation, that his wife Jessica and their children had permission to join him and would be arriving in Singapore on 9 November 1946.

S/Ldr Broom had never flown a Spitfire and had not flown any single-engined type for several years, but its reputation went before it like a bow wave. He welcomed the chance to fly this famous type and also to command an operational squadron again.

With Jess soon to arrive, happy days were clearly ahead even if he now had to accept the drop in pay from a Wing Commander to a Squadron Leader after having held the higher rank for over twenty months.

Ivor had enjoyed the experience of being a staff officer at a Command HQ. It gave him an opportunity to see how he could handle men and responsibility and neither had worried him. He had not been able to carry out any 'real' flying as he had known it before except for a period in June and July 1946 when he managed to get his hands on, and retain, a Mosquito VI TE 656 for some ten flights. On a number of local flights in this fine machine, he had, as usual, taken the opportunity to give members of his staff pleasant 'joy rides.' One beneficiary was a WRAF officer Flight Officer Arlette Harris, known to all as 'Harry.' She remembers it with great affection: as did all non-aircrew when given a chance of a flight. It has to be remembered that many in the RAF and even the WRAF would have liked to be aircrew but circumstances — education, physical requirement and, in the case of the WAAFs their sex — made them ineligible. Except for Air Tests or transportation such 'passengers' were not allowed and Ivor had to arrange for his passengers to board and disembark unobtrusively at the end of the runway or in similarly discreet locations.

Ivor also used this Mossie on one of his inspection trips to the out-stations of his huge 'parish', taking with him Warrant Officer Jones. The pair visited Butterworth, Rangoon and Pegu. This renewed for Ivor a brief taste of the joys of 'real RAF flying' but, as he was soon to find out, even a Mossie was a tame bird compared with the celebrated Spitfire.

CHAPTER FOURTEEN

No.28 Spitfire Squadron

Ivor Broom, back again to Squadron Leader after twenty-two months in a higher rank, knew that he would be taking over No. 28 Squadron and it flew only Spitfires. He was naturally reluctant to take command without ever having flown the type — it would start him off on the wrong foot. He was also very conscious of the fact that, although he had been in the RAF for over five years, he had never carried out any aerobatics and Spitfire pilots were renowned for their rolls and loops.

It was highly unusual for any pilot not to have learned elementary aerobatics. Usually they were shown these at an early stage of their flying training. They taught a pilot much, as during vertical banked turns and various manoeuvres when the aircraft would be upside down, the controls reversed themselves and it was necessary for a pilot to understand how they functioned under such conditions. However, at the time when LAC Broom was learning to fly on Tiger Moths, it so happened that there was a temporary ban on aerobatics. The aircraft were being kept out of doors and rain had seeped into the wings of some Tigers. The concern was that this may have caused structural weakness. The simple fix of drilling a few holes in the undersides of the wings to allow the water to escape had not then been carried out.

Accordingly the young Squadron Leader looked around and first got hold of a Harvard — an American single-engined training 'plane — and then a Griffon-powered Spitfire XIV, a fighter reconnaissance version. Although he could only manage to get in just under three hours flying in each, it did include some dual instruction in aerobatics on the Harvard. Pilots could not be given dual instruction in the Spitfire. An experienced pilot merely explained the various controls and gave a warning or two about its limitations and off the newcomer went. It posed no problems as the aircraft was a delight to fly with responsive controls, masses of power and a splendid performance.

By the time Squadron Leader Broom arrived at Kuala Lumpur to take command, he could claim some experience at both aerobatics and Spitfire handling. This was just as well as the news had got around that the new squadron commander was a Transport Command pilot (untrue) who had been 'flying a desk' at Singapore HQ, which was true: at least theoretically.

28 Squadron had been in India and Burma and consisted almost entirely of youngsters who had joined the RAF fairly recently but considered that they knew a lot about the Service by virtue of having attended a course at the prestigious Cranwell College.

One of their number was a youngster, aged twenty, P/O Ian Pedder who admits that:

It was a major experience to meet a married accompanied officer (Jess had arrived in November 1946), teetotal ex-Bomber Command pilot of mature years (all of 25!), who could take over a rather unstable squadron of bolshie, over-confident fighter boys and turn it into an efficient, cohesive unit within a matter of weeks.

Bob Wootton, one of the 'over-confident fighter boys', remembers Ivor's arrival. He, too, thought that the new CO was a former Transport Command pilot. In Bob's words:

Flying had been slap-dash and at once the new CO started a planned flying programme. 'Let him try it. It won't work here. He'll soon learn that his Transport Command stuff won't work with us', was the general initial reaction.

But to Bob's surprise, it did work. Bob was further surprised when Ivor personally led the Squadron to escort the arrival of the Duke of Gloucester and, like others, was even more surprised to discover that the supposed Transport Command pilot could display, on Dress nights, the ribbons of the DSO, DFC and two bars. Resentment soon changed to respect.

Moreover, the torch was being passed on. The good lessons which Ivor had absorbed from Hugh Pughe Lloyd, Mike Birkin, Roy Ralston and Don Bennett and which had become ingrained, was passed down by Ivor to the youngsters of 28 Squadron. Ian Pedder himself was to become Air Marshal Sir Ian and John Nicholls, another of the fighter boys rose to the same rank and title. By example so shall ye learn.

28 Squadron was one of the last two in the RAF to be still operating with Spitfires as later and faster designs had taken over. These included some of the first jet-propelled fighters. The squadron flew the Type XIV Spitfire and later also flew Mark XVIII Spitfires. Ivor Broom was to spend the next eighteen months and more working hard to ensure that this fighter/recce squadron was performing as the RAF expected it to do in peacetime.

Basically, fighter/recce squadrons had to prepare themselves for a war which, in theory at least, might break out at short notice.

The training programme which Ivor made the pilots of his Squadron carry out was:

— Formation flying of up to nine aircraft.

— Aerobatics and 'tail chase' dog fights.

— Interception, without radar assistance, of incoming aircraft.

— Photography at high and low levels: also oblique and mosaic pictures.

— Meteorological ascents.

— Low-level and dive-bombing practices.

— Air-to-air and air-to-ground firing with camera gun results.

— Co-operation with local Army and Navy units.

— Cross-country flights at high and low levels.

— Night flying.

— Instrument and cloud flying to Green Card (instrument) standard.

— Flapless and short-landing techniques.

There were also many flights to Air HQ at Singapore and it was not long before the Squadron moved to Singapore at Tengah airfield. In addition the Squadron had to take part, often a leading part, in 'Showing the Flag' special events. These included:

— Escorting the aircraft in which the Duke of Gloucester arrived.

— Leading thirty-six aircraft in a King George VI Birthday Parade.

— A formation display at Seramban.

— Air Display for visiting Siamese (Thailand) Air Force.

— Battle of Britain fly-past day.

— Air display for wedding of Prince Philip and Princess Elizabeth.

There was also the occasion when a formation went out to greet and lead in the aircraft in which the new C-in-C of Air Command SE Asia flew in. This was a great personal event for Ivor Broom as the incoming Air Marshal was none other than Hugh Pughe Lloyd, now Sir Hugh Pughe Lloyd, the former AOC Malta who had waylaid Sergeant Broom when he had landed in Malta only to refuel. Ivor welcomed the chance to serve again under his dynamic leadership.

Like all keen RAF pilots, Ivor was eager to fly a new type and when a Meteor visited Singapore for tropical trials he jumped at the opportunity of having his first flight in a jet fighter. Likewise when a friend from an aircraft carrier offered him a flight from the aircraft carrier HMS *Glory* in a Firefly.

The young officers of 28 Squadron and their likes in the Fleet Air Arm from the aircraft carriers HMS *Glory* and *Hermes* held several alcoholic-fuelled parties together. A feature was a form of skittles/bowls called Sembawang Skittles, using large shell cases which, when knocked over, made enough noise to wake up the entire station and probably half Singapore as well.

The youthful-looking Squadron Leader of 28 Squadron chiefly remembers two very special occasions when in charge of the unit. One was the occasion when it was decided to mount an exercise to find out if it would be feasible in an emergency to reinforce Hong Kong with Spitfires flown from Singapore. This was 'Operation Snapdragon.'

First the 'Spits' of 28 Squadron were fitted with 100 gallon overload tanks which, in theory would increase their short range to about 800 miles or more. One drawback was that the tanks had no fuel gauges and, to obtain maximum range, the only way was to use their fuel at an early stage of a long range flight and await until the engine spluttered from want of fuel and then, while saying a silent prayer, switch over to main tanks and hope that the engine would pick up quickly and no air lock or other malfunctioning would occur.

Even with their enhanced range, it was clear that a number of refuelling stops would have to be made to reach Hong Kong. The route selected was first to fly almost due east to Kuching in Sarawak. From Kuching to Labuan which is a small island off the coast of Brunei. Thence to Clark Field, the big US Army air base near Manila in the Philippines and finally the 600 miles over-water flight north to Hong Kong.

It would be no easy flight as the leader would have to carry out his own navigation without a vestige of navigational equipment on board and much of the flight would be over water with no visual clues as to where they were.

Fighter pilots are not experienced in long-range navigation, but in this case it was fortunate that the fighter squadron was being commanded by a pilot who had operated for four years in Bomber Command and who was also imbued with the will to lead from the front. Furthermore, 28 Squadron's CO had also taken the trouble, in the immediate post-war days in England, to take part in classes for the civil air navigation licence. The efforts now paid handsome dividends.

It also helped that, while operating Blenheims from Malta, he had learned to read the wind vector from observation of the wind lanes appearing on the surface of the sea. With the added knowledge gained when studying for his navigation licence Ivor also knew what factors to apply at heights above the water. Wind on the surface both veers in direction and increases in strength the higher one goes and does so by calculated percentages. A skilled man flying high can therefore obtain an approximation of what the wind over the sea would be just by observing the wind lanes and applying an approximate height factor. Much of the flight to Hong Kong would be between 10,000-15,000ft, ie. just below the height where normally a change from Low to Higher blower (supercharger) would be made. Maximum range not maximum speed was required.

Provided the compasses have been checked and compensated for both magnetic variation and deviation (another 'Second N' subject) and an allowance for wind drift applied, an aircraft over water can maintain a desired track satisfactorily. This would be the method that Ivor Broom proposed to use when leading his flock from Singapore to Hong Kong.

Another wise precaution was to ascertain, by a number of formation flights, exactly how far the overload tanks would take the Spitfires. It was confirmed that just over three hours in the air and a distance of about 800 miles could be safely accomplished.

The possibility of having to ditch in the sea due to an engine failure or other mechanical defect had to be considered and Ivor decided that every pilot should therefore practice getting into, and righting, the one-man dinghies that all would carry along with their 'Mae West' life-jackets. The drill was that each man would jump off the top board of the swimming pool with his dinghy and 'Mae West' and, as ever, Ivor would lead the way.

However, when on the top board, things looked a little awesome. 'I can't do that. You will have to kick me over,' said Ivor. Bob Wootton, who had been appointed the jungle Survival Officer and was behind him, duly obliged with a firm foot. As Bob has remarked, 'It is not often that a pilot is given an order to kick his CO up the arse and shove him into a swimming pool.' Bob confesses that he may have over-exerted himself as later Ivor advised him, 'From now on, you will have to take the penalty kicks.'

The Squadron had been offered the services of a Mosquito to lead and navigate the formation on its over-water flights but, after some consideration, Ivor decided that it was better if he navigated and used the Mosquito to trail behind the formation just in case a Spitfire might have to ditch. The Mosquito could then carefully pinpoint where the aircraft had gone down and inform the Air Sea Rescue services. He also arranged for a Sunderland flying boat to be trailing further behind so as to be able to pick up any such unfortunate chap. However, no one saw the Sunderland as it lacked the speed to stay with the others. It was also agreed that the Mosquito, crewed by Flying Officer Price and his navigator Sergeant Bail, would be available on the radio in case Ivor felt the need for navigational checks or aid. It would be keeping in sight behind the formation and would check on how the formation was proceeding and could interject advice. It was hoped that this would not be needed as 28 Squadron had already developed a pride in itself and confidence in its leader.

There was not all that much confidence in the overload tank as it was reckoned that, as this became empty causing engine splutter, a loss of height was inevitable. Also, on one of the training formation exercises, one had come off Ivor's 'Spit' during take-off and had gone bounding down the runway on fire.

The precautions and exercises to prepare for Operation Snapdragon had impressed all. The Squadron was clearly in good hands. Yet it was not all hard work for while Britain froze in one of the coldest winters on record and was plagued by strikes and ever more severe rations, there was plenty of sunshine and everything in Malaya and Singapore. The CO along with the rest of 28 Squadron lost no opportunity of a party, a picnic or a bathe in the warm seas round them. Ivor was always delighted to be able to mix freely with the young officers and men under his command. With his boyish looks and trim figure, it was hard to believe that this fun-loving man was a dedicated Squadron Leader and in firm command of an important operational fighter squadron.

On the occasion of the actual reinforcement exercise to Hong Kong, all went as planned. The night stop in Sarawak was especially pleasant as the pilots were put up in one of the two palaces of the fabulously wealthy 'White Rajah' where every kind of food and drink was available 'on the house.' Bob Wootton recalls that while he was helping himself to one of the free drinks, Ivor as usual, was sticking to orange juice. He topped this up with water only to discover with his first sip that he had topped it up with gin! Rather than reject it openly, he quietly put it down and when they all trooped into dinner he managed to slip it to Bob Wootton and suggested that 'to preserve the honour of the RAF and 28 Squadron' he drink it down. Just as Tommy Broom had likewise preserved Squadron honour in the past, Bob found himself able to comply!

On the final long, over-water, leg from Clark Field near Manila to Hong Kong Bob Wootton had a frightful scare. He was flying as 'Number Two' in the loose formation they were keeping during the period when the overload tank was liable to run dry. When Ivor's did so, instead of the usual loss of about 300ft in height, Ivor's main tanks took ages (so it seemed to Bob) to cut in and his leader was dropping closer and closer towards the sea. As Bob has put it 'As he fell away he kept getting smaller and smaller below.' If Ivor went down Bob would have to lead and not only had he no idea where they were, but also he lacked navigational experience and, to cap it all, his radio was 'on the blink.' After a loss of height of about 1,500ft, Ivor's machine was functioning normally again and Bob Wootton breathed a sigh of relief as Ivor's 'Spit' again began to appear larger and larger as it rose to greet him. His praise for Ivor's navigation throughout is unstinted for they hit Hong Kong right on the nose at the expected time.

By a remarkable coincidence, on the day before the six Spitfires successfully arrived in Hong Kong, the British Consulate in nearby Canton, was burnt down by an anti-British mob. The arrival of the Spitfires was thus hailed as some kind of immediate response and the Hong Kong papers had banner headlines about 'Britain's swift reply'! The locals were much impressed. Ivor kept quiet about the weeks of preparation and the three to four days that it had taken to complete Operation Snapdragon.

After the 'Spits' had first carried out some local exercises with Army and Navy personnel, the success was later marred by losing two aircraft which ran into one another on the ground. One pilot, Ian Hart, was lucky not to have been killed as the five-bladed propeller of the one behind sliced clean into his cockpit. With their long upwards slanting nose, Spits were notoriously 'blind' ahead when manoeuvring on the ground.

The return journey also had its difficulties. Tropical rain storms plagued them on landing at Kuching. This was a former Japanese grass field which, unknown to Ivor, had been turned into a bog by some three and a half inches of rain the night before. He, leading as usual, touched down first but ran into a patch of soft ground. The aircraft sank up to its belly and pitched forward onto its nose resulting in a write-off. Fortunately the radios, which were apt to be very unreliable, were all working and Ivor, having quickly checked the area for a harder landing surface, was then able to talk the others down to safe arrivals. Bob confesses that Ivor first waved him off, but he pretended not to have noticed. He did touch down safely, but nearly decapitated his CO when being waved off to go around again.

This reduced the formation to three with Ivor now leading in another aircraft. The storms for the final leg back to Singapore were of major magnitude and Ivor had to use all his skills and wits to avoid leading his reduced flock into a massive cumulo nimbus cloud or line squall. The rain reduced visibility to almost nil and Bob Wootton recalls that at this time the three aircraft had closed up to tight formation in order to keep their leader and sole navigator in sight. At times Ivor led them down to 50ft in attempts to fly under the storm clouds. The visibility was occasionally so bad that Bob could not even see the other wing man on the other side of the tight formation. It was as, Bob Wootton admits, a time when their aerobatic formation practice paid off.

The visibility was so poor and the tropical storms so intense that the Mosquito, which was still acting as a kind of shepherd watching over the flock of (now three) Spitfires, never managed to land at Singapore, but diverted to Butterworth, near Penang. The sheep, in fact, got home but the shepherd didn't! As well as dropping down to 50ft, Ivor also made attempts to climb up over some of the menacing clouds. It must have been about his worst moments in the air with the added responsibility of having Bob Wootton only a few feet from him on one side and Flying Officer John Phipps likewise on the other. If he had gone down, there was little chance for the other two. Bob's praise for Ivor's navigation throughout is unstinted. On that final leg home when the leader had to dodge around vast billowing clouds and when visibility in tropical torrential rain was reduced to a matter of only feet, he somehow kept in mind where their position was and guided them safely back to Singapore.

Another of the young pilots of 28 Squadron — and he was one of several who had first attended a short university course and thence been granted a Cranwell course and a permanent commission — was 20-year-old Pilot Officer John Nicholls. Like Ian Pedder he was later to have a distinguished RAF career retiring as an Air Marshal after having been appointed Vice-Chief of Air Staff and given a knighthood. In spite of his tender years (hardly a month went by in 28 Squadron without a 21st birthday celebration!) he had been appointed Squadron Adjutant. He also recalls the reinforcement flight to Hong Kong although his part terminated at Hong Kong when his Spit and the other collided on the ground. Sir John reaffirms that Ivor, when he first took over, had a lot to overcome. The youngsters such as he who knew that they had been more or less hand-picked to form a future backbone to the RAF, took a very dim view when first finding out that they would be commanded by a pilot who had never before been in Fighter Command. They remained in ignorance about their distinguished Second World War leader until the first 'dining-in' night.

In the tropics, all aircrew wore khaki drill without Wings or medal ribbons. It was only when more formally attired for this dinner that all came to appreciate that their Station Commander (they were still at Kuala Lumpur) was not just Wing Commander H Edwards but was THE 'Hughie' Edwards VC, DSO, DFC, formerly of 2 Group and that their own CO — falsely alleged Transport Command pilot — was displaying, as Bob Wootton has put it, 'the DSO and more DFCs than the rest of the highly decorated top table could muster between them.'

In addition the young officers quickly came to admire the charisma of their Squadron Commander and, as Sir John Nicholls is pleased to confirm, they learned much from his inspirational leadership. In the undefinable way that natural leaders somehow manage to bring out the best in others, Ivor soon had 28 Squadron one hundred percent behind him. It was much to Ivor's advantage that although the previous CO was a brilliant pilot with a distinguished war record, and had been awarded both the DSO and DFC he rarely flew with them or led them. Ivor's determination to lead from the front was in sharp contrast and an inspirational touch.

Ivor soon also showed that, although they regarded themselves as some kind of 'hot rod' fighter boy pilots, he knew, as Sir Ian Pedder has put it, 'Far more about this art than any of us was ever likely to know.' Like Sir Ian, Sir John Nicholls learned from their CO, what to do and what not to do when later put in charge of a squadron in the RAF. Doubtless they in turn passed on the lessons learned and today, some other young Squadron Commander may yet be benefiting and some young sprog, quite unknown to his CO, may be absorbing the lessons learned for the time when he might be put in charge.

Sir John adds several stories to the epic Operation Snapdragon. One is that, on one of the practice flights to ascertain the range of the Spitfire, one aircraft's overload tank (he thinks they were less than 100 gallons) ran dry and the main tanks failed to cut in. The pilot then decided to bail out. With impenetrable jungle underneath, this was to risk death. However, luck went his way and he landed in one of the few clearings and was soon able to catch a bus to a village where he was greeted as a hero with strong local drinks. By the time that the rescue services caught up with him, he was almost paralytic.

Sir John also recalls that when they landed at Kuching to refuel on the way to Hong Kong, they used a short grass landing strip which the Japanese had once prepared and which had received virtually no servicing since. However, isolated as it was, the ubiquitous Shell organisation had fuel ready for the squadron's next leg although it had to be hand-poured from 50-gallon drums and entered the tanks, via the usual over-wing orifices, with chamois leather acting as filters.

While in Hong Kong both he, and most of his fellow young

pilots, learned that there was a Chinese bank which would cash their cheques, and that the cheques would be unlikely to be debited to their accounts. On their poor pay, this seemed an opportunity too good to be missed and after successfully cashing one cheque, they tried it again with equal success. No explanation was forthcoming and the cheques never were debited. China was in turmoil with raging inflation. A cheque from a British Officer was held in high regard, rather as some hoard gold in similar circumstances, and it was believed the cheques were used as valuable currency. Strangely he believes that this bank, despite its 1947 generous habits, is still in business.

John Nicholls, like Bob Wootton, was very conscious at the time of Snapdragon, that the fate of Hong Kong then was precarious as the adherents of Mao were in the process of getting the better of those of Chiang Kai-Chek whom Britain favoured. It was for this reason, with the thought that a possible forced landing in Chinese territory might occur, that before arriving in Hong Kong, the Spitfires had all their guns removed. The British were not going to give the Chinese any excuse for military counter action.

Like everyone else who knew the Brooms out in Singapore, Malaya or elsewhere, Sir John Nicholls had nothing but praise for Jess Broom. She may have been delighted to get away from the restrictions of the Britain of 1946 and 1947 but she had other problems. Her journey out from England even had its awkward moments. In her own words:

I was not at all worldly wise when I married, hardly ever having been out of East Anglia. My life was centred around the church and youth activities.

In Bicester, where we started off married life (aged 19) after Ivor's first tour of Ops on Blenheims, we again entered into church activities and helped to run a youth group with the assistance of men from the Pioneer Corps unit nearby. Food rationing was very sparse and as I did not eat meat, I changed my meat ration (about three to four ounces per week) for cheese and extra butter. I think we lived on macaroni cheese for the first year of our marriage and unlike Maconachies 'meat and veg' (on which, in Malta, Ivor mostly lived and which he now will never touch) we still enjoy cheese.

After Ivor went back for a second tour of Ops with 571 Squadron, Jess and her young baby returned to Ipswich and resumed a life centred round church and now children. Then, in 1946, Jess was amongst the very first to be allowed to travel to Singapore to be near her husband.

Travelling on a troopship finished my education. I had led a sheltered life until then. I was invited to see a young subaltern's etchings while the two children had an afternoon nap and survived unscathed. I think he was as naive as I was because on going into his cabin, I asked where his etchings were. He replied, 'Well, actually, I haven't any but this is a photograph of my fiancée.'

Jess goes on to explain that it was only some weeks later in Singapore that someone on a boating party, told a joke about etchings followed by raucous laughter that she asked Ivor what was so funny about it as she had been invited to see someone's etchings! It was all then explained to her and to make matters worse, Ivor proceeded to tell the rest of the party about her boat 'adventure' that never was.

In Singapore, separated from Ivor within a week or two of arrival when he was posted to Kuala Lumpur, she made the best of part of a house which had been a temporary officers' mess and which was then under the control of the 'Custodian of enemy property.' The house was converted into three flats and two colleagues of Ivor rented the two other flats. From time to time someone would come along with an official and claim a piece of furniture which was then quickly removed. Another drawback was the fact that the house was overrun by large rats which in the evenings would run around the picture rails from room to room. However, she recalls that 'For the first time in seven years I saw fruit such as bananas and pineapples and after wartime England, it seemed like paradise.'

When Ivor and 28 Squadron moved to Tengah airfield at Singapore two months later there were no officers' married quarters so the Brooms settled in one of the only two Warrant Officers' quarters at the airfield. Jess recalls her first night there — the only occupant of the married quarters as the squadron was due to arrive the next morning. There was a prisoner-of-war camp on the airfield as the Japanese were building a new runway and when after dark some firing started, she says 'I was convinced that some Japs had escaped and sat up in bed all night fearing the worst!' Later it transpired that it was only activity on the firing range.

It is no part of Jess's story but the move of the squadron from Kuala Lumpur to Tengah was not without its own adventures. Ivor had put Bob Wootton in charge of the train carrying all the men. He remembers it well as it was his 21st birthday. Hot water for making tea during the journey was not available, but Bob found some way of getting it from the engine's boiler. The RAF's wartime motto about getting things done however difficult or 'impossible' was still carrying on. When later Ivor asked him if he had been worried about impurities in the water he replied 'Of course not. It came from a boiler so it must have been boiled!' At a level crossing near Tengah airfield Ivor arranged for the train to be stopped so that the chaps (as he called the airmen) could disembark and continue their journey by trucks. This shortened the overall journey by a couple of hours. Bob was thus able to celebrate his birthday with his fellow pilots.

Jess clearly blossomed out in Singapore. Living on a RAF station must have been a broadening experience. By the time that Christmas came around, when the station decided to put on its own pantomime, it was Jess who played Cinderella and who sang the lovely songs of the day made famous by Frances Day and others. The Station Commander's wife played the Fairy Godmother and, as can be imagined, burly airmen played the Ugly Sisters to the merriment of their colleagues. The show was so successful that the C-in-C suggested they take it on tour. However, it proved impossible to take the pantomime on tour because of the props and costumes, and another production was quickly organised with a smaller cast. By then Jess' third child had arrived and she had a very capable *amah* so was able to enjoy a well-earned break in Penang. Prior to acquiring a Chinese cook and *amah*, rather to her alarm the station had provided her with two Japanese officers who behaved like the traditional Japanese of the films — bowing every time they entered the room and always backing out of it hissing and bowing — rather as they would probably have expected our officers to behave if they had won the war.

Many a CO's wife does a great job looking after the men and their families and does so from a sense of duty, but in Jess Broom's case, this was her natural way and her upbringing. Taking care of others had been ingrained in her ever since she had helped to look after the junior boys of the Boys Brigade at Ipswich — a job which endeared her to those boys to such an extent that when she was married they formed a Guard of Honour when she and Ivor left the church.

As an RAF officer's wife, usually a Commanding Officer's wife, she fell easily into the required routine of wives' club, thrift shops, amateur dramatics, Brownies, coffee mornings, welfare work, etc. Jess found it a pleasant, fulfilling life and at risk of making a charming, modest lady blush, it should be recorded that no less than five observant persons who were contacted about the career of Air Marshal Sir Ivor Broom volunteered comments about Jess:

In this he was always supported superbly by Jess and together they were regarded as an ideal couple....

It is said that behind every successful man, there is a helping woman. This is certainly true about Ivor and Lady Jess....

Jess was a thoroughly charming lady who gave every support to Ivor and who was the sort of station commander's wife who played a very active role, particularly on the families side....

I am sure throughout his career Ivor received the unstinting support of his charming wife, Jess. She played a vital role in helping to achieve such a happy station — notably among the wives which is by no means the easiest of tasks....

Her quiet and gentle way was so unobtrusive that we didn't at first realise what a calming influence she was. Her Sunday curry lunches were a treat to look forward to....

Apart from Operation Snapdragon, the most memorable event of Ivor's career while in south-east Asia was when, out of the blue the C-in-C, Sir Hugh Pughe Lloyd, informed him that he, along with the GOC General Redman and the Admiral Caslon, had been invited to tour both Australia and New Zealand as guests of their governments and that he wanted Ivor to be the Staff Officer to the group. He added 'If anyone asks about Malta, you will have to do the talking.' These were odd words from the man whom many regard as the true saviour of Malta and one who was there for over a year compared with Ivor Broom's few months. Squadron Leader Broom had no idea what duties a Personal Staff Officer had to perform and no time to find out.

Together they flew in a York first to Darwin in the north tip of Australia, and from there to Sydney for a brief stop before starting the New Zealand part of the journey; first to Auckland and then, in a smaller 'plane, to Ohakea and Taupo, famous for its hot springs and trout fishing. Just before flying to Taupo it was discovered that one 'briefcase' had been left behind in Singapore. Ivor swiftly learned that a Personal Staff Officer was responsible for correct baggage arrival! Worse still, the 'briefcase' turned out to be a bag containing the C-in-C's fishing tackle. As Ivor recalls 'Hugh Pughe didn't speak to me for twenty-four hours.'

After stops at Wellington, Dunedin, Christchurch and Whenuapai, the distinguished party left New Zealand for Melbourne, Canberra, thence back to Darwin and Singapore. They had been away for nineteen days and had seen much. Qantas carried them several times, but Squadron Leader Peter Helmore in a York MW 325 had covered most of the long journeys. Another thing that Ivor learned about being a Personal Staff Officer was the need to carry with him plenty of local currency as whenever the party stopped for sufficient length of time, both Sir Hugh and especially Lady Lloyd, went shopping — and it was Ivor who had to do all the payments! All that the C-in-C said after this interesting glimpse of another continent at the end of their journeys was 'How much do I owe you?'

Ivor and Jess also saw another beautiful glimpse of the world when they spent a leave on the island of Penang where the Services kept the Runnemede Hotel for rest and recuperation.

All good things come to an end and after having been in charge for over eighteen months, Squadron Leader Broom's period with 28 Squadron and his longer period in this interesting corner of the world came to an end. Not only was he posted back to the UK, but for the best part of a year he never once had an opportunity to fly an aircraft. This, inevitably, was the lot that all permanent peacetime officers had, from time to time, to endure.

A highlight of the return journey by boat was the formation of a dance band for entertaining the troops. When the organiser discovered that he had no 'crooner', it was the wife of the Squadron Leader who had been appointed OC RAF contingent, who stepped into the breech or to be more accurate who 'was volunteered by my husband!' All in all, says Jess 'I arrived back more worldly wise than when I left England.'

Back in Britain the crooner and her husband found life rather different as they no longer could call upon Japanese house boys or Chinese *amahas*. Instead they were keeping chickens to supplement the miserly rations which still persisted in the UK; although the war had been over for more than four years.

But what was Squadron Leader Broom returning home to do? In spite of all that he had achieved since joining up in 1940, he still only held the firm rank of a Flight Lieutenant. Moreover, the RAF was being steadily reduced in numbers. The future suddenly did not look too bright.

CHAPTER FIFTEEN

Back in England:
Back in Pay, too!

Ivor Broom's first assignment back in England after
his year and more in command of Spitfire Squadron
No. 28 in the Far East, could hardly have been of greater
contrast. He was appointed a Schools Liaison Officer and his
daily task was to give talks about the RAF and his own
experiences in it, to boys in schools scattered around East
Anglia and beyond.

The principal asset about the job was that it held a Squadron
Leader's establishment and it enabled him to retain this acting
rank. His basic rank was still that of only a Flight Lieutenant
and the difference in pay and status was considerable. It also
helped that East Anglia was his principal 'parish' and that he
could establish Jessica in Ipswich in a rented house close to
her family.

In some respects the RAF could hardly have chosen a more
suitable man. Ivor's RAF experiences were the kind that thrilled
schoolboys and his row of gallantry medals was proof of the
genuineness of his tales.

In one way a spin-off of this appointment was to help Ivor
in latter years, right up to present times. Public speaking is an
art which is largely developed by experience of facing an
audience and hearing one's own voice. Experience breeds
confidence and it is the confident speaker who best holds an
audience. Having to deliver addresses to fidgeting schoolboys
twice a day and then to answer their questions must have helped
much to make Ivor Broom the excellent speaker that he is today.

Acting S/Ldr I G Broom, in spite of his DSO, DFC and
two bars, might have remained in this necessary but uninspiring
(to an active pilot) job for years if he had not taken the trouble
to prepare himself for a new examination which the Service
had just started. This was one which all who aspired to become
senior officers had to take. It was designed to sort the sheep

from the goats among those with high rank in mind. To pass did not mean that promotion would follow. It was an exam to create a list of names who would thereafter be considered both for promotion and entrance to the RAF Staff college. To fail meant that the likelihood of ever rising above Flight Lieutenant was slim.

Ivor duly passed this vital test. Although the ranks of Flight Lieutenant and Squadron Leader are next to one another, a wide chasm between the two exists both in pay and status. The majority of RAF officers do not get beyond Flight Lieutenant. There they stay until retirement — usually getting out at a fairly young age. If able to make the jump to Squadron Leader, prospects thereafter are good.

The result of overcoming this new hurdle — and Ivor was among the very first to sit the exam — was not long in forthcoming. After having lectured the schools for only six months, Ivor was posted to attend the RAF Staff college at Bracknell.

While this was the kind of upward step that all young officers almost prayed for because it meant that the way forward was now open — especially for one who had never been to the RAF's college at Cranwell — in Ivor's case it caused him such personal financial problems that he tried to resign his commission!

The RAF rule is that when an officer is on a course, he cannot be given any acting rank. This meant that Ivor's 'elevation' to Bracknell would drop him back to his basic rank of Flight Lieutenant. The posting came in April 1949 and seemed a harsh demotion for one who ever since 1944 had been wearing the rank badges, and had been paid accordingly, as a Wing Commander or a Squadron Leader. He knew that the Staff College course would last for nine months and that during this period he would be paid approximately HALF the pay that he had been receiving when in late 1944 he had taken command of 163 Squadron and when prices of essentials were considerably less. With now a wife and three children to support, he found himself in serious financial difficulties.

It now struck him forcibly that, whereas he was being paid

the low sum that the RAF paid for its Flight Lieutenants, his fellow Flight Commander of 128 Squadron, Cliff Alabaster DSO & bar, DFC & bar — a pilot who had also studied for the civil aviation licences when Ivor had been doing so — was now a Senior Captain with BOAC* and was earning three times or more the salary that Ivor was receiving. Moreover 'Alaby' (as all called him) was daily in command of fast modern aircraft and spending nights in five star hotels in glamorous places overseas while Ivor had to be content to 'fly a desk' at Bracknell.

To add to Ivor's woes at that time, he was disappointed to learn that, having accepted a permanent commission from the RAF, he was not allowed to resign.

Ivor is now mildly surprised that, although he had given as his reason for wanting to resign 'financial difficulties on a Flight Lieutenant's pay', no one even hinted to him that he was likely to be promoted to a basic Squadron Leader at the end of the course. Ivor accepted his fate and set about to get the most from the course.

The Staff Course at Bracknell was designed to prepare middle ranking officers (many 'pupils' were substantive Squadron Leaders and even Wing Commanders) for subsequent Staff appointments, right up to highest ranks. While there, having rented a flat at nearby Ascot for his family, Ivor was taught a number of essential 'office' administrative methods. They included such things as how to establish an efficient filing system; how to move a body of troops by air to 'foreign parts', how to move a squadron from one airfield to another. The course gave him an excellent grounding in man-management and office routine which was to stand him in good stead both for the rest of his RAF career and in business life after retirement. He also learned how to write better reports and it concluded with the writing of a thesis. For the first time Ivor learned about the exact structure and administrative machinery of the RAF, although in point of fact, he had managed

* Cliff Alabaster had, along with several fellow Pathfinders, joined Don Bennett's British Latin American Airways. This soon became British South American Airways. However, the airline ran into difficulties and was then merged into British Overseas Airways Corporation (BOAC).

successfully to look after flights, squadrons and departments, both home and overseas, without this background.

The course made no provision for any flying and it was up to pupils who wished to keep their hand in to scrounge whatever they could. Most did not try to do this and it certainly was not required. But Ivor had not flown for almost a year since leaving Singapore and was determined not to allow this lapse to continue. Thanks to using initiative and finding friends, he managed to average about two hours in the air in command of an aircraft each month. Virtually all took place at the same White Waltham airfield where in autumn 1940, with the contrails of the Battle of Britain visible overhead, he had first been taught to fly by the RAF.

Although Ivor once managed to get his hands on a Spitfire, which developed engine trouble and nearly caused him to force land in a field, the rest of the seventeen to eighteen hours which he scrounged were in slow, easy-to-fly types such as the Avro Anson twin-engined 'flying classroom' or the single-engined trainer the Percival Proctor. It was better than nothing but must have been a bit gruelling at a time when the jet-powered Comet airliner (soon to be in Alaby's hands) and the RAF's first jet bomber, the Canberra, were making first flights. It may also have galled him that, while he attended his lectures on filing and the like, Mao Tse Tung had taken charge of all China and was posing a threat to the Hong Kong colony which Ivor and the Spitfires of 28 Squadron had once reinforced.

It could not have been a happy posting and it reduced the quietly living Brooms to almost penury but it was one which paid handsome dividends in the years to come. In retrospect, Ivor is grateful that the RAF did not heed to his attempts to resign his commission and, at the back of his mind, there was always the thought that just to have been selected to attend a Staff Course implied that someone 'upstairs' must have had half an eye on him.

The nineteen fifties started better for Ivor Broom. Having completed the Staff Course to the satisfaction of his superiors, he was promoted to the full peacetime rank of Squadron Leader, with effect from 1 January 1950. The promotion came just two days after he had been posted to No. 1 Initial Training School where he filled the post of a Flight Commander. The drawback was that it was yet another ground job: moreover, it was one which was to last for almost two and a half years.

The ITS (Initial Training Schools) had taken the place of the wartime Initial Training Wings. Both were places where new intakes into the Service were first posted. The school contained over 600 cadets, divided into four squadrons: one of which Ivor now commanded. The courses lasted sixteen weeks.

Ivor Broom pitched into this new activity with his customary energy and enthusiasm. Although it meant that every four months he had a new intake of over 150 cadets, he trained himself to memorise every one by name. It was an accomplishment which also was to pay handsome dividends in later life and one which, when in higher command, was to earn respect from others.

Although flying training was no part of the curriculum, cadets were taken aloft for 'air experience.' An Avro Anson was available to take navigators and a Percival Proctor for pilots. S/Ldr Broom missed no opportunity to give the youngsters a ride.

At first the ITS was at Wittering in Lincolnshire, but within a few months of joining it, Ivor and the school moved to Jurby in the pleasant Isle of Man where he found a house to rent at Ramsay.

As might be expected from one who had been brought up in the Welsh valleys, Ivor paid particular attention to the ITS rugby team. He helped to referee games. When matches with mainland teams were arranged, he used the Anson, into which only about seven passengers could be crammed, to fly the team over. It therefore took two flights (all 'Air Experience') to get fourteen of the team across, so Ivor always made up the team for such away matches.

Thanks to making friends with colleagues at RAF Valley (on the Isle of Anglesey), S/Ldr Broom also managed to wangle a few flights in the RAF's two jet fighters, the Gloster Meteor and the de Havilland Vampire. As ever he was determined to keep his hand in.

The cadets were also taken gliding in two-seater 'planes and, during his period with 1 ITS, Ivor managed over 200 winch launchings. His checking out for his first flight in a glider was as brief as could be. After one winch launch and a hasty circuit back, he was told: 'You'll manage all right' and was left on his own. As he was about to be winch launched, a F/O Thompson of the RAF Regiment strolled by. These officers did not fly as the RAF Regiment is the 'army-like' unit which guards RAF airfields.

'Any chance of a flight, sir?' inquired the RAF Regiment officer.

'Hop in,' was the answer.

After the launch, which is the most hair-raising part of the flight, the passenger remarked: 'Do you know, sir, this is my first flight in one of these things.'

'Mine too!' was Ivor's reply.

A break from routine was when Ivor, near the end of his time at Jurby, got hold of a Harvard at the RAF airfield of Morton-in-Marsh and, in the course of a few days, carried out a dozen concentrated instrument flights, mainly with instructors. This was to enable him to take and pass the RAF's coveted Green Card Instrument rating.

Strangely one of the incidents which is most remembered by Ivor Broom during his two years at Jurby, concerns the popular but rather saucy comedian Frankie Howerd. A cadet informed him that the comedian was on the island and as it was the time of an end-of-course farewell dinner, it was suggested that the radio and TV star be invited as a guest speaker. Ivor readily agreed. He can still remember, almost verbatim, what Frankie Howerd said when rising to speak:

I hear that you will be receiving the results of your final examination in a few days. The vast majority of you will, no doubt, pass and proceed to your flying training ... A few may fail and will think that their lives are now in ruins ... As a young man, I wanted to be a serious actor. I went to the Royal Academy of Dramatic Art (RADA) but I failed to make the grade. This completely demoralised me. What could I do? … Well, you all know what I now do, and believe me, it pays well! If you should happen to fail, I urge you to pick yourself up and seek new opportunities for careers in other walks of life.

As Ivor recalls, it struck exactly the right note.

Bearing in mind he spent the period from 1948 to April 1952 on a number of purely ground assignments, it speaks well for Ivor's determination to keep abreast of flying developments that by the time he came to be posted away from 1 ITS, he had, whilst being 'chairborne':

— several times flown the RAF's two latest jet fighters,

— acquired the coveted Green Card Instrument rating,

— become an accomplished glider pilot

and, for old times sake, occasionally scrounged flights in a Spitfire and a Mosquito. In all, largely on 'Air Experience' flights for cadets (and also mainland rugby matches!), he had added another 200 hours to his considerable total, NOT counting any time spent in the air on gliders.

It is truly said in the RAF, 'You can't keep a good man down!' and the posting in April 1952 to attend the RAF Flying College at Manby came as a welcome relief. As the name implies, this was definitely a posting which officially included flying: and not just ordinary flying in slow types or gliders.

The RAF Flying College had been set up in 1950 in order to bring selected middle-ranking officers up to date in air warfare. In the process the students had to fly the RAF's latest aircraft. For the most part these were by then jet powered.

To have been selected was an honour. Each course contained only sixteen students. Ivor's course was only the College's third and it lasted a whole year. The students were divided into two groups of eight and held the ranks of Squadron Leader or Wing Commander (with one or two Group Captains) so there was a relaxed atmosphere between instructors and pupils since many were of similar seniority.

Basically, the students flew on one day and were attending lectures or seminars the following. The flying either took place in the jet fighters: Meteors and Vampires or in the larger piston-engined Valettas and Lincolns. The former was a military version of the Vickers Viking twin-engined airliner which had replaced the DC3s in BEA. The Lincoln was Avro's replacement for the wartime Lancaster four-engined bomber but it never quite achieved the fame nor affection that the Lanc had gained. In a world of increasing jet-powered aircraft, it began to look out of date. Even the US-built B-29 bombers of the Second World War were considerably more advanced.

Students emerged from the Flying College with a much broader knowledge of the RAF and its commitments overseas, its overall strategy and an enhanced knowledge of the finer points of flying. Latest bombing and air firing techniques were also covered and the growing importance of radar and electronic approach-and-landing aids was additionally hammered home.

It was heartening for Ivor to be thrust into the forefront of all these developments after his years in the background dealing with schoolboys or raw recruits. Seldom was aviation developing faster and while he had been refereeing rugby matches at Jurby, both large jet airliners and jet bombers had come into being. Now at Manby, Ivor and fellow students were learning much about the mighty four-engined jet 'V' bombers which would later become Britain's principal air strike deterrent. Also while he was there an RAF Canberra made headlines by flying from Northern Ireland to Newfoundland where it refuelled and back in a minute under eight hours.

A lowlight for Ivor was to be assessed, at the end of the course, as only 'Average.' This quite normal rating would have satisfied some but for a pilot who for many years had always been either rated as 'Exceptional' or 'Above Average' it was a retrograde step. The four years when all flying had to be scrounged and when most of it had been carried out in slow training 'planes could hardly have polished Ivor's flying skills.

A highlight was the visit that the course, in a RAF Hastings transport aircraft, paid to the USA. They flew out by way of the Azores and Bermuda. The RAF and the USAF kept in close contact and already the latter had supersonic fighter aircraft, the F-86 Sabres, based in the UK. While in the USA, Ivor managed brief flights in their jet trainer the T-33 and also in their venerable twin-engined bomber, the B-25 Mitchell.

The significance of the explosion by the USA of the first hydrogen bombs was not lost on the instructors and advanced pupils at Manby. Air power now definitely held the keys to world stability ... or otherwise. As wars flared up in Korea and elsewhere, the enormous impact of even conventional aircraft and weapons was reinforced in the minds of many. Few could now doubt that it was the RAF, and not the traditional Royal Navy, which had become Britain's premier shield.

A near personal disaster struck the Broom family while at Manby. Ivor had rented a pleasant sea-side bungalow near Sutton-on-Sea. Jess and her three children were there when, in January 1953, a North Sea gale struck with such force that the sea defences were overcome and the water poured in across the flat Lincolnshire lands.

When the defences were breached, Ivor was on a golf course and, try as he did, he found it impossible to find a road through which he could drive home. In the bungalow, Jess was alarmed both for her family and for the elderly owners who were living temporarily in what was little more than a summer house in their own garden. One owner was an invalid and the best that could be done for him was to bring him into the house and lie him on a stout kitchen table — he was unable to climb up to the loft.

Ivor eventually managed to reach his family but by then it was midnight and he had been struggling for eight hours: much of the time on foot with water waist high. The old man survived on the kitchen table, which could float, but by the time that Ivor arrived Jess and the children had taken refuge in the rafters of the roof.

As Jess has remarked: 'These things always seemed to happen when Ivor was away.'

Although much has been written about the RAF and its best pilots, the lot of their wives remains largely unrecorded. With their constant moves, school difficulties and the nagging fear that the latest RAF disaster, always over-publicised by the Press, might have involved their man, the wives had to cope with plenty.

Ivor's 'schooling' over the last few years had taught him plenty. First the Staff College at Bracknell had brought him up to date about how to manage the ground side. Now the Flying College at Manby had added an air dimension. It was more obvious than ever that some people high up in the RAF hierarchy had their eyes on him but for what was S/Ldr I G Broom, with his wartime decorations and fine record, being prepared?

CHAPTER SIXTEEN

Squadron Commander Again

At the end of an interesting year at the Flying School at Manby, S/Ldr Ivor Broom, to his great delight, found himself posted to 231 Operational Conversion Unit at Bassingbourn, Cambridgeshire. There he would be taught to operate the English Electric's splendid twin-engined jet bomber — the RAF's pride and joy — the Canberra. He was also advised that, after the month-long conversion course, he would be posted to take command of a new Canberra squadron. This would be the third such to be formed and would be No. 57 Squadron.

Nothing could have pleased him more as it had rapidly become apparent that, in the Canberra, the RAF had found itself a worthy successor to the war-winning Mosquito bomber which Ivor knew, and flew, so well.*

In view of the Canberra's potential operating height of up to 50,000ft and its limited flight compartment pressurisation, Canberra crews had to breathe oxygen under pressure and to wear a special pressure breathing waistcoat. They also had to pass an extra medical examination — a High Altitude Selection test — which happily caused Ivor no difficulty.

He was also required to pass, at the end of his conversion course, a 'Canberra B2 Instrument Overshoot Procedure' test. With high-speed sophisticated aircraft now costing millions each, the RAF was making sure that those who flew them were physically and operationally capable of coping with all that might be required. Gone for ever were the wartime days when both aircraft and pilots were being mass-produced by the thousand and when a tragic accident rate during training had to be tolerated with the sad result that fatalities running into thousands became inevitable without the enemy having to fire a shot.

---

* The Canberra was one of the very few British aircraft ever to be produced in large numbers in the USA. The Glen Martin Company built it under licence, where it became the B-57.

Although it was being envisaged that relatively small aircraft such as the Canberra (the dimensions of which were markedly smaller than the wartime four-engined bombers) could be adapted to carry atom or even hydrogen bombs with destructive powers far in excess of those of whole squadrons of Lancasters carrying the largest of wartime bombs.

Pilot training costs had also escalated enormously. It was not quantity which counted but quality. Britain's strike force would be in the hands of only a relatively few young men who had been trained and tested to the highest standards. They alone would be allowed to operate the deadly modern aircraft which the manufacturers were producing in strictly limited numbers.

After about eight hours of dual instruction and eighteen hours solo flying in Canberra B2s — a far more thorough training course than any which Ivor had before received on a new type — S/Ldr I G Broom was passed out as a fit person to operate the RAF's much cherished latest bomber in Service. Ivor must have been relieved to note that he had reverted to a more familiar assessment of 'Above Average'; which in peacetime was about as high as was given.

On 15 May 1953 Ivor was posted to Coningsby to form the third Canberra bomber squadron in the RAF — No. 57 Squadron. He wasted little time for almost at once he personally started to check out the few pilots already posted to the Squadron. Whereas wartime squadrons contained as many as twenty-four aircraft, with a ready reserve at hand to make good a night's losses, 57 Squadron's establishment was just eight aircraft. Also the position of Squadron Commander carried the rank of Squadron Leader. Consequently Ivor found himself in a lower rank than that which had been given him when taking command of No. 163 Squadron in January 1945.

As CO, Ivor also now had to run the office in the prescribed manner as taught at Bracknell. In the heat of war, paper work came very much secondary to operational results but in peacetime there could be no excuses for not complying fully with required procedures.

A glance at the log book of S/Ldr Broom shows that a greater emphasis was now being placed upon night flying training and upon instrument let-downs. The extreme paucity of Ivor's night-time training during the war almost implied that it was too dangerous to attempt. It was better left to front line units to find out who could, and who could not, cope with the hazards involved — truly a case of survival of the fittest. Otherwise the tactics had not changed overmuch. There were cross-country flights to levels of at least 40,000ft. There were visual and blind bombing practices; the latter carried out with the aid of GEE-H sets, as per wartime: plus some night navigation using astro shots. There were also formation practices in preparation for displays on such occasions as the Queen's birthday and Battle of Britain Day. A break from routine would be visits to friendly European airfields in Holland, Germany, Scandinavia, etc, in keeping with Britain's NATO role.

As the CO, Ivor had to live on the station. There were no officers' married quarters but he was allocated quarters for Jess and the children in a Warrant Officer's married quarter. During the war married quarters for officers, quite naturally, were not built and even by 1954 the RAF had barely started to add these to the relatively few of the hundreds of the UK airfields which the RAF still occupied.

Just after leading a fly-past formation of Canberras for the Queen's birthday, in May 1954 No 57 Squadron was moved to Cottesmore as Coningsby, and other bomber stations, were having runway extensions built in anticipation of the mighty four-jet 'V' bombers which would soon be arriving. These Valiants, Vulcans and Victors, carrying the latest nuclear weapons, would become Britain's principal deterrent during the Cold War pre-Polaris era.

At Cottesmore, in the County of Rutland, which now no longer exists, Ivor and Jess were delighted to find a few pre-war officers' quarters and, as he puts it 'For the first time in twelve years since joining the RAF and taking a bride, we were actually accommodated in an official officer's quarter.'

The highlight of 57 Squadron's stay at Cottesmore was when Ivor was ordered to take six Canberras on a tour of several Arab states with which Britain had treaty relations. This prestige exercise was timely as it coincided with the seizure of power in Egypt by a belligerent Colonel Abdul Nasser following upon Britain's withdrawal of troops from their Suez Canal bases.

The Canberras flew first to Iraq, then ruled by an Arab Regent, by way of El Aouina then to Nicosia in Cyprus where the RAF had one of its largest of all operational stations. The next stage was to Habbaniya in the Arabian Desert where the RAF had been firmly entrenched long before even the Second World War and thence to Baghdad. At Baghdad the Squadron performed their well-practised display which ended by a low high-speed pass in an aircraft flown by F/Lt Shrivell. It was an impressive display and lasted for thirty minutes. Doubtless the hard work that the Squadron had put in during practices and their excellent UK displays were factors in determining the selection of 57 Squadron as the one to show the Arab leaders the might that Britain and the RAF possessed. It was a period when ex-Colonial countries were finding pleasure in 'twisting the lion's tail' with apparent impunity.

After the thunderous beat up by F/Lt Shrivell, Ivor asked the young Crown Prince ruler of Iraq if he would like a flight. The youngster readily agreed and suitably attired in RAF gear, Prince Abdul Illah was given a short trip by Ivor. He later took up the GOC General Hakim but oddly the Chief of the Iraq Air Staff declined the invitation.

That busy day, 8 November 1954, ended with another demonstration display over the city. It was Ivor's fifth flight on that date.

The Squadron next flew to Amman, Jordan, where a similar routine was followed: an impressive display followed by an invitation to the young King Hussein to go flying with Ivor: an invitation which was accepted with alacrity by the British-trained air-minded Jordanian ruler. Not many people could claim to have flown two foreign and regal rulers in a jet bomber within the space of a couple of days.

The Canberras then flew back to Habbaniya for another pleasant night stop before proceeding on to Idris, Tripoli, by way of El Adem, Tobruk. Over Tripoli they gave their final display and these exhibitions of power and precision over the capitals of Arab rulers with whom Britain then had treaties, may well have caused Nasser, who had open ambitions to become the ruler of all Arabs, to think twice before trying to extend Egypt's boundaries.

With much regret Ivor Broom had to hand over his command of 57 Squadron, and leave his married quarter, in late November 1954. He had been in command for eighteen months and he had, as he had done before with the Mosquito, come to love the graceful Canberra. It cruised at Mach 0.74 (ie. seventy-four percent of the speed of sound). It could climb to about 50,000ft and could carry about three tons of ordinary bombs over a range in excess of 1,000 miles. Without bombs, it clearly had a considerably greater range potential: as yet not fully determined.

Canberra B2s normally carried a crew of three with a navigator seated adjacent to the pilot and a bomb aimer down in the nose with all three having ejector seats. The aircraft was capable of being modified to carry a nuclear weapon and, as history shows, with instability in Vietnam, Korea, Egypt and elsewhere and with the constant threat of the USSR looming over Europe, only a nuclear deterrent seemed likely to prevent the Third World War from erupting with terrifying global consequences.

Ivor Broom for the third time in his life had successfully commanded a RAF Squadron and, although still only fuelled by nothing stronger than orange juice, he had led it from the front. He never believed in asking aircrews to do what he himself was not prepared to do. His acknowledged skill as a pilot commended itself to all aircrew and his self-taught habit of remembering almost every NCO and humble 'erk' by their names brought out the best in them. It made them feel that they were not just small cogs in a big soul-less machine, but people doing a worthwhile job.

Ulf Burberry, who was one of Ivor's Flight Commanders, has described Ivor's influence as follows:

He was a fine and much-respected Squadron Commander,

apart from being an exceptional pilot. He did not drink nor smoke but, apart from these drawbacks [sic] he always definitely led from the front whatever the occasion.

Ulf goes on to add that at Coningsby the Station Commander was an even more highly-decorated Second World War pilot. This was 'Tirpitz' Tait: one of only two pilots ever to be awarded FOUR DSOs as well as other medals. Willie Tait became known as 'Tirpitz' after he had led the Lancaster bombers which finally sank the giant German battleship *Tirpitz* in a Norwegian fjord. The only other pilot to win FOUR DSOs??? Basil Embry. Who else!

Ulf recalls that with such distinguished officers, and with Wing Commander Woodruffe DSO, DFC as Wing Commander (Flying) at Coningsby, he and the others *had* to respond. Ulf Burberry mentions that Ivor enjoyed organising Squadron outings. One was to Skegness where, after enjoying a show in which Michael Bentine starred, they all went backstage for a party. 'Only Ivor remained sober which was just as well as he had to drive the bus back.' On another occasion the Squadron visited London:

Where we had *carte blanche* until midnight when the rendezvous would be Trafalgar Square. One of our members had tipped a gallon of TEEPOL — a strong aircraft cleaning detergent, into the famous fountain: suds, suds and more suds everywhere.

Again Ivor led the gallant band back to Coningsby at a rate of knots. The papers in the morning were unable to apportion blame.

By coincidence two of the senior commanders where 57 Squadron was based also had Malta wartime connections. Willie Tait had earned an early DSO in Malta when in February 1941, he led a flight of Whitleys on Britain's first Commando-type airborne raid. Nigel Maynard, who was Wing Commander (Flying) at Cottesmore, had been a Sunderland skipper earlier in the war and had occasionally dropped anchor there. At the time his father, Air Commodore 'Sammy' Maynard, had been the AOC Malta prior to the arrival of Hugh Pughe Lloyd's dynamic period in that post. When Nigel Maynard also reached Air rank, he and his father became the only father and son who rose to become Air Marshals.

After building up 57 Squadron to the point where it became the unit which the RAF chose to show off its authority in the troubled Arab world and, after commanding it for eighteen months, Ivor again found himself back at the RAF Flying College at Manby. This time, however, he would be going as an instructor and not as a student. He had been posted to be one of the College's two Syndicate Leaders.

CHAPTER SEVENTEEN

Memorable Moments at
Manby and West Malling

O ne important difference between the courses at
Manby of 1952 and December of 1954 was that, by
the time that Wing Commander Ivor Broom returned there at
the end of 1954 as a Syndicate leader, the splendid Canberra
had taken the place of the now totally obsolete Lincoln bomber:
although a few of this propeller driven aircraft were
occasionally used by Ivor and others.

In all, Ivor served as a Syndicate leader for over two years
and towards the end of this time the College also introduced
the trans-sonic* Hawker Hunter fighter aircraft. However most
of the flights in fighter type aircraft were still being flown in
the earlier Meteor jet fighter.

A curiosity was that Ivor and his colleagues quite often
flew the obsolete Avro Anson — dear old 'Faithful Annie.' It
was used for journeys to Hendon, Farnborough and the like
and as a communications aircraft for the Commandant, Air
Commodore 'Gus' Walker, and other staff members. 'Faithful
Annie' had been hopelessly outdated even at the start of the
Second World War when it was the most numerous aircraft in
Coastal Command in spite of its deficiencies in range, carrying
capacity, speed, defensive fire and armour. Twenty and more
years after its first flight, it was still soldiering on in the RAF
although all the types with which Coastal Command had
hurriedly replaced it, the Blenheim, Hudson, Wellington,
Whitley, Halifax, B 17 and Liberator, had faded into RAF
memory: the tortoise and the hare again.

Moreover 'Faithful Annie', due to her reliability, extreme
simplicity and commodious fuselage, was to remain in use for
several more years to come. Once, during the war, two collided
and embraced one another in mid air. Yet so great was the

* A trans-sonic aircraft is one which can exceed the speed of sound, ie. it can cross the sound barrier
(Mach 1) in a dive.

safety margin of an Anson that the pair landed safely, one on top of the other.

Ivor's two years at Manby were also a blessing for Jessica. Like many other Service wives, she found the constant moves disturbing but now that the children required schools, it was they who concerned the Brooms most. By the time that their son, Ian, was eight he had been to nine different schools. As a result he had taken some subjects more than once, jumped over some subjects yet taken others more advanced. For example, Ivor discovered that Ian knew how to do and set out a long division sum but had never been shown the simpler short division method!

After about a year at Manby, Ivor Broom was promoted to the rank of Wing Commander more than eleven years after he had first been given this acting rank. In peacetime they were rarely given and double acting ranks almost never. It was largely a wartime device to reward outstandingly successful operational pilots and to fill vacancies in a rapidly expanding RAF. The pay as well as the promotion was welcomed and soon both boys were safely ensconced as boarders at Dean Close School in Cheltenham.

As well as bringing specially selected middle rank officers up to date in modern air warfare, and so preparing them for potentially high ranking positions in the RAF of the future, the Flying College at Manby also took opportunities to extend the frontiers of aviation knowledge.

The college at that time, in its studies of future operations, was constantly seeking to gain the optimum performance out of the RAF's first jet-powered bomber, the Canberra. It was also placing increasing emphasis upon the need of the RAF to become an 'All weather' force. As the Canberra was the RAF's first venture into the jet-bomber age and, in the knowledge that bigger four-engined 'V' bombers were being planned, the Service was anxious to prove its long range potential. Any lesson learned could then be tried with the future 'V' bombers and every opportunity was taken to show that this new generation of aircraft could operate safely in the kind of bad weather which had, so often in the Second World War, caused

Bomber Command to cancel operations.

The jets were operated from a satellite airfield of Manby, named Strubby, where a GCA (Ground Controlled Approach) radar team had become adept at talking down aircraft to safe landings in bad weather conditions, when aircraft at neighbouring airfields were grounded.

The attempts to advance the frontiers of aviation knowledge were made at Manby by the staff instructors in the intervals between courses. Unquestionably the highlights of Ivor's period as a Course Leader at Manby were the parts which he played in two such ventures into the unknown.

In one of these he played a leading role. This has resulted in his name appearing in the books of the *Federation Aeronautique Internationale* (FAI); this being the recognised international body responsible for recording aviation world speed and other aviation records.

There was also a valuable 'spin-off' for the RAF whenever it accomplished some outstanding feat. Governments were for ever trying to balance their budgets by reducing the size and efficiency of the RAF. For the RAF to create a world speed record, or to carry out successfully a speed and distance record, was excellent self-publicity. Politicians are swayed by people, and the public at large are influenced by the media's exploitation of such events.

One of the subjects taught to the selected middle ranking officers at Manby was how logically to present a case in its best light. This subject was useful to ensure that those at the top who had to deal with politicians made the most of their opportunities. In the last analysis it was the politicians, with control of the money, who determined whether or not the Services were adequately manned or equipped.

On the grounds that actions speak louder than words, what better way was there to present a case for continuing to order outstandingly successful RAF aircraft, such as the Canberra, than by making spectacular flights with it while ensuring that the press, TV and radio men were on hand to witness and record events?

Two birds were being killed with one stone: the RAF was

expanding its knowledge and at the same time was receiving the kind of favourable publicity that was necessary to keep it in the form and shape that its leaders considered to be essential.

Prior to Ivor's arrival at Manby, Canberra No. 699 which had been named Aries IV, after earlier record breaking aircraft also called 'Aries', had flown to Capetown and back with a minimum of refuelling stops, in record times. The aircraft was therefore in the public eye.

By the time that Ivor had been at Manby for a year and more, he had established himself as one of the staff's best pilots. Thus, when two more record breaking development flights for Aries IV were being planned, during a short mid-summer break between courses, Ivor was earmarked to take the lead in one and to play a supporting role in the other.

First Aries IV would be flown non-stop from an airfield in the north of Norway, over the North Pole, to one in Alaska in the extreme north-west tip of America. To anyone brought up to look (as most are) at the world in an Atlas drawn up on Mercator's Projection, this seemed to be an enormous non-stop flight by an aircraft type (ie. jet powered), which at that time was known for speed rather than endurance. Looked at in terms of longitude, it meant taking off from Bodo, which lies about 15° *east* of the Greenwich meridian and landing at Fairbanks in Alaska at about 150° *west* of Greenwich, literally flying almost half way around the world non-stop. This would surely impress all, especially those who were unaware of the false presentation of distances that the traditional Mercator's Projection maps depict.

The actual Great Circle distance to be flown would be only a little over 3,000 miles as both the airfields of departure and arrival lie within the Arctic Circle. A glance at a globe, rather than at a map, reveals the true nature of the flight. However, even 3,000 miles would be further than Aries IV, or any other RAF military jet had before flown non-stop.

The more spectacular feature of this Bodo-Fairbanks flight would be that the route had been deliberately chosen because it passed right over the North Pole. This not only posed major navigational difficulties which had to be resolved but it enhanced its publicity spin-off. The Poles have always been of great interest to the public at large, although the North Pole had before been overflown by the RAF in an earlier propeller-driven Aries when one crew member added to the public's interest by eating a banana when directly over it. However, it had not before been overflown by a jet aircraft making an international flight between Europe and America* nor had any jet powered aircraft attempted to do so. Both from an operational point of view and from the publicity which Britain and the RAF would gain, this would be a flight of great significance. It even paved the way for the many large civil jet airliners which nowadays make daily non-stop polar flights between Europe and north west America in a westerly direction, and Europe and Far East cities in the other.

W/Cdr I G Broom's role in this particular historic flight was that of a supporting player. He would get himself to Alaska in advance of the flight and from there would help to guide the incoming Canberra to its destination. Also he would, via an air-to-air R/T voice link, fly up to meet Aries IV in order to supply his colleague with the latest Alaska weather and Air Traffic Services information. Aries IV on this epic trans-polar flight would be flown by a crew consisting of Wing Commander Michael Lyne, the Senior Instructor at Manby, and two experienced navigation instructors, Squadron Leader Dougie Bower and Squadron Leader Bob Seymour.

Ivor, who had been flown to Alaska by stages in the College's Hastings transport, would help Michael Lyne by flying in the Hastings to a bare and barren gravel landing strip at Barter Island, situated on the extreme north coast of Alaska. There, with the aid of the radio mechanics with him, they would erect a portable radio beacon towards which the Canberra could be guided, using its directional radio compass; if uncertain of its position. The radio beacon was put up on the end of the gravel strip so that if, in an emergency, Michael Lyne had to land at Barter Island, due to fuel shortage or mechanical fault,

---

* As the flight terminated in the US State of Alaska, it received massive US as well as UK publicity. It may even have helped the Americans to decide to build under licence the 'record breaking' Canberra type!

he could come straight in.

This done, Ivor in the Hastings then took off and headed north towards where the Canberra was expected to be. At a predetermined time (1500 hours local time) he would call his Senior Instructor and hopefully make voice contact so as to be able to pass him all the information he might need to continue and land at the US airbase at Ladd, near Fairbanks, Alaska.

Meanwhile Michael Lyne and the two excellent navigators were proceeding apace. All had gone well with them at Bodo where, since they had departed late in the day of 24 June 1955, their only problem was that of getting accustomed to the midnight-sun's perpetual daylight. Another even more personal problem they faced was whether or not to accept a friendly farewell cup of tea or coffee. Because it was realised that they might possibly have to come down in Arctic waters, the crew had been dressed in special immersion suits — akin to today's wet suits worn by water skiers. Thus attired, it was very problematical whether or not they could possibly manage to relieve themselves in the confines of the cockpit *en route*. Hence the indecision about accepting a farewell cuppa!

Once airborne, all had gone well for Aries IV. Rather to their pleasant surprise they had managed to get a visual check of their position by overflying the Island of Spitzbergen in almost cloudless weather. Thereafter it had been hour after hour of flying without hope of any further visual verification of their position.

The flight had been deliberately chosen with a period of short duration when both the sun and moon would be visible to the aviators, as navigation over the vast polar region would entirely depend upon astro shots of these heavenly bodies. Normally, aircraft at that time depended upon the magnetic compasses which all carried. Only by steering a magnetic course with due allowance for wind drift could a track be maintained. However, when up into the Arctic circle, the magnetic compass became more and more untrustworthy. The difficulty was exacerbated by the difference in position of the North Pole and the magnetic (north) pole. The magnetic pole at the time of the flight lay about 800 miles from the North

Pole. It was in the neighbourhood of Ellesmere Island, one of the islands of the Canadian Queen Elizabeth group to the north-west of Greenland but its position was continually, although slightly, shifting.

After overflying Spitzbergen, the crew of Aries IV would have no land check for the next 2,000 miles or more, neither would they obtain any worthwhile information from their magnetic compass. They would be over an area where the ice pack never melts, and which maps define as 'an area of inaccessibility', being devoid of animal or plant life and certainly no radio, meteorological station, emergency airfield or navigational guidance. The aircraft was entirely dependent upon the sights of the sun and moon taken by the navigators inside the aircraft via a periscopic sextant. The beacon set up on Barter Island could have been of enormous assistance but, as it was, the skilled navigators had overcome their difficulties.

Ivor, in the Hastings, was scheduled to call Michael in the Canberra at 1500hrs local time. Bearing in mind that the arrangements had been made days before in a different continent and that there was much that could have gone wrong between two aircraft rushing towards one another at a speed of over 12 miles per minute — a mile every 5 seconds — it was a pleasant experience for Michael Lyne to hear Ivor's first tentative call 'as if the two had been talking together in a room.'

Soon the pair were chatting away. The fact that they were using a VHF frequency and that Michael by then was flying the Canberra at nearly 50,000ft was to their advantage as the range of VHF transmission is increased by height.*

The first question asked by those in the Canberra was about the weather in Alaska. Ivor was able to advise a delighted Michael Lyne that there was scarcely a cloud over Alaska and that the forecast for the arrival of Aries IV at Ladd was visibility of 60 miles and a temperature of 75F!

After the Canberra had shot past the Hastings, the latter returned to Barter Island to pick up their portable radio transmitter and later was able to join Aries IV at Ladd: where

---

* VHF transmissions are largely limited by 'line of sight' distance and, at low levels, are soon cut off by the curvature of the Earth's surface. At heights the distances are greatly increased.

it had landed safely.

At Ladd, Michael Lyne, with navigators Douglas Bower and Bob Seymour, found themselves almost besieged by an army of reporters, photographers, TV cameras and Pressmen. When Ivor and the Hastings later arrived he had to fight his way through in order to add his congratulations to those of the US media.

That night the US Air Force laid on a celebration dinner along traditional RAF guest night lines and, on US soil, the health of HM the Queen was duly toasted! Later still, although it was midnight, Ivor and others were taken to a daylight baseball game played under the midnight sun.

The US dinner was a splendid affair, but by then Ivor had already been indoctrinated into the eating habits of North America. On his way through Canada, the Hastings had stopped for a night at Edmonton, Alberta, where Ivor and his colleagues had been taken to a steak house where one ordered as much by the pound as by the ounce. The high point of the menu was a 72oz steak for C$9.50 with the note that if the customer could eat it, and all the trimmings, within one hour there would be no charge. The menu added 'Limit one to a customer'! It made Ivor recall that it was only a year or two after the tight meat rationing in the UK had finally ceased. This, and other rationing had persisted, almost in Britain alone, for many years after the war had ended.

One feature of the Canberra 699 flight over the North Pole was that it had overtaken the sun in its east to west passage. Although the crew had departed late evening on 24 June 1955, they had arrived over six hours later mid afternoon of the same day. For them, with no night visible in Norway, it had been a long thirty-five hour, or more, day.

The following day both aircraft flew to Vancouver where the Canadian Press were equally insistent and the RCAF (Royal Canadian Air Force) equally hospitable. On the 26th (next day) Ivor, who had taken over command of Aries IV, began preparations for his own special return flight.

Aries IV having flown to Alaska, the planners at Manby were determined to have it fly back on another special flight:

one which would also expand their knowledge of the aircraft's capabilities. This was a non-stop flight by a jet aircraft between the Canadian and UK capital cities. This time, to make it an official record flight, they made use of the *Federation Aeronautique Internationale* and arrangements had been made for official FAI observers and time-keepers to be at the airfield of both departure and arrival. Ivor would be assisted by the same two first class navigators S/Ldr Dougie Bower and S/Ldr Bob Seymour.

Ivor first flew Aries IV from Vancouver to Ottawa in 4.5 hours. The average speed was over 500mph and it constituted an unofficial record. Prior to departure from Vancouver, Ivor found himself being briefed by George Hutchinson, the George Medal holder who had been one of his navigators during his Blenheim period in Malta after Bill North had completed the normal stipulated thirty Ops on Blenheims. Post-war, George Hutchinson had transferred from the RAF to the RCAF and, having read about Ivor Broom's contribution to the first highly publicised flight, he had arranged matters so that he could be the duty officer at Vancouver, to provide the flight information for his former friend and Malta 'plane driver.'

Upon arrival at Uplands Airport, Ottawa, from which the record attempt would be made, Ivor decided to attempt the flight to the UK the next day. This was in keeping with the 'All Weather' aspects of these Aries IV special flights.

To establish this official capital-to-capital record, it was necessary for the aircraft to fly a distance equal to at least the minimum distance between the two cities. The official minimum distance ie. the Great Circle distance, was 3,330.416 miles. This gave rise to certain problems as the distance between Uplands Airport, Ottawa, and London's Heathrow was a few miles less than this due to Heathrow being west of London. Accordingly arrangements had been made for the aircraft to depart from Uplands, but to land in the UK at the RAF station at West Malling in Kent. Official FAI observers and timekeepers were therefore at both these airports to observe departure and arrival of Aries IV: also to put on board a barograph which would show conclusively that the aircraft had not landed to refuel en route.

The reason why Ottawa-London, rather than London-Ottawa was being attempted was that the distance of 3,330 miles was at the very extreme, or even beyond, the theoretical maximum range of the Canberra. However at the heights at which the flight would be made the prevailing winds between the two places were predominantly westerly. At times these upper winds could aid an aircraft at height by over 100mph. Such a boost would have given the Canberra a generous safety fuel margin. However, on 28 June 1955, the Met forecaster at Ottawa was expecting an average assistance of only 10mph. Some calculations showed that this was just sufficient assistance as it gave a small allowance for minor errors or miscalculations of fuel, speed and wind vectors.

The Met forecaster at Ottawa also warned Ivor that at his expected time of arrival (about 3am British Time) fog was expected to blanket out the airfields in the west of England where Ivor might have to head if finding his fuel insufficient for West Malling. However this didn't at the time unduly concern Ivor or his navigators. Compared with the trans-polar epic, the navigational problems were not too formidable. Although astro navigation would be required across the Atlantic, excellent aids existed at both ends of the route and Met forecasts covered the whole. It was only the 1,800 mile gap between Goose Bay in Labrador and Ireland that lacked navigational facilities where they would be entirely dependent on astro navigation.

Just as Michael Lyne had done in Norway for his departure, Ivor arranged for a fully fuelled Aries IV to be positioned near the start of the take-off runway. Jet aircraft consume fuel at a high rate when taxi-ing around an airport and it was a wise precaution to avoid any waste. Jet aircraft also use less fuel the higher they go and it was policy therefore to climb rapidly to the maximum altitude that could be sustained and then drift upwards, on what is known as a 'cruise climb.' As the aircraft consumed fuel *en route* this made it lighter and it could then progressively climb to a slightly higher altitude.

By such an operating technique the initial ceiling of about

43,000ft could, towards the end of the flight, have risen to about 50,000ft and once there in the rarefied upper thin air, the aircraft would be sustaining its higher speed at a relatively low rate of fuel consumption. As the Canberra for these flights would consume about 20 tons of fuel (about 5,000 gallons), the steady drift upwards would continually be self-rewarding in terms of range.

Initially all went well, and Ivor in Aries IV after a 4pm local time departure, had the pleasure of being accompanied by a Canadian CF 100 twin-engined jet fighter 'plane, flown by a pilot known to him, for the first few hundred miles. He was glad to be in the air as the final half hour on the ground had been spent being photographed and badgered by what seemed to be an army of press, radio and TV reporters. One even had the nerve, after Ivor and his crew had been photographed from every conceivable angle, to request that they get out and get in again because, when they had climbed aboard, the photographer had been changing a film magazine! When requested by the photographer, 'Would you please get out and get in again so that I can get my shots', Dougie's reply in basic Yorkshire was not reported ... nor was reportable!

The crew's last radio contact with Canada was with the big RCAF/USAF airbase at Goose Bay near the coast of Labrador. This is one of the bases which were exchanged with the Americans in the early days of the Second World War for a number of 'four-stack' US Navy destroyers used in the Atlantic against U-boats: Newfoundland and Labrador at that time being British Colonies rather than Canadian Provinces.

For a while as the sun rapidly sank below the western horizon, the crew had to depend upon a calculated position but this time, flying against the sun, it was not long before the stars became bright enough for the two Squadron Leader navigators to fix the aircraft's position from star shots taken by their periscopic sextant. For these Ivor had to hold the aircraft level and temporarily abandon the continuous cruise-climb.

Barely two and a half hours after seeing the last of the sunset in the west behind them, it started to rise again in the east as an enormous flattened orb in the eastern sky ahead, although those who might be on ships on the sea below would not have caught even a first glimmer of light nor for quite some time later. Operating at nearly 10 miles up in the sky the horizon stretches far into the distance. Another oddity at that height during the midsummer period of the year, is that it is noticeably lighter on one side of the aircraft than on the other, with the light from the northern 'midnight sun' on their port side never quite darkening that segment of the heavens. On the south or starboard side of the Canberra, the full blackness of the night — short though it was — obscured everything.

The navigation fix and the 'fuel used/fuel remaining' calculations, showed that they would have enough left to reach West Malling, make a normal approach and, if necessary, be able to overshoot and do it all over again.

Upon first making contact by VHF R/T with Scottish Oceanic Control at Prestwick, the weather ahead was checked. It was not a rosy picture. As expected the airfields in the west of England were fog-bound. The more ominous news was that West Malling was also affected and visibility there was being reported as only 500 yards. This was only marginally sufficient for the safe arrival of a tired crew and a pilot who had been flying without an autopilot for many hours, because the Canberra had none.

Ivor discussed this with the navigators but they both favoured a continuation. The only sure alternative was to land at Shannon in Ireland, which was reported as clear. However this was not what they had flown all that way, and prepared for so long, to do — it also fell far short of their mileage requirement.

As the aircraft carried on at 50,000ft over the Irish Sea, a snag arose. A substantial amount of fuel was sloshing about in two of the near-empty tanks and would not feed into the engines. Normally these particular tanks would be completely emptied before switching over to others. Now about 100 gallons could not be used and with the aircraft still using about 600 gallons per hour, the loss of this ten minutes meant that their reserve for a missed-approach and the circle around to make a second attempt was extremely slim. This, at a time when the weather forecast indicated a likelihood of fog at West Malling, was a serious snag. By then, still rushing on at 500mph, West Malling itself could read their transmission direct and control was passed to it.

In the UK it was now about 3am local time, with the airfields still in darkness and the fog thickening. Although it was the hour when senior RAF officers were usually well tucked up in bed, several now stood behind the West Malling Air Traffic controller. On their instructions the Met Office was issuing a steady stream of reports. These showed that the visibility was becoming steadily worse. Even without the knowledge that a now priceless 100 gallons was not feeding through to the Canberra's engines, several of the experienced pilots on the ground — and they included the Station Commander, G/Capt. Peter Hamley, Air Commodore 'Gus' Walker and Air Vice-Marshal Nicholetts — were in favour of ordering Ivor to divert to the RAF airfield at Biggin Hill, 14 miles away, which had slightly better visibility. It was an order that W/Cdr Ivor Broom could hardly have disobeyed.

One of the senior officers present was Wing Commander William Hoy. As well as being a fellow syndicate leader with Ivor at Manby, he had been, until of late, the Wing Commander (Flying) at West Malling. As such he possessed an intimate knowledge of the conditions in which Aries IV and its crew now found themselves. William Hoy was against Ivor being ordered to divert to Biggin Hill. Quite apart from the knowledge that all shared, namely that any diversion away from West Malling would negate the record breaking attempt because it was only at West Malling that the FAI had placed official observers, his local knowledge of the area and its weather, inclined him to think that if West Malling had poor visibility, then Biggin Hill was liable to be much the same. But what really dominated William Hoy's thoughts was the knowledge that, in his opinion, the West Malling GCA talk-down team was 'the best in the business.' Although almost every Met report gave an ever reducing visibility, William Hoy was convinced that the GCA controllers on duty would nevertheless talk Ivor and his crew to a safe arrival.

Air Commodore Gus Walker, the then current Commandant at Manby, knew Ivor's capabilities and was a person who knew better than most how to overcome adversity. Gus was a legendary wartime bomber pilot. He had played rugby for England, and was a former Captain of the RAF XV. He earned a DSO and DFC commanding No. 50 Squadron in 1941, but lost his right arm when a Lancaster exploded on the ground later that year. Despite this terrible accident he became a top class one-armed rugby referee and a very good one-armed golfer. He also returned to flying duties, with an artificial right arm, and was a qualified captain of the Canberra. He was therefore well placed to size up the situation from his own practical experience. He, like William Hoy, had given up a night's sleep in order to be at West Malling to greet the Canberra. It was Air Commodore Walker who made the decision. 'Let's give him all the facts we can and leave it to him to decide what best to do.'

Gus Walker himself took over the microphone and talked direct to his syndicate leader. In reply to Ivor's question of 'What is the visibility with you?' the Air Commodore replied 'About one hundred yards', adding that 'Biggin Hill was reporting three miles.' After what seemed a long pause Ivor was heard to ask, with obvious incredulity in his voice. 'Did you say ONE hundred yards?'

Gus had to confess that this was so but added that the fog was fluctuating and the approach lights were now clearer since he had spoken. Meanwhile, Ivor and the team above were again conferring. Both of the navigators were keen to put their trust in Ivor continuing. All their hard work to help make this a record breaking flight would have been wasted if a landing had to be made at Biggin Hill. Although Biggin Hill appeared to be well within normal landing visibility limits, all knew that fog was an unpredictable topographical phenomenon which came and went at will. Also by then there was also a slight element of doubt that Aries IV could even reach Biggin Hill, only 14 miles from West Malling. Ivor decided to take a calculated risk and to continue. If his companions had that much faith in his abilities, he was determined not to let them down. He advised Air Commodore Gus Walker accordingly.

Ivor also had great faith in the West Malling GCA team. The Senior Air Traffic Controller, a character who went by the name of 'Fiery' Phillips, was known to him personally and Ivor knew that 'Fiery' had trained his team well. Let 'Fiery' now continue his recollections of the drama. He had known Ivor ever since 1943 when both had been instructors at 13 OTU at Bicester, where 'Fiery' had taught navigation. He knew that Ivor was an exceptional pilot, he also knew that he had a good GCA talk-down team and the latest MPN 11 radar. He knew well that the flight was something special.

I selected my 'talk-down' controllers, F/Lts Bill Smith and Kim Hall, and briefed them how I was going to handle the approach … I realised that there would not be a lot of fuel left to spare. Much to my consternation, the Control Room filled up with very senior officers, the BBC and others whom I didn't know. About two hours before the Canberra's ETA (Expected Time of Arrival), the visibility dropped to 25 yards. Even the sodium lights (alongside the runway) were not visible from the Control Tower. Through London Airport and our own Met, I established that the fog was widespread.

'Big Top' was Ivor's call sign but we failed to contact him on our approach (radio) frequency. The only common frequency we had was 121.5 m/cycles; the Distress one. I advised London Airport I would be using this for approach and talk-down. They were quite happy as all their flights had been cancelled.

Having established contact with 'Big Top', Air Commodore Walker then asked to speak with him, told him about the deteriorating visibility and painted rather a gloomy picture. I then gave him an alteration of course and greatly exaggerated the visibility. I believe I told him it was 500 yards. At this moment the BBC commentator stuck his microphone into my face when I was transmitting, and I quietly informed him where I would stick his microphone if he persisted.

In all his transmissions, Ivor's voice was cool and calm as if he was on an exercise. A controller of my experience can tell by the voice, no matter how it is disguised, the state of mind of the pilot, and Ivor was confident, which was a great relief to me.

Meanwhile inside the Canberra, Ivor and his navigators had been working out how best to descend into West Malling, hopefully with enough fuel in hand for a second try or a diversion to Biggin Hill. They would stay at their vast altitude of 50,000ft for as long as possible, as at that height the aircraft was eating up the miles fast whilst consuming minimum fuel. Then at a point calculated by the navigators, they would shut down one of the engines to conserve fuel and glide down on the other engine to West Malling. It had to be a precise calculation as if brought down too early, the engines would devour their meagre supply of fuel at a fiercely uneconomical rate.

Upon being advised by Dougie Bower to 'descend now', Ivor shut down one engine completely and told his crew that he would relight it when 5 miles from touch-down on the final approach — thus giving himself complete control for those critical last few miles.

From inside the aircraft Ivor had continued to glide down passing over London at about 10,000ft. Within seconds of this the GCA controller at West Malling had come on the air and had begun to issue directions. His voice was calm and radiated great confidence to the Canberra's crew. Ivor began to feel more assured, especially when he heard that the visibility had gone up to 500 yards. ('Fiery' Phillips's kindly 'white lie'!) At around this time Dougie Bower had wriggled his way from his navigation compartment in the nose and perched himself on an aluminium frame alongside Ivor. There, he would act as a forward look-out to enable Ivor to concentrate wholly upon his instruments, while obeying the controller's steady flow of instructions from the ground. Dougie was perilously placed should the aircraft strike hard, nor could he have got back to where his ejector seat and parachute were if, on trying to reach

Biggin Hill, the engines cut out.

Soon Ivor was on final approach, with the steady stream of directions coming to him via his head-set. He had by then remembered to relight the engine which, to save fuel, he had stopped.

'Fiery' Phillips continues:

I had planned to descend him on a course to enter the radar pattern of the GCA. As soon as they (the GCA operators Bill Smith and Kim Hall) picked him up, I handed him over to them. We all then listened with bated breath to the 'talk-down', but Ivor's responses remained quite cool and calm until, of course, the final talk down when (because a non-stop stream of instructions being given) the pilot does not answer.

The instructions were now non-stop:

Left a little … straighten out… five degrees to port. Increase your descent a little, you're above the glide path. Check wheels down … steady your descent you're approaching glide path … another three degrees port. Steady on centre line … two miles to go … you're lined with the runway … one mile to go … left a little … you are over the threshold.

Ivor sneaked a quick glance up to look ahead but, although the airfield's intensity approach lights were at full power (for the first time in the station's history) all he could discern was a glow ahead. At least he was pointed at a lighted area — which in all probability was the runway. Dougie on his aluminium perch had recognised nothing visually so Ivor had to switch back swiftly to his flight instruments.

Back to 'Fiery' Phillips's recollections:

When the controller said he was over the threshold, we listened and heard the wheels hiss onto the runway. He was completely invisible, but a hearty cheer went up from those present. I didn't know that the BBC had their microphone 'live' and I just said 'Thank God', which came over very well on the broadcast.

As the controller commanded 'Touch down now!' Ivor again looked up. He could see a glow equally from lights on either side. That meant he must be on the centre of the runway. The flaps were already in landing position and the green lights had earlier assured him that main wheels and nose wheel had satisfactorily dropped and were locked down. His speed was a correct 110 knots. All he had to do was to close the throttles and then wait for the sound of the wheels as they crunched sweetly on to the runway.

They had arrived ... and all in one piece, too. However, the fog was so thick that he was literally 'lost' on the runway. He slammed hard on the brakes for fear of over-running the end of a runway he could not see. This caused both navigators to pitch forward and Bob Seymour's helmet hit the instrument panel ahead of him.

The Canberra was soon stopped and, at the radar controller's instructions, Ivor was turned onto an intersecting runway to his right. The next transmission from Ivor was typical of the man. 'I've not been lost all the way from Canada,' he announced 'but I'm lost now!' Eventually he managed to inch his way slowly towards the parking ramp. The ground crew then 'dipped' the fuel tanks and found only 1,400lb of fuel was left — enough for another five to ten minutes flying at low level.

A 'Follow me' jeep had been sent to guide Ivor to the ramp, but as this had gone to the end of the runway and Ivor had turned off on to the other runway 100 yards before the end, the two had never met. This as much as anything else gives a picture of how poor the visibility was.

Ivor and his crew lost no time in personally thanking 'Fiery' Phillips and the GCA talk down team of Bill Smith and Kim Hall, into whose hands they had placed their lives. The many senior officers present were also lavish with their praise. Perhaps only William Hoy had remained unmoved throughout, so great was his confidence in the GCA team at the station which he had so recently left.

In all, Aries IV had been flown 3,361.989 miles (31 more than the minimum distance between the two Commonwealth capitals), in 6 hours 45 minutes and 1 second. Aries IV had done it again at an average speed of 496.825mph.

This contrasts sharply with the speed at which A V-M Nicholetts — one of those present at West Malling — had once taken part in a record flight. This was between the UK and South Africa. The year was 1933 and the speed record? It had taken the Fairey long-range monoplane 52 hours and 25 minutes to reach Walvis Bay non stop, at an average of just over 100mph!

'All's well that ends well' but with the benefit of hindsight it would seem that the flight would have been a lot less demanding if delayed for a day or two, or even if departing a few hours later, by when the early morning June fog would probably have lifted. However, Ivor is swift to point out that, as well as establishing a first ever capital-to-capital record in a jet 'plane between America and Europe, the ability to complete the flight *in spite of the adverse weather*, went a long way to prove that in the Canberra bomber, the RAF truly had an 'All Weather' aircraft with sufficient range to reach almost any target, and still get back.

The BBC who had recorded the talk down and later interviewed the crew soon after landing, broke into the 'Housewives' Choice' programme that morning to broadcast the last ten minutes of the talk down. When the people in the Control Tower heard the wheels of the Canberra hiss onto the runway (although none could see the aircraft in the fog), a loud cheer and 'Fiery's voice saying 'Thank God he's down', could be clearly heard in the recording.

Not too surprisingly, this splendid feat of cool-headed precision flying, coupled with the official breaking of a Trans-Atlantic air-speed record, resulted in W/Cdr Ivor Broom DSO, DFC & two bars, being awarded an AFC (Air Force Cross). This is an award given for outstanding performance in the air, although NOT in active operations against an enemy. Ivor Broom is one of only six persons who have been awarded a

DSO, three DFCs and an AFC. One of the other five is Air Commodore Ted Sismore. Ted and Ivor were in Singapore together just after the Second World War had ended and a photograph of them exists which is perhaps the only one to show two of the six together.

To have broken into such a popular radio programme as 'Housewives' Choice' was almost unique. Seldom, if ever, did the RAF in peacetime receive more favourable publicity than it received over these two early jet bomber flights. Moreover, the operational information gained is still relatively valid today. Namely that the RAF, if needed, can reach its targets no matter how difficult it may be to get there, and regardless of the worst that the weather can produce.

CHAPTER EIGHTEEN

A Valiant Broom at BCDU

After his eventful period at Manby, which he left with the rare distinction of being assessed 'Exceptional', Wing Commander I G Broom was once more posted to a conversion unit where he would be taught to fly one of the latest RAF types. This time he was to spend six weeks at No. 232 Conversion Unit, learning to fly the impressive Vickers Valiant, the first of the RAF's mighty 'V' bombers.

An invaluable training aid had by then been introduced. This was the Flight Simulator. These amazing realistic devices enabled crew members to learn to operate new types of aircraft (and later to be checked out on them), at a fraction of the cost of the real thing. The new four-engined bombers consumed thousands of gallons of fuel during even relatively short flights, so any device which could achieve the same results by simulation rapidly paid for itself. Another advantage was that in a Flight Simulator, dangerous situations could be induced that never could be attempted when actually flying. To suddenly cut two engines on the same side immediately after take off would be to risk disaster, but this could be tried in a Simulator if only to see how the pilot reacted. Simulators could, and did, 'crash' without the slightest damage!

The key to a Simulator was to produce it so that it was as real as possible. While the windows were opaque as if flying in a cloud, everything else was genuine. Every nut, bolt, instrument, piece of furnishing etc, was identical with the front part of the aircraft. The pilots had the same headsets, radios and received instructions via these as if on a real flight. There were even realistic engine noises and the soft squeal of tyres hitting the runway could be heard on 'landing.' Rocking movements could be introduced whenever the 'flight' encountered turbulence and, not only was every flight instrument and control identical but, on an instructor's plotting table out of sight of the crew, the track of the aircraft would be faithfully depicted. So realistic are Simulators that experienced pilots have been known to panic inside them and, after a gruelling session coping with emergency after emergency, the crew would emerge dripping with sweat and feeling mentally and physically exhausted. By comparison, flying the actual aircraft without induced emergencies was relatively easy.

Although the thorough Valiant conversion course lasted for six weeks, Wing Commander Broom's real flying times on the Valiant were only twenty-two hours and this included nearly fourteen under dual. However it was ample, and he was duly passed out as 'Proficient' to handle the large bomber both by day and night. He also acquired a Master Green Instrument Rating.

At the end of the course, Ivor was posted, not to a Valiant squadron as might have been expected, but to the Bomber Command Development Unit (BCDU) at Wittering, near Stamford in Lincolnshire. He was to stay there for two years, and he personally regards it as one of the most fulfilling and interesting of all his RAF assignments.

Manufacturers produce military aircraft; usually to meet an RAF specification. However, it is then up to the Service to get the most out of their modern machines. This is where units such as the BCDU enter the picture.

When Ivor Broom joined BCDU there were two squadrons based there. One was 100 Squadron equipped with Canberras. This whole unit was allocated to BCDU for trial purposes. 138 Squadron equipped with Valiants made four of these, with crews, available whenever trials by BCDU were required.

The unit worked in conjunction with RAF Boscombe Down, where advanced designs were flight tested, and also with the Royal Aeronautical Establishment at Farnborough, where the technical frontiers of aviation, both civil and military, were further explored.

One reason for the four Valiants being available for the BCDU, was that it had been decided to subject the type to a 1,000 hour intensive flying test programme, in order to establish the spare parts and back up requirements. Every minor deficiency was recorded and every flight was scrutinised in detail. Only by such measures could a Service know what might be required in the event that the aircraft might have to be used on a continuing basis.

Problems which could be resolved by Canberras were normally dealt with by trials in these aircraft rather than by using the more expensive to operate Valiants. However, each aircraft posed its own individual problems. For example, it was decided to try to reduce the take-off distance of Valiants by providing a lot of extra thrust via additional rocket motors. This could also allow more fuel or bombs to be carried from small airfields. Accordingly, Rocket Assisted Take Off (RATO), motors were affixed to a Valiant. This shortened the take-off distance, but raised the problem of what to do with the motors, now useless and weighing near two tons, after take-off? Drop them hopefully in a field? Dangerous, especially at night. Make them retractable, or leave them as they were under the aircraft, where they created extra drag as well as adding weight? Only by actual flight trials could such a problem be resolved. In this case the disadvantages outweighed the advantages. Air-to-air flight refuelling trials were also carried out with Valiants: this time with more satisfactory results.

As often was the case, 'V' bomber trials would be carried out by a designated squadron, although the results were monitored and evaluated by BCDU. At the end of the trials recommendations would be made by BCDU to Bomber Command.

In the case of the very successful Flight Refuelling Trials, these were carried out by Valiants of 214 Squadron, under the energetic leadership of W/Cdr Michael Beetham, a man whose abilities later enabled him to climb to the top of the tree. Flight refuelling became a vital service some twenty-four years later during the Falkland Islands campaign when, by coincidence, the man in charge of the RAF as its Chief of Air Staff was Air Chief Marshal Sir Michael Beetham GCB, CBE, DFC, AFC who has kindly written the foreword of this book.

Many of these trials with both Canberra and Valiant were carried out only by code names, and Ivor's log books are full of 'Trial 258', 'Trial 356', etc., with strange annotations, like '14 manoeuvres' and '6 passes' added. Several trials were repeated a number of times.

Another unusual feature is that the crews seldom contained an officer of lower rank than Flight Lieutenant. Originally when the jets first came into being with their considerably faster speeds, the thinking was that only the young quick reacting pilots should fly them, but it was soon discovered that most pilots could master the faster speeds, and that what was wanted was calm experience rather than youthful exuberance. In BCDU a number of civilians often flew during flight trials. These were 'boffins' and manufacturers' representatives of latest gadgets.

One important development which Ivor well remembers were the flights to try out a novel way of delivering bombs. It was realised that if it ever came to a third World War, then the aircraft would be required to drop atomic, or even more deadly, bombs. To avoid enemy defences, and to make certain that these terrible weapons were dropped as accurately as possible, a low level method of release was required. However, it was soon realised that the pilot was, in such circumstances, as likely as anyone to be the victim of the explosion or the radiation fall-out. Consequently the LABS (Low Altitude Bombing System) was developed. This consisted of approaching a target at about 250ft at high speed of 420 knots and then start to pull the aircraft up into a loop. However, when at a vertical angle of sixty degrees the bomb would be lobbed forward. At the top of the loop, the aircraft, now upside down, would do a half roll so that it would regain a normal flying attitude and be travelling away from the target at high speed, even before the bomb could strike the ground. Provided correct allowance was made for drift due to cross wind, the method proved in practice to be remarkably accurate. It became known as Over-the-shoulder bombing and, to ensure greater accuracy, arrangements were made by which the bomb would be released automatically as soon as the aircraft reached the sixty degree point of the loop.

In between flights on these high speed jet bombers, Ivor

carried out a number in Chipmunks, a monoplane which replaced the Tiger Moth, and ... dear old 'Faithful Annie', which was used to carry the senior officers to such places as Boscombe Down and Farnborough. Ivor's first three flights at BCDU were in an Anson, a Valiant and a Chipmunk*. The contrast must have been astonishing.

The other two 'V' bombers also visited Wittering, and Ivor made flights in both the Victor and the Vulcan, but not as a first pilot. These expensive and formidable aircraft — both Vulcan and Victor cruised at about Mach 0.87 — could only be captained by persons who had passed an official conversion course on such sophisticated machines.

New navigation methods, new bad weather let down and landing procedures were also tried out, and Ivor now became familiar with the ILS (Instrument Landing System), and Decca navigation. It was all helping to ensure that if war was to break out, then the RAF would have been able to operate efficiently in all kinds of weather. Aviation then, as now, seldom stands still. Not to keep abreast of developments was to fall behind.

Ivor had been lucky. Although the RAF was developing the policy that a flying job was normally followed by a ground job, Ivor Broom had been given a succession of interesting flying jobs. However, all good things come to an end. His fascinating period at BCDU terminated in April 1959, after which Ivor would have to spend the next few years sitting behind a desk at the Air Ministry. It was a position that every senior officer with life-time prospects in the RAF was bound, sooner or later to occupy, and many were content to hang up their flying helmets and leave the ever faster, and extremely complicated (and expensive) aircraft for other people to operate.

Ivor's position became even more secure after July 1960 when, still 'flying a desk' at the Air Ministry, his promotion to Group Captain came through. To have attained this rank was literally another feather in his cap, as Group Captains could edge their caps with a fringe of prestigious gold braid; generally

---

* On a few Anson and Chipmunk flights, a 'Cadet Broom' was listed as a passenger. This was Ivor's son who also enjoyed nearly two hours on a Canberra Flight.

referred to as 'Scrambled Egg'! To have become a Group Captain meant that he had gone far. He could have happily stayed there and retired at a respectable age with a fairly decent pension. Also, since Ivor and Jess had produced their three children while still young, part of their expensive educational years were, by then, behind them. The road ahead beckoned smoothly. Financial problems would be unlikely again to recur.

However, Group Captain Ivor Broom was not content to rest upon his laurels. He knew that the RAF would never cease to face new problems and to explore new frontiers. He could hardly wait until he could face up to these new challenges for, clearly, the supersonic age was only just around the corner and he was determined to try to enter into this advanced realm of flight. He also reckoned that the bombers which carried the nuclear weapons were Britain's and NATO's best answer to the overwhelming size and might of the Soviet tanks, men, nuclear submarines etc, which posed an ever present threat to Western civilisation. His hat might now have gold braid upon it but he was far from content to hang it up and to retreat quietly behind one of the many desks of the Air Ministry.

CHAPTER NINETEEN

Brüggen at the Brink

After a little more than three years at the Air Ministry, Group Captain I G Broom arrived to take command of the RAF station at Brüggen, situated on the Dutch German frontier. The date was 28 October 1962, and it was the moment in history when the USA and the USSR had come closest to a nuclear war. A time when the Allied forces in NATO had a vital deterrent role to play in avoiding a nuclear holocaust. In that role, Brüggen was a key element and the new responsibilities of G/Capt. Broom were awesome.

To have been given a plum posting after having only officially 'flown a desk' for a mere three years, was, in part, due to Ivor's own initiative. Thanks to the goodwill of Bomber Command in general, and of RAF Bassingbourn in particular, he had managed to maintain proficiency on the Canberra by flying this splendid machine on two or three sorties per month. This had enabled him also to keep his Instrument Rating up to date. He had even managed to fly himself on a tour of overseas RAF bases, by giving talks on latest Air Ministry policies, in Cyprus, Bahrain, Aden, Kenya and Rhodesia on the way out, and at Khartoum and Libya on the way back. In all during this hectic eleven day tour, he personally added another thirty-one hours to his already large Canberra total. Ivor was a believer of the dictum: 'The only way a visiting senior officer should arrive at a station was down the centre of a runway.'

Brüggen formed a part of the RAF contribution to NATO's 2nd Tactical Air Force. Two Canberra squadrons were based there. One was No. 213, a low-level strike squadron equipped with twelve Canberra B(1)6 aircraft capable of carrying either conventional or nuclear (which were then called 'atomic') weapons. The other Canberras were PR 7 aircraft of 80 Squadron. They had an important photographic reconnaissance (PR) role to play. 80 Squadron was supported by a mobile unit which was capable of developing and producing prints within just a few minutes of a photographic aircraft landing. It was a facility, as will be seen, which Ivor made the most of when wanting to impress VIPs.

The station, in common with the other RAF bases and Allied Forces in Germany, maintained a very high state of readiness, and could have been involved within minutes of the start of any hostilities. No. 213 Squadron always kept two Canberras (known as Quick Reaction Alert aircraft), ready for immediate action with nuclear weapons loaded in their bomb bays: and with air and ground crews living and sleeping alongside the aircraft, in a special hangar. The two crews could become airborne within fifteen minutes of an order being given; with the rest of the Squadron trained to follow up swiftly.

The nuclear weapons were American and there was a small American detachment under the command of a US Major, permanently based at Brüggen, to service and safeguard these weapons of mass destruction. To prevent a nuclear war being accidentally started, no aircraft could have taken off with active nuclear weapons unless *both* RAF and USAF commanders at the highest levels had so authorised it.

The final act of 'triggering' the nuclear weapons was the responsibility of the USAF Detachment Commander. No action by the RAF station commander, or by the senior American in charge alone, could initiate the final decisive order to drop the deadly bombs; although the pilots knew in advance what their particular targets might be. If, as seemed quite likely in late 1962, the world was about to be devastated by a rain of nuclear bombs, then the Canberras of 213 Squadron, backed up by the PR ones of 80 Squadron, could have been swiftly involved. As a further example of how the British and Americans worked in harness, the special hangar in which the Quick Reaction Alert RAF crews lived and slept was guarded by US personnel.

The cause of the international crisis between the two superpowers lay in events which had begun in late September 1962: a month before Ivor was placed in command. US spy 'planes over Cuba had brought back conclusive evidence that bases in that Communist controlled country were being prepared to receive Soviet-built missiles, and that they soon would be in position ready to be fired at the USA. No one doubted that if these missiles were ever to be fired, they would likely contain nuclear warheads. America, under President Kennedy, was not prepared to live with this threat perpetually overhanging its cities and citizens.

There was also not the slightest doubt that if any Soviet nuclear missile were to land in the USA, NATO would immediately retaliate by launching a nuclear air strike upon Eastern Bloc targets, and that such a strike would be launched from a base such as the one Ivor was being sent to command. The RAF Canberras of 213 Squadron were there specifically for such a retaliatory purpose.

By 26 October, the date when Ivor officially took command, after having completed a short Canberra refresher course at Bassingbourn and passed further medical and Rapid Decompression tests, the crisis had come to a flash point. By then the Americans had published, as proof of their anxiety, clear photographic evidence of the work going ahead at the Cuban missile sites. The Soviets, in rebuttal, had protested against the actions of US spy 'planes which had violated Soviet air space while taking photographs of key USSR installations.

The Americans then imposed a comprehensive shipping blockade on Cuba, and were able to maintain it thanks to their naval superiority in the Atlantic and Caribbean waters. Soviet ships carrying missiles and launch equipment had been stopped at sea and ordered back home. The question during the last week of October 1962 was: 'How would the USSR leaders in the Kremlin react to this open violation against the established Laws of the Sea?'

Neither side seemed willing or able to back down and for days it looked as if a Third World War, which had hung in the air ever since the much earlier Berlin Blockade, might erupt at almost any minute. This would have been a war between sides both of which were well stocked with nuclear weapons, and possessed many times the destructive power of the atom bombs which had destroyed the cities of Hiroshima and Nagasaki. The world also had few illusions about the massive radiation fall out which, carried by the wind, would remorselessly spread its way around the world to peoples far removed from the combat zones.

Then on 28 October, almost before Ivor could have had time to explore his new 'parish', Chairman Khrushchev of the USSR backed off, and people all over the world breathed a massive sigh of relief. NATO's policy of having a retaliatory deterrent had succeeded.

Khrushchev promised that the USSR would dismantle the bases in Cuba, and return all its equipment to the USSR. It was a promise that he knew he had to keep, as daily the USAF was demonstrating that it had the capacity and will to photograph any part of Cuba in the most minute detail.

By 2 November, the US photographs showed that the Cuban bases had been destroyed. As a secret *quid pro quo*, not announced until a month later, the Americans had agreed to remove their missile bases in Eastern Turkey. These threatened the USSR as much as the Cuban ones might have threatened the USA. The USSR's vital oil fields were probably within their range.

By then the Cuban blockade had been lifted and the world suddenly seemed a safer place. Perhaps few were more relieved than the crews of 213 Squadron. Although none would have hesitated for a moment to carry out the missions for which they had been so thoroughly trained, the ultimate consequences did not bear thinking about. For one thing their airfield would immediately have become a prime target. It had been brinkmanship played for the highest stakes imaginable. President Kennedy had emerged a winner, but Chairman Khrushchev also came in for praise. It could even later be argued that he, too, had been a winner, especially when it was revealed that the American bases threatening the southern flank of the USSR had been dismantled.

The immediacy of the crisis into which Ivor Broom had been dropped was not lost on the new Station Commander at Brüggen. For the next two years he worked ceaselessly to ensure that if a similar situation was to reoccur, then strike and reconnaissance Canberras could be launched, with whatever kind of bombs his superiors decided, within the shortest practicable space of time.

Only two persons at Brüggen could initiate an alert. One was the Group Captain himself and the other was when a visiting team of inspectors would drop in unannounced. In neither case would the air and ground crews, while responding with alacrity, know whether it was a practice or 'for real' until quite late in the exercise. As one who had to respond has commented, 'Ivor seemed to like to sound the alarm at about 2am!'

The many wives who lived in the camp also learned to play a part. While their husbands were struggling to get themselves dressed, they would be out in their night clothes starting cars and generally gathering their husband's equipment together.

One of the methods by which precautions were taken to ensure a Third World War was not started accidentally, was that there were a number of alert stages and these followed one another in a step-by-step sequence. It was not until a very late stage of this logical process that the final triggering of the nuclear weapon was done and, by then, both US and RAF commanders had become fully involved.

Apart from the two aircraft in the special hangar, dummy nuclear bombs would be used during training and practice sessions. They were known as 'Shapes', and were identical in size and weight to the real thing. The manhandling and loading of these provided the armourers with the realistic training which they also required.

Only when arriving at their aircraft could personnel possibly know whether it was 'for real' or not. One armourer who knew Ivor's keenness for sports at the station was quite convinced that it was 'for real' when Ivor sounded the alarm only a few hours before the start of the 'RAF in Germany Inter-Station Sports Day.' 'My God, this must be IT. He would never call us out at this time otherwise!'

Although the principal purpose at Brüggen was to serve as part of the NATO deterrent, in order to make the Soviets think more than twice before ordering their vast army and array of military might into action — and this raises the question of:

Would Khrushchev have backed off if there had been no NATO bases armed with nuclear weapons? — Ivor was also conscious that the RAF might at any time become involved in a war with more conventional weapons. During his term of office at Brüggen (October 1962 to November 1964) troubles flared up in Cyprus, where Britain retained a huge air base, in Rhodesia and along the China/Indian/Tibetan border, as well as between Malaysia and Indonesia — in all of these places Britain had Commonwealth interests. Outbreaks of fighting also occurred in the Belgian Congo and in Vietnam; all conceivably inviting United Nations intervention. The need for Britain and her Allies to maintain large effective conventional Air Forces was as great as it had ever been in the so called post-war era of peace.

The RAF also had to keep in mind the fast rate of progress that aviation was making. During Ivor's term at Brüggen, the 2,000mph huge American B-70 experimental bomber was flown, and the agreement between the French and British jointly to develop a supersonic airliner to fly at more than twice the speed of sound was signed. This Concorde project almost made the excellent Canberra look old-fashioned, and emphasised that civil aircraft were now as much in the vanguard of development as were their military counterparts. Certainly the hundreds of fast, pressurised jet airliners which, by then, daily crossed the Atlantic with 160 or more passengers on board, were an advance upon anything that RAF Transport Command possessed.

Perhaps the most poignant memory for Ivor at Brüggen came on the evening of 22 November 1963. He was presiding over a Ladies Guest Night in the Officers' Mess where some American officers and their wives were present. During the meal an orderly passed him a note which announced that news had come over the radio that President Kennedy had been assassinated.

Ivor received the news with no obvious emotion and did not announce it to his guests until they had completed their meal and the port had gone around. He then broke the tragic news and the Americans all swiftly left.

Mention of Guest Nights reminds Ivor that one lasting taste which he developed while at Brüggen was for European wines! No longer was his personal motor, which never seemed to run down, fuelled by nothing stronger than orange juice. However, as could be expected, his intake of this stronger stuff was only moderate and even today, while enjoying a glass of white wine, he still refrains from both beer and spirits.

Ivor may not have minded too much therefore when being unexpectedly robbed of his wine! The occasion was when a young Air Traffic officer, new to the Mess, came in at a time when an AOC was visiting. When the man came up to Ivor, the Station Commander at once pointed to the AOC to indicate that he should first acknowledge him. To do this he swung around on his heels, a characteristic move, and pointed with an outstretched arm. The Air Traffic officer misunderstood the gesture, smiled with mild surprise, took the wine which Ivor happened to have in his hand; and thanked him for it!! While at Brüggen, Group Captain Broom maintained his friendly man-to-man approach with all and sundry but not to the extent of giving glasses of wine to newcomers.

As Wing Commander Norman Searle had written:

I arrived at Brüggen to take up the post of OC Technical Wing. I was replacing a Flight Engineer with a DFC who had been on the famous Dambusters raid. It was a very hard act to follow as he had been a great character. You can imagine how heartening it was that Ivor had recognised this fact when, with a friendly hand on my shoulder, he advised me not to be overawed by my predecessor's reputation and to do things in my own way.

Ivor welded the station into the happiest on which I have been privileged to serve ... the flying and engineering staff worked with complete harmony.

W/Cdr Searle also comments upon the free and easy manner in which Ivor chatted with all and sundry around the station.

Ivor by then had also developed a tactful way of advising a department head that all in their domain was not a hundred percent to his liking. He would telephone. 'Arthur' (he liked to use first names with department-head officers), 'I've just been around your section. Do you know what I found?' To which the only answer had to be 'No, sir.' Ivor would then mention the deficiency and conclude the phone talk with 'I thought that you would want to know.'

That was all. It generally was quite sufficient*.

One of Norman Searle's requirements was that two-thirds of the aircraft always had to be ready for immediate action. This meant that at times work might have to be carried out all through the night; even to air testing in the small hours of the morning, when the noise from the screaming jets would waken the entire station and half the countryside beyond. He mentions that Ivor's action of talking to the wives and explaining why this had to be, did much to soothe the anxiety they felt for themselves and their children.

Ivor, as usual, took a keen interest in sporting activities. At Brüggen there were facilities for almost every kind of sport. The men had even built a Go-Kart track, and a gliding club thrived. Ivor's daughter Diane joined this and made her first solo flight from Brüggen. There was keen rivalry between Brüggen and the other stations at Laarbruch, Wildenrath and Geilenkirchen. The exceptional enthusiasm that the men at Brüggen displayed is mentioned by Norman Searle who recalls that when they played an away rugby match against RAF Laarbruch, the Brüggen supporters outnumbered those of the home team. Ivor recalls that a visiting rugby team from Llanelli came to play matches against the RAF and Combined Services in Germany. G/Capt. Broom was the referee. Almost at once he called a penalty against the visiting hooker for a blatant infringement and quietly whispered. 'There is no need to do that today ... and in any event you are going to win by about

---

* Someone who knew of this habit, and who also knew that Ivor had taken part in the raid of the Knapsack power stations, Cologne, visited the area in 1993. Ivor was advised by postcard: 'Knapsack seems undamaged. I thought you would want to know'!

thirty points', to which the Welshman replied: 'If I didn't do that in Wales ref, I'd never get the … ball.' Llanelli did win by a hatful of points and later that evening at a concert, entertained their hosts by singing traditional Welsh songs and other airs as only a Welsh choir could.

Both Ivor and Jess took a great interest in the social life of the personnel. Including the many families, RAF Brüggen had a population of about 3,000, and Ivor likens their positions as being akin to the Mayor and Mayoress of a small town. The camp included a good Junior School, with a kindergarten and nursery school run by the wives. There were three churches, an eighteen-hole golf course within the perimeter and, in all, thirty-six clubs and societies run by the residents and their wives. So many babies were born that a roster of wives was prepared so that those in hospital would be visited. The WVS was also active, and played a major part in the smooth running of this 'small British town' on foreign soil.

There was also a large civilian work force under the highly disciplined direction of a splendid ex-Luftwaffe officer, Herr Reinhart: one of but many former enemy air force personnel working for the British. Many were highly decorated but only Herr Reinhart was prepared to admit that he had fought valiantly against the RAF. The others gave the impression that they had earned their medals fighting solely against the Russians!

When important visitors came to Brüggen, Ivor found a unique way of showing off the 'quick-print' capabilities of the photo-recce squadron. They prepared in advance sets of book-matches, the covers of which were made of stiff photographic paper. As the visitor arrived, say for lunch, they would be surreptitiously photographed. After a welcoming pre-lunch drink, they would sit down to eat and find, on the table, a collection of book-matches which showed their own photograph on the front and a pre-printed, 'With the compliments of the Station Commander, Brüggen', on the reverse. They were always delighted to take away examples to show their friends. Alternatively, Ivor would welcome them with a cup of coffee, and almost before this was served, they would be presented with an enlarged photograph of themselves, at times taken by a low flying Canberra, as they stepped out of the 'plane or car in which they had arrived! Either way, it was proof positive that the mobile ground reproduction unit was wonderfully efficient. It also raises the point that, if by chance Ivor's flying career might have been curtailed due to accident or illness, then he would have made a success as a Public Relations expert.

A supreme example of this came when Marshal of the Royal Air Force Lord Tedder, with Lady Tedder, came for a visit and enjoyed a luncheon in the Officers' Mess. During a pre-lunch chat with Ivor, the Tedders mentioned that they were building themselves a house for their retirement at Uist, a remote town in the Outer Hebrides islands off the Scottish coast. By some excellent navigation, a swift flight by a Canberra of 80 Squadron, accurate photography and lightning quick developing and printing, Ivor was able, at the end of the afternoon, to give his distinguished guests a photograph of how the builders were progressing! This most eminent of Air Force Marshals — the man who never once seemed to have put a foot wrong throughout the Second World War — went away highly impressed. It could have done G/Capt. I G Broom and his prospects no harm at all.

The RAF saying: 'If a job is very difficult it will be done at once' was being maintained in peacetime as well as it was during the 1939-45 war.

Another who served under Ivor Broom at Brüggen and who knew him well was his Wing Commander (Flying), Wing Commander Frank Bowen-Easley. He mentions the difficulties that the RAF personnel had to face because of having to integrate into NATO procedures allied to those of the USAF. These were not always those to which they had been accustomed. Both squadrons were proud of their achievements but would have preferred to do things in the RAF way.

Some idea of how keen the squadrons were can be judged by the information that, although no one likes to be called out on a practice emergency at 2am, nevertheless the Wing Commanders in charge of both 213 and 80 Squadrons almost vied with one another as to who could get to their aircraft soonest. Married or not, there are things, other than hastily throwing on clothes while a wife warmed up a car, that some men prefer to be doing at that silent night hour!

Although Ivor, as the 'Town Mayor' had a thousand things to do, he was determined to get airborne at least once a week. His efficient 'office manager' and Personal Assistant, Flight Sergeant McInnes, was instructed to keep Thursday mornings free of all appointments so that the Station Commander could keep his hand in and up-to-date. Both with 80 and 213 Squadrons — and he used to alternate between them — Ivor took a place on the usual exercise being carried out on that morning. He was gratified to note that both the LABS method of over-the-shoulder bomb release, and the low altitude Decca navigation method, in regular use, were systems which he had helped to develop when serving with BCDU.

To improve efficiency, RAF squadrons in peacetime take part in bombing, gunnery and other competitions, and any trophies won are prominently displayed in their Messes. No. 213 Squadron, in 1963/4 and 1964/5, won RAF Germany's Salmond* bombing trophy, and 80 Squadron may have gone one better by winning a NATO photographic-reconnaissance competition for which PR squadrons of many nations had taken part. This competition went by the name of Operation Royal Flush. It so happened that at some time thereafter HRH Princess Margaret came to Brüggen to present 213 Squadron with a standard. As was usual, the ladies loo was tarted up for the occasion. With their NATO victory in mind, you can guess what the sign on the door said, instead of the usual 'Ladies'!

Generally the visit of HRH was a huge success. Air Marshal Sir Ronald Lees, the Commander-in-Chief, who had presented the trophy to 213 Squadron was present but, as a break with tradition, it was decided that when they all sat down to lunch, the Princess would sit between the two Squadron commanders, Wing Commanders Dickie Arscott (213 Sqdn) and Bob Simpson (80 Sqdn), with their four Flight Commanders

---

* Named after former Air Marshal Sir John Salmond.

opposite. Ivor and the Air Marshal took up minor places. However, those who sat close to the royal visitor at lunch were not invited to the Ball in the evening at which HRH scarcely missed a dance, while showing herself to be an accomplished performer. It seemed a fair arrangement, but Ivor was given a mild rocket by the Princess who had hoped to meet her young lunch companions on the dance floor!

Although 213 Squadron was at Brüggen principally because it formed part of NATO's deterrent, it kept itself prepared to act for Britain in a conventional bombing role. As part of their intensive training, visits were paid to RAF bases in Cyprus and North Africa.

For their main task, the LABS method was practised on the bombing range, using ordinary practice bombs, until all were proficient, but once a year crews were allowed to try it out realistically with 'Shapes.' Prior to Ivor's arrival, the crews were also allowed one realistic 'Shapes' practice at night. However, accidents happened and this was stopped. The Canberra can be thrown about almost like a fighter in daylight, but night aerobatics in a jet bomber proved to be beyond the capabilities of some pilots.

Just prior to the end of Ivor Broom's full and demanding two years spent at Brüggen, he made a farewell visit to the NAAFI and was enjoying his now customary glass of dry white wine when an airman apologised that their glasses were not of high quality. This was the lead-in to a presentation which they then gave him of Belgian cut glass wine glasses and a decanter, with the expressed hope that when in future he used them, pleasant recollections of his period with them would come back. Ivor has confirmed that this is the case and that the glasses are still in use thirty years later.

From several accounts received, it seems evident that G/Capt. Ivor Broom made an excellent station commander of a huge RAF/NATO base. It was not the easiest time for Britain in Europe, as it coincided with the period when General de Gaulle was successfully preventing Britain from joining the European Common Market, and when British prestige, already weakened by the disastrous Suez campaign of a few years earlier, was further damaged by the Profumo/Christine Keeler scandal which rocked the Conservative Government then in power.

From the accounts of those who served under him, and from the successes which were achieved in competitions by both Canberra squadrons, all the evidence is that Ivor Broom made an excellent RAF station commander: and that his wife Jessica gave him just the right kind of support and, it being in her nature to help people, she enjoyed her time at Brüggen as thoroughly as Ivor did.

Mixing with both air and ground crews in an informal manner may have been the key to his success. This, and his determination to fly alongside his aircrews, earned him the respect of all. In some inexplicable way, the groundcrews at RAF stations could always tell between the able and less able pilots. The complete absence of side — that assumption of superiority — may have stemmed from Ivor's Malta days, when Hugh Pughe Lloyd treated the young Blenheim pilot almost as an equal. Men in authority who treat their staff in this manner, stand the best chance of getting the most out of them.

Ivor Broom throughout was determined that he would keep himself up to date in the air, no matter what ground or other jobs he was given. He could hardly have not noticed the almost awe with which Don Bennett was regarded in 8 Group because of this very feature. Many have shining examples presented before them, but not all manage to copy the good and discard what is not. Also not everyone keeps to the principles which are learned when young. Authority tends to blur ideals.

The odds against G/Capt. Ivor Broom being able to emulate Don Bennett by continuing to fly the latest operational types were great. It seemed inevitable that after his tenure at Brüggen was over, he would in all probability find himself again behind a desk. Also he knew that the next era of flying would include the RAF's venture into the supersonic age, and would involve the operation of aircraft with ever more electronic and other sophisticated gadgetry. The days of thousand bomber raids, or of huge wings of fighters climbing to defend, were over forever. The future lay in having a few extremely fast and terrifyingly potent aircraft capable of operating in every kind of weather, and carrying bombs which could eliminate a whole area, and missiles to fire by radar and electronic means at enemy aircraft which, perhaps, might never be seen visually.

Already he was beyond the age of forty. Both his career and his family were firmly established. Time alone would tell whether he could possibly continue to be active in the great advances yet to come. Circumstances would also play a part but, if the past was any guide, Ivor Broom would not allow mere circumstances to keep him from getting his hands on the RAF's latest and most deadly machines.

CHAPTER TWENTY

From Ground to Air

After his interesting two years with 80 and 213 Squadrons at the RAF/NATO base, G/Capt. I G Broom finally had to come down to earth and had to stay down for quite a while. He took his last flight from Brüggen on 4 November 1964 and did not find an opportunity to get airborne again until January 1966 when he managed to arrange a Canberra refresher course at Bassingbourn. As, by then, he had amassed well over 1,000 hours in these splendid aircraft, the three weeks refresher course must have been akin to reminding an Anglican Minister of his Protestant faith. However, he revelled in the chance to be flying again.

The RAF, as with the other Services, has a large administrative machine, with a number of important jobs which can best be done by senior officers, and Ivor Broom again found himself behind a desk in the Air Ministry in London. Some proof that he could cope as well on the ground as he did in the air came on 1 July 1965 when, exactly five years after having been made a Group Captain, he was promoted to the rank of Air Commodore.

After the short Canberra course, it was another two and a half years before a more active flying appointment was to come his way. This was in July 1968 when he was appointed the Commandant of the RAF's celebrated Central Flying School (CFS), where selected pilots learn to become instructors.

The RAF's CFS is the oldest Service flying school in the world with a reputation which stands literally sky high. At the time when Ivor was in charge, it could proudly proclaim that national Air Forces from fifty-five countries had already sent their best pilots there in order to hone their skills to a sharper degree. With the new nations which have since emerged, doubtless the number is now well beyond this.

Prior to taking up his appointment Ivor, who had not flown regularly since November 1964, put himself back to almost square one by attending a Jet Provost refresher course at the same Manby where he had, a few years earlier, achieved international recognition (and a well earned AFC) for his epic Ottawa-West Malling record flight. The Jet Provost is a small training aircraft on which newcomers to the RAF learn to handle jet powered aircraft. It was a bit like going back to Prep School after having graduated from a University, but having been out of touch for so long, it made sense to take the course.

At Manby it all came flooding back and in less than a month, Ivor was fit and ready to take over as an active Commandant of CFS. This famous school, founded in 1912, had its headquarters at Little Rissington in Gloucestershire and it was from there that most flying took place. However, there was a helicopter section at a smaller airfield at Ternhill, just across the Shropshire border, and a special unit which flew very special aircraft from Kemble also in Gloucestershire.

The special unit was the RAF's famous formation aerobatic team the Red Arrows which, operating from Kemble, came under the aegis of the CFS. One of Ivor Broom's responsibilities was the management and operational control of the nine Folland Gnat light fighters, which then comprised the unit; also the selection/training of their pilots.

Pilots who flew these daring displays stayed with the team for three years but it was policy to retire three of the nine every year. Consequently three newcomers had to be integrated annually and a new leader chosen every three years. The training of the new team took place during the winter months when, normally, no displays were given. At first the newcomers were used in only small formations of three or four aircraft. This was then extended to six and eventually to the full nine. During all this while, the team would be practising and working up at a safe height. Ivor periodically would fly with the team as an observer and when he considered that the pilots were sufficiently proficient, the heights would be progressively lowered until the Red Arrows reached the point where the nine could safely carry out their formation aerobatics and spectacular high speed cross-overs at very low heights where spectators could best see them.

When the team flew off to give their displays, a spare Gnat always flew with them. Within a few days of Ivor arriving at CFS, he had himself checked out to fly the Gnat and thereafter, in keeping with his policy of always being in the air as 'just one of the boys' regardless of his high rank, it was the CFS Commandant who occasionally flew the tenth Gnat to the summer displays: But not, of course, ever joining in the daring formation aerobatics. That would have been too much even for Ivor Broom!

Another early action of the new Commandant, and one which kept him up to date with the shifts of emphasis which were constantly occurring within the RAF, was to get himself checked out on helicopters. Prior to arriving at CFS, he had never even sat in one. During a busy two weeks at Ternhill, he first learned to fly and control the small trainer Sioux machine and then progressed to the RAF's standard one, the Westland Whirlwind. It proved to be a busy but fruitful August 1968. During this, his first full month in charge, he flew thirty-two sorties in all. He was in his forty-eighth year but it was the most sorties that he had flown in any month during the whole of his long career in the RAF. By the end of August he emerged fully competent personally to handle both the Red Arrow's Gnats and the School's rotary wing machines and had accompanied the formation team, flying the spare aircraft, to a display over Biarritz. There, from his spectator's vantage point, he was pleased to observe that the Red Arrows drew more applause from the French crowd than did the formation display given by the French Air Force aerobatic team.

Ivor's active participation in both the Red Arrows and helicopters did not go unnoticed by either the air or ground crews under his command. Everyone likes to follow a leader who leads from the front and who is therefore prepared to expose himself to risks.

The helicopter programmes were completely foreign to everything which he had known before in the air. His flights included instructions on how to carry out such manoeuvres as spot turns; sideways turns; carrying underslung loads as well as both wet and dry winchings. He also took part in a road traffic review over Cheltenham and several exercises dubbed 'Mountain Flying' as the RAF 'choppers' were available to pick up any injured climbers who might need transporting from the steep slopes of the Welsh or other hills. To manoeuvre a helicopter in a wind when hovering perilously close to hill sides required courage and skill. Ever willing to share the risks to which others were exposed, there was the unusual sight of an Air Commodore dangling at the end of a winch wire suspended over the sea in a realistic Air Sea Rescue exercise.

Overseas visits were made to many of the countries which had sent their best pilots to CFS. On one such visit to Indonesia, Ivor delighted their Commander-in-Chief, who had been a former CFS student, by presenting him with a CFS tie and other embossed regalia. While there, Ivor also managed to get flights in the Russian Mi-4 'Hound' helicopter and a Czech made L-29 Delphin.

Air Commodore Broom was flying the tenth (spare) Gnat on his way to Germany where the formation was to give a display when, on 13 June 1969, this usually very reliable type started to play up. The controls of the snappy little Gnat fighter were normally power activated but there was a manual back-up system in case of emergencies. This required muscle but it was a sufficient reserve to enable a landing to be made. The trouble in Ivor's Gnat was that the power system was cutting in and out and that there was a big difference in trim between the two systems which seemed determined to operate alternately no matter what Ivor did. He decided to land as soon as possible and headed for Fairford. When at about 300ft on approach with the power controls temporarily behaving themselves, they again abruptly cut out. Before Ivor could adjust the trim, the Gnat pitched into the ground.

The Gnat is a two seater aircraft and as a 'perk', Ivor was giving an airman a free ride to Germany. He was, as ever, pursuing a policy of treating men of all ranks as friends. Both men were seriously injured and the airman, SAC Williams, helped to pull Ivor clear, as he had broken both legs and was immobile.

Ivor's left leg suffered only a minor fracture but the right one had a more serious break. However, the left ankle was also badly damaged. Part of the next few weeks was spent by the Commandant at the RAF rehabilitation centre at Headley Court where he had to carry out a rigorous series of exercises. When first arriving there he had reached a stage where he could hobble about aided only by a stick. Headly Court advised him that he must either have two sticks or none as they did not want patients to develop a limp. In all it was twelve weeks before Ivor could again be passed fit to fly but, thanks to Headly Court, he came through without any limp and suffered no ill after effects. Twenty-five years later he still gallops around golf courses, in spite of having a four-inch screw in his left ankle, with no ill effects or visible impediment.

Only ten days after this calamity, the CFS was greatly honoured by a visit from many members of the Royal Family. The occasion was that HM The Queen was to present a Queen's Colour to the famous school. Prince Philip, Prince Charles and Princess Anne, along with the Queen Mother, were also in attendance, making it an almost unique occasion.

Ivor arranged for the stretchered airman, who was also involved in the accident, to view the event from the Control Tower. He himself left hospital in a wheelchair in order to be able to greet the Royal visitors on their arrival. He was also present to see them depart but otherwise left the job of looking after the Royal visitors to his deputy. Once the formalities were over he and SAC Williams returned to hospital.

Air Commodore Broom had been at CFS for about six months when, on 1 January 1969, it was announced in the *London Gazette* that he had been made a Companion of the British Empire (CBE), Military Division.

Another most welcomed piece of news was that, upon relinquishing his command at CFS, he would be posted to become the AOC of 11 Group — the same famous Group of Fighter Command which had distinguished itself during the Battle of Britain. Then, during the summer of 1940, the 350mph Spitfires and Hurricanes had successfully defeated the bombers and fighters of the Luftwaffe and thereby stopped Hitler in his tracks. That event was now thirty years back in history and, by 1969, 11 Group operated aircraft many times faster, as it had recently been equipped with another of Britain's outstanding aircraft. This was the English Electric Lightning which, with a maximum speed of over twice the speed of sound, was probably the fastest production fighter aircraft in the whole world at that particular time.

But could the forty-nine-year-old Air Commodore still manage to adhere to his desire of flying whatever type the pilots under him were flying? Could he even be allowed to attempt to handle the Mach 2.0 Lightning?

CHAPTER TWENTY-ONE

Sonic Boom Broom

For a Sergeant pilot who had hesitantly taken to the air during the closing months of 1940 to have reached the stage where he was appointed to command 11 Group was a remarkable achievement. This was the famous Group which, under Air Marshal Keith Park, had valiantly defended southeast England during the Battle of Britain when Ivor had been a raw RAF recruit awaiting his first flying lessons. 11 Group now formed part of a newly-named Strike Command with responsibilities for the operation of all UK air defence units.

Ivor Broom took this honoured position on 2 February 1970. By when, since 1 January, he had been promoted to the rank of Air Vice-Marshal. However, this elevation to the upper hierarchy caused not the slightest deviation from his self-avowed policy of not distancing himself from those whom he commanded. Although he was within six months of his 50th birthday, he soon set about the task of personally learning to fly the magnificent supersonic English Electric Lightning fighter which comprised the backbone of his Group.

Before February was out, A V-M Broom was being given dual instruction in a Lightning T5 and by 10 March had made his first solo flight in one. It was only nine months since he had broken both legs in the Gnat accident.

While satisfactorily solving this purely personal challenge, Ivor was also having to give much thought to another pressing one: one which concerned the honour and reputation of the RAF.

During the initial briefing about his new appointment, Air Chief Marshal Sir Denis Spotswood, the Commander-in-Chief, had advised Ivor that one of his first tasks was to win the NATO Air Defence Competition being held only three months hence. The C-in-C went on to say that the Squadron which had been nominated to represent the RAF, over a year earlier, had since 'fallen by the wayside' and was now one of the weakest in the

Group. A quick investigation showed that a new Squadron Commander was wanted and George Black, a Wing Commander with an outstanding record on Lightnings, was put in charge. With the help of excellent engineering staff, the Squadron rapidly came up to scratch and duly went on to win the 1970 NATO Air Defence Competition. Ivor can still vividly recall with much pleasure, visiting the Air Defence Radar Station at Patrington on the last night of the competition to witness the final interception which ensured victory.

The Lightning's magnificent performance did not belie its name. On take-off it reached a lift-off speed of about 160 knots in approximately fourteen seconds and would soon be roaring upwards at an angle of about forty degrees while maintaining a speed of Mach 0.9. By the application of reheat* at take-off and throughout the climb this remarkable machine could reach 30,000ft (higher than Mount Everest) in less than two minutes although it weighed more than a fully-laden DC3-Dakota. With reheat on, the Lightning was easily capable of reaching a speed of twice the speed of sound (Mach 2.0).

Lack of fuel limited its endurance to little more than one hour without flight refuelling but considerably less than this when using reheat continuously. However, a Lightning could maintain a speed in excess of the speed of sound without reheat, which was more than any contemporary US, Russian or French fighter of that time could accomplish.

Although the AOC of 11 Group flew Lightnings on forty occasions, he only twice exceeded one hour in the air. The role of this aircraft was strictly to hasten-off, climb at a phenomenal rate, overhaul, intercept and destroy any incoming raider, using air-to-air guided missiles and then to hasten back.

One reason for its remarkable performance was that its wings were swept back at an angle of sixty degrees. This was far more than any other design and allowed a fast approach speed of 175 knots (nearly 200mph) with the controls both positive and crisp. Moreover, thanks to being fitted with a large braking tail parachute, which was streamed immediately after

---

* Re-heat — the re-fuelling and re-igniting of its exhaust gasses — doubled the power of the Rolls-Royce Avon engines to give about 15,000lb of thrust (each) but at enormous cost in fuel.

landing, and with the benefit of anti-skid brakes, the landing distance was similar to earlier slower aircraft types.

RAF aircraft had to have 'All Weather' capabilities and the Lightning could be brought down by either GCA or by the ILS (Instrument Landing System) which the pilots could operate themselves. Several of Ivor's Lightning sorties ended with a GCA or ILS practice but although he was qualified to fly solo supersonically, he did not tempt fate too far and, since he could never give sufficient time for continual flight practice, he would usually take an experienced pilot with him in the two-seat training version of the Lightning, the Mark T5. On a few occasions he also flew the previous RAF trans-sonic fighter the highly regarded Hawker Hunter but, by comparison with the Lightning, it seemed almost pedestrian.

When Ivor became AOC of No. 11 Group it was policy to keep a small number of Lightnings, known as the Interceptor Alert Force, continuously at two minutes readiness on two aerodromes — one in the north, one in the south. Like the Canberra crews in Germany the pilots and groundcrew on immediate readiness slept fully-dressed in the Alert hangar near the end of the runway and could always be airborne in two minutes. When Ivor took over Command he found that the fighters were only scrambled to intercept any unidentified aircraft which was seen on radar if that aircraft approached within 100 miles of the coast. He decided that excellent training was being lost if his fighters were not being scrambled until the unidentified aircraft had come so close. Liaison was developed with the NATO Early Warning Radars, particularly in Norway, who were the first to identify Russian aircraft proceeding westward around the north of Norway. He therefore decided to scramble Lightnings to identify the 'unidentified' aircraft at the earliest possible opportunity.

When advanced notice was received, flight refuelling Valiants would back-up the Lightning pilots, who were then able to fly alongside Russian aircraft flying through the Iceland–Faroes gap *en route* to Cuba. Lightning pilots would photograph the Russian aircraft — and vice versa — and the crews of each aircraft frequently waved to one another, bringing back photographs to prove it! Apart from being excellent training for the Lightning pilots it showed the Russians that the RAF knew when they were over the high seas some 500 miles or more away from the Scottish Air Defence base of Leuchars — all part of the deterrence policy which has given the country the longest period of peace since the Battle of Waterloo. Pilots at Leuchars kept 'league tables' of interceptions in their crew room.

Ivor, as Air Defence Commander, or his Senior Air Staff Officer as his deputy, were required to be within twenty minutes of the Air Defence Operations Centre at Bentley Priory to handle any sudden emergency. They shared this task twenty-four hours a day, fifty-two weeks a year and the one on duty always kept the Operations Centre aware of their location. They therefore had little private life. Personal communications — such as mobile 'phones — were very primitive in the early 1970s when compared with the 1990s but Ivor had a good two-way short-range radio in his car which was most useful — but no two-way mobile telephone.

When not at the end of a telephone or in his car Ivor could usually be found playing golf at Stanmore. On these occasions he would strap to his golf bag a fairly large radio receiver which buzzed him if he were needed. He could not speak on that radio so had to rush to the nearest telephone when the buzzer sounded. One Saturday afternoon the buzzer went while playing golf and he found he was urgently needed at the Operations Centre. Three Russian Bear aircraft were flying down the North Sea — and four Lightnings had been scrambled to keep them under observation. If they entered UK airspace Ivor, as Air Defence Commander, would have been the person to authorise his pilots to take appropriate action in accordance with the agreed 'Rules of Engagement.' Fortunately, on this occasion they never came closer than 20 miles off the Scottish Coast — on a day when the Open Golf Championship was in progress at St Andrews in the presence of the Prime Minister — and then they turned away and cleared the area.

As well as their squadrons of Lightnings, the RAF also had a squadron of US-built Phantom fighters in Scotland and, as can be imagined, it was not long before the Air Vice-Marshal was also flying this foreign supersonic aircraft. It proved to be a reliable and popular machine but lacked the supreme performance of the Lightning. On its credit side, the Phantom had a greater range than the Lightning and all of Ivor Broom's sorties in it, during a concentrated week of flying from RAF Leuchars, were between 1.20 and 2.00 hours.

For personal transport, Ivor used the pleasant four-seat piston-engined Basset aircraft but he also made sure that he kept himself familiar with helicopter operations and made many a visit to the several RAF units within his Command in Westland Whirlwinds. He also made the most of every opportunity to fly his favourite 'taxi', the great Canberra and, during his nearly three years as AOC 11 Group, added to his already large total, another fifty hours on this type. He delighted in flying a Canberra to visit his squadrons when they were on detachment overseas at the RAF stations at Luqa in Malta and Akrotiri in Cyprus. He reached Malta in only three hours which contrasted markedly with his 1941 visit in a Blenheim which took him three days and included two seven hour flights as he first had to refuel at Gibraltar. Strangely enough, those two flights seem to have been the longest that he ever made during his many years in the RAF.

As A V-M Broom had done at both Brüggen and at CFS, he made sure that he renewed his Instrument Rating Certificate as without this he was restricted to good weather: once cruelly dubbed 'Group Captain's weather.' The ability to cope with bad flying weather came in handy for once, when flying to Sweden in a Lightning on a goodwill visit, he had to arrive with clouds almost 'on the deck.' Sweden, not being a NATO country, had no formal links with the RAF but this visit brought the two Air Forces closer together. For Ivor, now 50 years of age, it was the opportunity to fly two of Sweden's home-produced jets: the SAAB 105 and their Draken fighter.

Because 11 Group included the RAF station at Leuchars in Scotland Ivor, as AOC, became indirectly responsible for all activities at that northern airfield. This also included an RAF Mountain Rescue team which was based there. During one of their tough training exercises a curious incident took place in which Ivor was indirectly involved. A storm blew up and the team took refuge in a lonely mountain hut. Judging by the amount of rubbish lying about it was one in which tramps, or the like, had in the past taken shelter or even lived a while. As the team awaited for the storm to abate, something on the ground caught the eye of a Flight Sergeant. It was a copy of the Socialist *Daily Worker* more than twenty-five years old in which there was an article about the 'hush-hush' awards of their DFCs to S/Ldrs Ivor and Tommy Broom!

The Flight Sergeant brought back the paper which, now almost fifty years since issued, is still in Ivor's possession. 'I think it is the only time that I ever read this particular paper!' Ivor has remarked. The term 'hush-hush' had been used by the journalist because the citations of the awards, which were immediate ones, gave no details of how the 'Flying Brooms' had blocked up the Kaiserslautern tunnel.

Generally, when decisions concerning flying operations had to be made, the opinions of those who were actually flying the aircraft were sought. This called for visits by senior HQ officers to the squadrons and, of equal importance, the presence of squadron officers at HQ for conferences. This essential cross-fertilisation of ideas has helped to keep the RAF among the vanguard of Air Forces of the world. A memorable moment for Air Vice-Marshal I G Broom, CBE, DSO, DFC & two bars, AFC was that he discovered that his former chief and mentor at Malta, the now-retired Air Chief Marshal Sir Hugh Pughe Lloyd lived reasonably close to his HQ. Hugh Pughe in retirement had set up, and looked after, an efficient pig farm at Chalfont St Peters in Buckinghamshire. Ivor therefore invited him to be a guest at a home dinner party. At first his old Malta chief demurred: 'I'm too old; I don't go out at nights now. I dislike night driving.' However, Ivor persevered and eventually the man, who had been his former AOC in both Malta and Singapore, accepted with Ivor arranging for him (Lady Lloyd was unwell) to be picked up by car.

During the evening, Hugh Pughe gradually became his old dynamic self and soon had the table listening with pleasure to his rich fund of stories about the war. It was a dinner party which went famously and, as the retired Air Chief Marshal came to leave in the highest of spirits, with a broad grin on his face, he pointed at Ivor, remarked upon his high rank and roared: 'To think that I'm responsible for THAT!!'

Moreover, he was right for as Ivor himself has written:

I look back now on my Malta times and wonder what would have happened to the course of my life had Air Vice-Marshal Lloyd not 'hi-jacked' me at Malta. Many of those [in the other Blenheims] who went on to Malaya spent most of the war — if they survived — in a Japanese POW camp. I, on the other hand, returned home to marry the girl to whom I have been married ever since.

Also with Hugh Pughe much in mind Ivor has posed the question, 'What would have happened if the loss rate in Malta had been much less and I had not been commissioned there but had remained a Sergeant pilot? Would I have stayed on in the RAF and retired as an Air Marshal? Were these events, and others, such as when my Blenheim Squadron colleague asked me to change places in the formation on that fateful day in October 1941 and, of the three of us who set forth, only I returned. Were these events really acts of chance or is there a divinity which shapes our ends; rough hewing them as it may? I believe the latter to be the case.'

This reunion with the man who had done more than anyone else to shape the destiny of Ivor Broom is clearly the right place to end the operational chapters of this biography: not that it was anything like the end of a remarkable career of the lad who had come from the Welsh valleys.

The officer of Air rank would achieve much more both in the RAF and after retirement. As the saying goes: 'You can't keep a good man down' and nowhere can it apply more literally than for one, such as Ivor Broom, who had found his true vocation and a fulfilling life in the air: as the last chapter will show.

CHAPTER TWENTY-TWO

Ivor Controls

A nyone who has followed the progress of Ivor Broom since May 1945 when the war in Europe ended, is struck by the suspicion that a possible career in civil aviation always occupied a small corner of his mind.

There were the classes for civil aviation licences which he inaugurated in 163 Squadron, almost immediately after VE day, and which he also attended. At that time, knowing as he did, that he held no permanent commission, the scales could have been tilted either way. Much would depend upon what was offered: what might turn up. It was a period when the future for millions lay in the lap of the gods. Fortunately, for the RAF, two events tipped the scales towards a Service career. Ivor failed one of the written subjects of his Commercial Navigation Licence and, thanks to Roy Ralston and Air Commodore Boyce, he was offered a posting thousands of miles away from war-torn Britain (and Don Bennett!) which enabled him to retain for over a year the rank and pay of a Wing Commander.*

The posting to Singapore meant that at the time when Don Bennett was recruiting pilots for his British Latin American Airways — which soon became the ill-fated British South American Airways — Ivor was 'out of sight and out of mind.' Later, when back in England, and back to his basic correct rank of Flight Lieutenant, Ivor would have been quick to apply to virtually any airline, the moment that his resignation from the RAF was accepted. However, again fortunately for the RAF, it was not accepted.

Finally, Ivor is quick to point out without a trace of sadness and with some pride, that during his long career in the RAF,

---

* Later, when Ivor was promoted to permanent Squadron Leader, he was delighted to receive a letter from Air Marshal Sir George Pirie, who had been Ivor's first C-in-C in Singapore. 'Pleased to note that you have stopped going down and have started to climb the ladder again.' Sir George was clearly one person 'upstairs' who was keeping a fatherly eye on the post-war career of Ivor Broom.

he was only given an Air HQ desk to sit behind on three occasions: twice in the Air Ministry in London and a third in Singapore. His *métier* was in flying and personally looking after others on an operational station and none could scarcely have done the latter job better. That he would have much enjoyed being a commercial pilot is obvious and that he would have made a good one is equally so. However, the RAF gained themselves a winner; so all was well in the end.

It was therefore with pleasure, rather than with regret, that in November 1972, after handing over 11 Group to Air Vice-Marshal Bob Freer, Ivor learned that he was to become, although still in the RAF as an Air Vice-Marshal, the Deputy controller of the National Air Traffic Services (NATS). By then the *London Gazette* had also announced that he had joined the distinguished ranks of those whom Her Majesty had appointed a Companion of the Order of the Bath (CB).

NATS is a joint military and civil aviation organisation which looks after all air traffic in the airspace over the UK and its adjacent boundaries. In 1962, long before air traffic had grown to its present volume, the Government decided, after studying the recommendations of the 'Patch Committee Report', that due to the limited area of the UK, it would be inefficient and inflexible to allocate specific portions of the airspace for military aviation and another portion solely for the ever-growing number of civil aviation movements. A prime task for NATS was, and still is, to see that both military and civil aircraft use the airspace over the UK efficiently and without risk or hindrance to either.

Arnold Field, a civilian who was then in charge of the London Air Traffic Control Centre, remembers well the impact that the highly-decorated and very senior RAF officer 'new boy' made upon arrival. He writes:

It was apparent that, from the very first days of his appointment, Sir Ivor was not going to be just a desk warrior. For example, he immediately set about an extended tour of the 'sharp end' of the service by visiting not only as many of the military and civil units throughout the United

Kingdom as possible but also those adjacent authorities such as France, Belgium, Holland and Eurocontrol, with whom co-ordination of the airspace and its operating procedures are inextricably linked.

I was privileged to accompany him on a number of these tours and it became immediately apparent that here was no AOC doing a courtesy visit but a man who had the rare quality of talking to an airman or his Station Commander or an air traffic controller or his Senior Controller, as if it were of prime importance to the unit's operational responsibility. It is interesting to observe that throughout the years I have known Sir Ivor I have yet to meet anyone who has taken advantage of this approach. In other words respect is engendered, not familiarity. The other feature which was equally evident was that he really had a genuine interest in what he saw and what he heard and, to the intelligent observer, one knew that the questions to those in command would come later.

Starting from this thorough basis, it was not long before Ivor had a complete picture of his new duties and was on top of the job.

In 1974 — the year when his promotion to a full Air Marshal was announced — Sir Ivor took over as the Controller and Arnold Field, as Joint Field Commander, became one of three Director-Generals and the man directly responsible to Ivor for the day-to-day operations of both military and civil air traffic. As Arnold Field has written:

Ivor did not suffer fools gladly but nonetheless had a charming way of conveying his concern. In my case this took the form of a phrase well remembered by me. He would look directly at me from beneath those bushy eyebrows and say in a most conciliatory tone: 'Arnold, I don't think that we have got this quite right.' But I most certainly knew that what he really meant was: 'You have made a right pig's ear of this brief, take it back, revise it completely, no hurry *but* I want it back as soon as possible, like yesterday.'

In 1974, by which time Ivor had become Controller, I became more aware of his meticulous attention to detail and the manner in which he carefully assessed and balanced the differing requirements of the two prime contenders for the use of airspace. It has to be appreciated that the airspace over the UK is probably the most crowded in the world. Co-ordination, integration and co-operation are therefore vital to air safety. The fact that Ivor Broom was held in high regard by the RAF [to which he still belonged] and also accepted by the civil air authorities as a fair-minded and knowledgeable arbiter had undoubtedly been fundamental to the success of the safe and efficient regulations of air traffic within the UK. The high regard in which today's UK NATS is held by other international authorities owes much to the manner in which he discharged his duties as Head of the volatile mix of professional disciplines.

It is not always the case, when civilian and military powers meet on common ground with different objectives, that harmony rules. Ask any Council which has military firing ranges or training areas within its boundaries!

Working for Ivor Broom meant just that: WORK. Arnold Field quotes an example:

Shortly after he had taken up his post of Controller, I accompanied him on a three-week tour of air bases, civil airports and Area Control Centres in USA. This meant criss-crossing the continent east to west and north to south, flying in medium/light aircraft, often piloted by himself; flying in advanced simulators, attending military and civil briefings and dispensing [and coping with] American hospitality.

Night stops were spent at USAF bases or airport hotels. I well remember awaking in an airport hotel and being initially at a loss whether I was in Los Angeles, Washington DC or Tulsa. Not so Sir Ivor — when I staggered down for an early breakfast, there he was on his last cup of coffee greeting me with: 'Come along Arnold quick as you can. We've a busy day ahead of us.' As for me I was still mentally writing the 'action notes' for three days before.

Finally when the tour ended and we were safely on our way eastwards across the Atlantic, I climbed the stairs of our 747, settled myself down for a quiet few hours when suddenly the 'Welsh Terrier' was saying: 'Now Arnold, how about those procedures for helicopter operations in the New York Terminal area.' So, there we were at thirty degrees west, high over the Atlantic, still working away!

The highly efficient and wonderfully safe separation of the vast volume of air traffic over the UK — and it never ceases to increase — owes much to the dedication of men such as Arnold Field, OBE, and his one-time boss, Ivor Broom.

It is with little wonder therefore that the efficient ever-cheerful Air Marshal Ivor Broom became on 14 June 1974, Air Marshal Sir Ivor Broom KCB, CBE, DSO, DFC & two bars, AFC.

Ivor received his knighthood at Buckingham Palace with Jess and his two eldest children present as his daughter, Diane, had flown over from Canada for the occasion. Her Majesty had done her homework well and Ivor, along with others at the investiture, received relevant comments during the time-honoured rituals.

Ivor also recalls that when he received his CBE, the Queen Mother, who was standing in for her daughter, was equally impressive. It was after he had broken both legs in his Red Arrow Gnat's 'prang' and had been obliged to welcome the Royal Party from a wheelchair. She at once inquired how his legs had recovered.

Ivor's eventual retirement from the RAF came on 6 July 1977. It was thirty-seven years after the young clerk in the Ipswich tax office had offered his services to the RAF after having been inspired by the sight and sounds of the low-flying Blenheims roaring overhead as they went their ways from their East Anglian bases. He was 57 and about to draw an adequate index-linked pension. He and Jessica were happily still together and in excellent health and their three children were off their hands and safely on their respective ways. Some, at this point in their life, having put so much into whatever had come their way, might thankfully withdraw from the spotlight and find fulfilment in gardening, golf, bridge, travel or even a dog and cat. However, this was not the Ivor Broom way.

The good work that Ivor had achieved as Controller of NATS had not gone unnoticed and, upon retirement from the RAF, he was offered by Nigel Foulkes who had taken over as the part-time Chairman of the Civil Aviation Authority (CAA), the post of Deputy Chairman. Ivor, being full-time, would bear much of the responsibility for ensuring that the various aspects of civil aviation in Britain; licensing, air traffic control, safety etc, were functioning to the public's interests and liking. Ivor was delighted to be offered such a plum position (awesome responsibility never seems to have worried him a scrap) and a salary of £14,000 per annum was agreed. The past few years of working with NATS had given him as good a ground of the civil aviation picture in the UK as any retired Air Marshal could possibly have.

At this point, however, the Treasury reared its disapproving head. It had a policy that retired Servicemen should not be appointed to the boards of national organisations while enjoying their [hard-earned] pensions *and* a full salary. They decreed that Ivor could only take up the appointment if the salary were to be reduced by the *full* amount of his pension! This meant that he would be holding down an arduous full-time job in the CAA for less than half the amount which had been agreed. It is not surprising that Ivor declined this 'kind' invitation and, instead, he set himself up as an aviation consultant, operating from his delightful house in Hertfordshire. Here he faced new challenges for no longer would he have a skilled staff, headed by a SASO, to carry out research or to deal with the nitty-gritty of the variety of subjects that might come his way. He would have to prepare his own briefs and, in a constantly changing industry, it was still necessary to keep himself thoroughly up to date. No aviation manual lasts for long without the need for tedious amendment and, in such matters as global navigation and air traffic control, startling developments are always 'just around the corner' opening up studies for scientific advancements.

By the time Ivor became a high-powered consultant, he had acquired a reputation of getting things done. Also he had countless useful personal contacts in both the civil and military aviation fields and, as a result, within a short time, had obtained a number of lucrative contracts which generated work in fourteen different countries. He was finding himself as busy as he ever had been with the additional benefit of being paid more than previously: plus, of course, his Air Marshal's pension! His decision not to work for the CAA for next to nothing had been a wise one.

While carrying out his role as a consultant, Sir Ivor quite naturally came into contact with board members of many companies and it was not long before he was invited to join in a non-executive role. In that capacity he became a director of Plessey Airports Ltd until that company merged with another Plessey company some four years later. In 1982 he became Chairman of Gatwick Handling Ltd, which handles much of the passenger and freight business passing through that busy airport. During his eleven year tenure, he saw the company double in size. The author suspects that he is not the only one who has marvelled at the manner in which Gatwick, with just its single main runway, handles such a vast number of passengers.

An amusing story is attached to the time when Sir Ivor decided that he had had enough of being a consultant. He mentioned that he was giving up this line of business to an American associate whose advice was: 'Don't give it up, just double your fees and keep on doing so until you have no business.' However, Ivor decided against this — it seemed slightly unethical!

Later, when the famous Farnborough airfield opened its doors to civil aviation, the Carroll Group set about making it a Business Aviation Centre for London. They looked around for a Chairman for its Carroll Aviation Corporation and Sir Ivor quickly filled the bill.

Among the many big firms, such as BP, which keeps its fleet of swift business jets at Farnborough, there was one alleged millionaire who owned not just one of the large Gulfstream private jets but two: both a G-2 and an even larger more up-to-date (and more expensive!) G-4. These are aircraft capable of carrying a load of forty or more passengers non-stop across to America. Who was this profligate? None other than Robert Maxwell!

On top of all else Sir Ivor was, for many years, a Vice-President of the Royal Air Forces Association (RAFA) and Chairman of its Council. In this honorary position he played a major part, ably assisted by Lady Broom in her secretarial capacity, in chairing the appeal to turn a derelict prep school in Moffat, Dumfrieshire, into sheltered housing for former members of the RAF and WAAF, and their families, in need of this kind of support.

It makes an appropriate venue as the school had been founded by the father of Lord Dowding who, as Air Chief Marshal Dowding had been the saviour of Fighter Command during 1939-40 when it won eternal glory during the Battle of Britain. Lord Dowding was born in the school which now serves as a kind of living memorial to his name. The appeal, ably ministered by Air Commodore Ian Atkinson, raised £1.75 million and its total overheads were less than five percent. In keeping with the heroics of the Battle of Britain, the appeal used the slogan of: 'Honour the dead by helping the living.' By being called 'Dowding House', the successful project will ensure that the name of the man to whom the RAF and Britain owe so much will be remembered, hopefully, in perpetuity.

Although Ivor is no longer Chairman of the Council of RAFA, he is now a Life Vice-President of this Association, the President of the Blenheim Society, the President of the Mosquito Aircrew Association, Vice-President of Bomber Command Association, a Vice-President of the Air Crew Association (ACA), the President of Moor Park Golf Club, the Rickmansworth Society and the Rickmansworth & District Residents' Association. He is also a Past President of the Pathfinder Association and Wales Area of RAFA.

As a result scarcely a month goes by without Ivor being asked to grace some special occasion and he gives his time most willingly. Such as the occasion when the Pathfinder Association organised a reunion in 1992 to commemorate the 50th Anniversary of its formation. Former Pathfinders came from all parts of the world and it turned into a six-day reunion with over 1,200 former members and their families attending the service in Ely Cathedral. As Ivor was President of the Association at that time, he was heavily involved in the organisation which was masterminded by Air Vice-Marshal Mike Hedgeland.

Sir Ivor was also invited to lead the RAFA contingent in 1990 on the occasion of the Battle of Britain 50th Anniversary March Past of Buckingham Palace.

As this is being typed, Sir Ivor and Lady Jess are about to embark upon another invited tour in the USA. Well past their Golden Wedding anniversary, they seem as active and interested as ever.

Looking back and wondering at what qualities enabled the lad from the Welsh valleys to rise to such heights, one is struck at once by several facets of his make up:

He, like almost every really successful person, was imbued with an extraordinary amount of energy and never seemed to tire or lose interest in what he was doing.

He had a sound education but not, it is thought, to the point where he was always top of the class. But, nonetheless, he writes excellent English and knows better than most how to marshall the facts and to present them in a logical, very readable, order.

He has always been quick to note and emulate the good ideas of others. We all see shining examples before us; at school, at work and at play but not everyone has the ability to spot the good: also to note, for future reference, how not to proceed.

Perhaps most of all Ivor has always had a determination to live his life in accordance with sound Christian precepts. He treats all men as equals, plays hard and fair with his colleagues, keeps both body and mind free from the many unworthy distractions which surround us and was always prepared to share the risks and pleasures which have become part of aviation folk lore. Although virtually steering clear of both tobacco and alcohol, he seldom misses an opportunity to join in any convivial occasion.

As well as these characteristics, he surely 'struck oil' when, returning from the maelstrom which was wartime Malta, he married a lovely lass who so mirrors his own likes and beliefs.

Many who came to know both Ivor and Jess at various stages of their lives, have described them as an ideal couple.

Although now well past the traditional three score and ten years of age, it would not surprise any of his many friends to learn that Ivor had launched himself, ably aided as usual by Jess, into some new activity. Long may it be so.

Appendix A

Citations (and/or recommendations) for DFC, DFC bar,
DFC second bar, DSO, AFC.

DISTINGUISHED FLYING CROSS
*Pilot Officer Ivor Gordon BROOM (1252084) Royal Air Force
Volunteer Reserve, No. 107 Squadron.*

This officer has completed forty-five sorties, involving 170 hours
flying. He has participated in attacks on a wide variety of targets with
much success, obtaining hits on a factory at Catanzaro, on military
barracks at Buerat and on mechanical transport and barracks near
Tripoli. On 17 November 1941, near Cephalonia, he bombed and
machine-gunned a 4,000 ton ship setting it on fire. This officer has at
all times displayed great leadership, courage and determination.

BAR TO DISTINGUISHED FLYING CROSS
*Flight Lieutenant Ivor Gordon BROOM DFC (112392)
No. 571 Squadron, 8 Group (P.F.F.).*

Flight Lieutenant Broom was captain of a Mosquito aircraft
detailed to lay mines in the Dortmund–Ems canal on the night 9/10
August 1944. This mission he completed successfully with the utmost
skill and daring in spite of weather conditions which were far from
ideal. He brought his aircraft down to a height of only 100 feet above
the water at exactly the correct speed before releasing his mine at the
place detailed. The attack was made with such swiftness and precision
that the defences were surprised completely and the mine was laid
before they could take action. The return from the target was made
with equal skill using cloud cover and variations of height and speed
to outwit the fighter and gun defences. His attack was a complete
success.

This pilot has now completed twenty-six sorties on his second
tour including seven to Berlin. He has shown at all times a high sense
of duty and leadership, and I strongly recommend him for the
immediate award of a bar to the DFC.

SECOND BAR TO DISTINGUISHED FLYING CROSS
Acting Squadron Leader Ivor Gordon BROOM, DFC and bar
(112392) No. 128 Squadron, 8 Group (P. F. F).

Squadron Leader Ivor Gordon Broom, Distinguished Flying Cross and Bar to Distinguished Flying Cross, was the pilot of a Mosquito aircraft of 128 Squadron detailed to place a 4,000lb bomb up the mouth of a railway tunnel near KAISERSLAUTERN on 1 January 1945, an operation requiring the greatest of skill and precision on the part of the pilot. In spite of the fact that he was followed by two enemy fighters, this officer, with tenacious determination, bombed his target from low level with great accuracy.

This officer has shown outstanding ability as a leader and as a determined and courageous operational pilot. Since the award of a Bar to his Distinguished Flying Cross he has successfully completed a further twenty-two operational sorties, each of them with a cheerfulness and enthusiasm that have set a very praiseworthy example.

DISTINGUISHED SERVICE ORDER
Acting Wing Commander I G BROOM DFC,
RAFVR No. 163 Squadron.

Since the award of a second Bar to the DFC this officer has completed numerous sorties, many of which have been directed against Berlin. Throughout he has displayed the utmost fortitude, courage and determination. At no time has enemy opposition deterred him from completing his allotted tasks. Wing Commander Broom has at all times set a high standard of devotion to duty.

AIR FORCE CROSS
Acting Wing Commander Ivor Gordon BROOM DSO, DFC
(112392), General Duties Branch, Royal Air Force Flying College.
(a) 2700 (b) 266 (c) 169.

Wing Commander Broom has been a syndicate leader at the Flying College since December 1954. Immediately on arrival his detailed knowledge of his aircraft, and his energy and example, combined to raise the standard of flying not only in his own syndicate, but in the College as a whole. In spite of a number of incidents, he has always shown an enthusiasm for flying, even in the admittedly difficult position in which an instructor was placed before a dual conversion of the Canberra was made available. At the same time, his personality and originality of thought have made him an outstanding instructor on the ground in the many subjects covered in the Flying College Course. This officer's courage, determination and skill in the air was exemplified in the highest degree in June 1955, when he piloted the Canberra 'Aries IV' on the world-record flight from Ottawa to London. Faced by mechanical failure, which meant that he had practically no fuel reserve, and by the prospect of fog at his destination, he refused to be diverted. Shutting down one engine to conserve fuel, he carried out a confident instrument approach and made a successful landing in conditions which compelled the official observers to rely on hearing rather than sight. Wing Commander Broom also participated as pilot of a Canberra in a series of high-latitude navigation training flights from Bodo, Northern Norway, in December 1955, for student navigators on the Flying College courses. This officer is an outstanding pilot of modern operational aircraft and he has the determination, courage and ability to fly these aircraft to their operational limits. His high standard of personal example in the air at all times, makes him an ideal instructor to students on Flying College courses. He has displayed great devotion to duty and has made a notable contribution to the advancement of modern aviation.

Appendix B

EXTRACT from *Thanks for the Memory* compiled by P B 'Laddie' Lucas CB, DSO, DFC, in which Sir Ivor Broom is writing about his wartime Malta leader and mentor Air Marshal Sir Hugh Pughe Lloyd.

Hugh Pughe Lloyd, who as a very junior pilot in World War I earned the Military Cross and Distinguished Flying Cross, was 45 years old at the outbreak of World War II. From May 1940 to late May 1941 he was the Group Captain Senior Air Staff Officer in No. 2 Group of Bomber Command, which at that time operated mainly Blenheim aircraft from United Kingdom bases. Ten days after leaving No. 2 Group he arrived in Malta as an Air Vice-Marshal — rapid promotion by any standard — to command the Royal Air Force in Malta.

Historians have, justifiably, written at length about the remarkable defence of Malta during World War II, but Hugh Pughe, as he was affectionately known, was never purely defensively minded. He regarded the island as being in a strategically perfect position to harass and sink shipping carrying supplies to German and Italian troops in North Africa. He was the ideal man to implement that part of his directive which said, 'Your main task is to sink Axis shipping sailing from Europe to Africa.' The outstanding defence of the island by his very limited fighter force provided the capability for his bomber and reconnaissance aircraft to seek the enemy by day and night. So successful were he and his small force that Malta eventually became the springboard for the first assault on Nazi-occupied Europe by Allied forces.

It was in September 1941 that I was first to learn of the decisive manner in which he commanded his forces — without always paying too much regard to normal staff procedures. My crew and I (all sergeants at the time) were flying a Blenheim en route from England to the Middle East and thence to Singapore, and landed at Malta for a refuelling stop — but we were to go no further. His two Blenheim squadrons, which were on detachment to Malta from his former Group in England, were suffering heavy losses in their mast-high attacks on ships carrying supplies from Italy to Rommel's forces in North Africa. He replaced those losses by 'hi-jacking' aircraft and their crews who landed to refuel. Within forty-eight hours of landing for our refuelling stop we were operating with the Blenheims based in Malta.

The squadrons under his command in 1941 were a mixture of day bombers, night bombers, reconnaissance and the wonderfully effective fighter squadrons, so activity continued on a 24-hour basis. I don't know when Hugh Pughe ever slept. He never seemed tired, and his bulldog manner bred a similar spirit of resolve in his air and ground crews. Nothing seemed to shake him personally. He instilled confidence in his men and developed the spirit, ability and determination to overcome odds which any rational person might have been excused for considering overwhelming. I always felt that he had a special regard for the Blenheim squadrons, but I learned later that other squadrons also felt he had a special regard for them — the art of a true Commander, who made each unit feel special.

One day after we had suffered some heavy losses he visited the squadron at Luqa airfield (now Malta airport). We were lined up for a pep talk when an air raid warning sounded. Calmly he went on talking. The camp siren sounded, but he continued talking until his aide said, 'They are diving on the airfield, sir.' He looked up, and then casually and slowly said, 'I think we had better take cover.' The bombs fell as the crews dived for cover almost before he had finished his sentence. Within seconds he was back on his feet and quickly started touring the airfield to inspect the damage.

He exhibited a delightful human touch one day when my observer and air gunner, both sergeants in uniform, were walking from Luqa to Valletta. A car stopped, a corporal driver got out of the car, and told them to get into the car. Inside the car was the Air Vice-Marshal, who, when he found they were a Blenheim crew, immediately started talking about the important role of the Blenheim. He took from his briefcase a signal of congratulations for the Blenheim crews which he had received from the Air Ministry that day and showed it to them. My air gunner was not wearing a hat and in response to Hugh Pughe's question he replied that he had lost it and the storekeeper would not give a replacement unless an old one was produced. Immediately the Air Vice-Marshal produced a sheet of paper, wrote an instruction to the Stores to issue my air gunner with a new hat, signed the paper, handed it to my air gunner and asked if that would satisfy the pedantic storeman! My air gunner, a cheerful Londoner, replied 'I hope so, sir, but they are a strange lot in Stores!'

I only served in Malta under Hugh Pughe's command for four months, but as a 21-year-old sergeant pilot I first learned from him the importance of senior officers identifying themselves with their units. In 1941, Malta was in the midst of a life and death struggle, yet I felt no apprehension about the future. He generated both individual and collective courage and a trusting faith that we would win through. Defeat was not a serious option, and it was fitting that this very operational commander should be knighted by King George VI in a tent in Tunisia in 1943. He was the first Air Marshal I had ever met and he not only altered the whole course of my life, but gave me, by example, my first lessons in leadership and the role of a commander. Having hi-jacked me in September 1941, he commissioned me in November 1941, when my squadron had lost all its officers except the Wing Commander and later in life our paths continued to cross at brief intervals.

In 1947-48, when he was the Commander-in-Chief of the South-East Asia Air Command, I commanded one of the two Spitfire squadrons in Singapore (the last two Spitfire squadrons in the front line). He never forgot that I had been one of his pilots in Malta in 1941— and I was merely one of many hundreds who served under him. In 1948 the three British Service Chiefs in Singapore were invited to Australia and New Zealand as guests of the Governments concerned. He plucked me out of my squadron for a couple of weeks, made me Staff Officer to the parry, a role about which I knew absolutely nothing, and said that if anyone asked him to speak about operations from Malta he would hand over to me. That was my briefing. Short and sweet. I fear I was a very inadequate staff officer on that trip, but I had the great privilege of being with him for two whole weeks.

In the early 1950s he commanded Bomber Command. At that time, bombing accuracy fell short of his high standards and he set himself the task of improving the accuracy in all weather conditions. He constantly sought the precision with which a rapier strikes its target, and although he did not achieve his objective for all his crews, he set in train the groundwork for his successors to do so.

In those days Command Headquarters still had communications aircraft to keep staff officers in limited flying practice. He was always keen that his air staff officers should maintain close contact with stations and squadrons, and I recall him saying to me once, 'There is only one way for an air staff officer to arrive on a visit to a flying station — and that is down the centre of the runway.' He had little time for air staff officers who failed to maintain a practical operational approach to life. Paper tigers were not popular with him. I recall the occasion when he attended a guest night at Manby, in Lincolnshire, in the early 1950s shortly before he retired. He left just before midnight, and although he had a professionally qualified crew in charge of the aeroplane, he sat in the left-hand seat and taxied out for take-off.

We did not meet again until 1971, when I was an Air Vice-Marshal commanding No. 11 (Fighter Group) in Strike Command. He lived some 30 miles away and I invited him to a dinner parry. He demurred, and said he was now too old to go out at night, but I pressed him hard and insisted on sending a car for him. We had a marvellous evening, the old sparkle was still in his eyes, the quizzical look still present, and he kept my other guests enthralled with his stories at the dinner table. As we rose from the table he turned to my wife, pointed to me, and said with a grin, 'To think I am responsible for that!'

We never met again. My relatively lowly rank at the height of Sir Hugh's career meant that my personal contact with him was always fleeting, but the impact was always lasting. Most people meet in life a few — very few — unforgettable characters who make a big impact on their lives. Air Marshal Sir Hugh Pughe Lloyd, Air Force Commander Extraordinaire, was one of those for me.

Appendix C

From Tom Williams, then a Sergeant pilot, RAF, in 1941.
Tom is now Lord Lieutenant of Derbyshire.

My first encounter with Ivor Broom was whilst serving in Malta in September 1941, and I have very good reason to remember him.

On the afternoon of 22 September 1941, Blenheims from Luqa were attacking Barrack blocks and ammunition dumps at Homs on the Tripolitanian coast. On the final run in to the target, although formating on the aircraft on my left, for some reason (I don't know why) I looked to my right and saw a Blenheim turning towards me at the same height, very obviously on a collision course. We were at about 50ft and I decided the quickest way to avoid a collision was to climb steeply and risk the flack. At about 600ft the aircraft collided with me from underneath, resulting in both propellers being bent and knocking the pitothead off. I made for the shore hoping to keep the aeroplane in the air, and to my relief I found that by adjusting the throttles to minimise the vibration, she would still fly.

Gradually gaining height to about 2,000ft, I saw in the distance one of the tiny dots which were the rest of the squadron, detach itself from the rest and begin to fly towards me. The pilot was Sgt Ivor Broom. He circled around and underneath me and in response to my request gave me my airspeed and altitude. He indicated that there appeared to be some damage to the fuselage but that the main wheels seemed to be undamaged. He then flew on ahead on course for Luqa. Ivor must have known that we were within range of fighters and that had any or even one arrived, it would have been impossible for me to have formated with him to give each other defence. Typical of him he said afterwards, 'If I had not been on my first Op, I probably wouldn't have done it!' This I do not believe, even had he been operationally experienced I think he is the sort of man who would have done just as he did.

Talking of first 'Ops', Ivor was actually on his way to Alexandria, and was one of the crews who was stopped in his tracks and seconded for duty with the Squadrons operating from Malta. As you will no doubt recall, this often happened when there was a shortage of aircraft on the Island.

I next met Ivor some fifty years later. He had been invited to a RAFA New Year's party as a guest of honour of the Long Eaton Branch. I arrived a few minutes late and my wife and I were standing at the opposite end of the hall from which the President had just finished his welcoming speech. Sir Ivor spotted me and more or less ran the full length of the room. We embraced in what was a very emotional moment.

He then explained that only the previous day he had been preparing for a presentation in support of the Blenheim restoration fund, one of the objects being to show how tough the aircraft was, and he had used as an example my aircraft which had held together despite badly bent propellers which had turned the engines and airframe into a sort of vibration rig.

It was, as he said, a remarkable coincidence since he had no idea that I would be at the party.

Later the Chairman said that there was not a dry eye in the house.

Appendix D

Account of the Argostoli raid as written by P/O Len Williamson
(later Air Commodore Len Williamson, RAAF).

Attack on Shipping, Argostoli Harbour, Cephalonia

Awoken at 5, had breakfast and reported at the flight at 6.30. Briefed then driven down to the kites in the bus. Took off at 7.30. I was flying No. 2 in the first vic, and we went down to deck level in an open formation. Weather was dull with heavy layer cloud at 5,000ft — sun rose like a huge red ball on our right. 'Tallyho' was given but the machine was a long way off on the horizon. Kept the speed at 170mph and arrived in sight of the coast at 10.00. Increased speed to 185 and closed in the formation. Rounded the N tip and passing over the coast went through a little valley. I had to climb to get through as I was being squashed into the side. Over another hill and dived down the other side to deck level. The harbour was particularly smooth and very deceptive. Could not see any ships and for a moment thought we'd come on a wild goose chase. Ivor turned sharply to the left and hugged the side of the precipitous shore. We followed close on his heels and kept as close to the side as safe flying would permit. The leader had spotted the ships around in a small cove and was remaining out of sight until we burst out on top of them. It seemed hard to believe that were on a mission to destroy as the whole scene was one of quietness and beauty. Rounded the bend and right in front of us were two M/Vs close together and a further one hugging the shore. There were three destroyers to the right between the ships and the harbour entrance and two others across the bay. Ivor attacked one of the ships and overshot and I followed Ray in on the second. Pulled up sharply to climb over the masts which seemed to loom up with surprising suddenness. Dropped my bombs as I was going over the ship but that was too late. Everything was still peaceful until I was over the ship then hell broke loose. It seemed as if everyone was bent on shooting at little me. The destroyers and shore batteries opened up with machine gun, pom pom and heavy stuff. Dived steeply for the deck and as I did both motors cut out, Arthur was thrown upwards with all his navigation gear with the force of the bunt. The motors came on and I started to breathe again. Kicked on hard rudder and kept throwing the kite around as hard as I could. The tracer was cutting across my path, yellow and red lines of it and black puffs were bursting around. Had on full power and kept hard on the deck as I pulled up over the hill at the end of the harbour. Pushed her over the top and was out of the line of fire of the guns. Just breathing a sigh of relief and grinned across to Arthur when Harry reported a Macchi diving down on us. Kept the taps open and concentrated on catching the leader. Line of m/g bullets kicked up the water on my right and in front. Harry kept me informed as to its whereabouts. Caught up to the leader, who had slowed down slightly and formated tightly on him. Macchi made about three attacks but the boys put a few bursts across his bows and he sheered off to have a crack at the formation coming after us. The leader reported a lone Blenheim behind us so he turned the flight around and went back to help him. All settled in together and continued towards home. Harry dropped his bombshell by telling me the turret had been u/s since we took off, could not rotate it, only lower and elevate it. He certainly had learned his lesson. Sighted the other squadron going in high up. Spotted a 'Bogie' but it did not come near to us. The other kites had wireless trouble so we got the QDM. Came into the island, circled and landed. We lost two machines out of the second formation. The other Sqdn lost one but the crews got out. They reckoned that there weren't any ships in the harbour so couldn't have looked very hard.

2 x 500lb 11 sec delay

MALTA 13/12/41

Pilots involved in the attack on Argostoli Harbour

P/O Broom

P/O Len Williamson

Sgt Noseda

Sgt Lee — missing

Sgt Crossley

Sgt Gracey — missing